The Illusions of Progress

Georges Sorel

 The Illusions of Progress

translated by
John and Charlotte Stanley
with a foreword by
Robert A. Nisbet
and an introduction by
John Stanley

University of California Press
Berkeley and Los Angeles 1969

University of California Press
Berkeley and Los Angeles, California
University of California Press, Ltd.
London, England
Copyright © 1969 by The Regents of the University of California
Library of Congress Catalog Card Number: 69-16511
Printed in the United States of America

Foreword

Robert A. Nisbet

It is a pleasure to welcome this book into the English language, the more so for the general excellence of the translation and for the valuable introduction that Professor Stanley has given to Sorel's work. Not the most ardent of Sorel's admirers would ever have claimed lucidity of thought or felicity of style for him. His notable conflicts of life, purpose, and thought are only too well mirrored by the structure and manner of writing to be found in his books and articles. It is high tribute to the skill of the translators that they have managed to penetrate the sometimes tortuous recesses of the original and to give us a work that seems to me eminently faithful to both the meaning and the spirit of *Les Illusions du progrès*.

There is a kind of Gallic charm in the fact that a Frenchman should have been the one to expose the intellectual roots of an idea that is, for all its universality of appeal, French to the very core. The modern idea of progress—the idea that mankind has progressed in linear fashion in the past, is now progressing, and will continue to progress indefinitely into the future—came into being in the French Enlightenment. We find it stated with matchless assurance early in the eighteenth century by the Abbé de Saint-Pierre and with prophetic passion by the great Condorcet at the end of the century.

But, as Sorel makes superbly evident in the first section of *The Illusions of Progress*, behind eighteenth-century French insistence upon the inexorability of the progress of civilization lay an earlier and crucial seventeenth-century French insistence upon the inexorability of the progress of *knowledge*; knowledge alone. When such luminaries of French rationalism as Pascal, Fontenelle, and Perrault postulated the universality and inevitability of progressive change in time, they had in mind, not the institutions, polities, and morals of mankind, but solely what Fontenelle himself referred to as "the growth and development of human wisdom."

Moreover, as Sorel emphasizes almost gleefully, this insistence upon the certainty of progress in human knowledge rested, in the first instance at least, upon foundations no more substantial than the belief by Fontenelle and Perrault that the literary and philosophical works of their own day were superior in quality to those of Plato, Aristotle, Aeschylus, Sophocles, and others in the classical age. For it was squarely within that elegant donnybrook of intellectuals known to posterity as the Quarrel of the Ancients and Moderns that the idea of necessary, linear progress had its first statement. As Sorel shrewdly makes clear, there was a kind of circularity of reasoning involved among the rationalist defenders of the Moderns. Writers of the seventeenth century could be declared superior to writers of the ancient Greek and Roman world because of the natural tendency of knowledge to increase cumulatively in time, as does the growth of the individual human mind. And the reality of this postulated principle of progressive change could be proved by the evident superiority of seventeenth-century philosophers and dramatists over their classical predecessors. We can almost hear Sorel chortle as we read the opening, brilliant section of *The Illusions of Progress*. Parade all the "proofs" of progress you wish, he seems to be saying, but the irrefutable fact remains: the modern idea of progress arose, not as a summary generalization of historical conditions, but as a kind of rhetorical trick of some French intellectuals in the seventeenth century seeking to demonstrate their and their contemporaries' intellectual superiority to Plato and Aristotle.

There is much more to the matter, of course, than this—much more in Sorel's own book and much more in the larger perspective of the history of the idea of progress. It is one of the distinctive merits of Professor Stanley's exemplary introduction that he has gone into this larger perspective and has, with fine scholarship, shown us the deeper roots of the European idea of progress. It is not only the scholarly literature on Sorel that has been enhanced by Stanley's introductory essay, but the literature generally of the history of the idea of progress. He makes very clear indeed that a belief in the progress of knowledge and culture, far from being a monopoly of the modern mind, had a good deal of philosophical understanding and also prestige among the classical thinkers of Greece and

Rome. It would be impossible to praise too highly Stanley's treatment of the roots of the idea of progress in Western thought; brief
as it must necessarily be, it casts illumination well beyond the scope
of its few pages.

Equally important is the longer and more detailed analysis that
Professor Stanley gives us of the relation of the idea of progress to
Sorel's own age in European thought. He shows us some of Sorel's
own ambiguities and misconceptions, especially with respect to the
concept of ideology. Sorel persisted in the belief that progress was
an ideology; an ideology, as we have seen, which arose first among
some seventeenth-century intellectuals, but which has depended
upon the bourgeoisie for its continuing popularity. His purpose indeed, Stanley tells us, was rather less to deal with the idea of progress
than it was to take on the bourgeoisie and to use his attack on the
idea, as he found it, as one more attack on the bourgeoisie. There is
also the fact that Sorel was himself far from denigrating the philosophy of progress. It is, as Professor Stanley notes, one of the more
striking paradoxes of an exceedingly paradoxical mind that "a
thinker who sets out to debunk the modern idea of progress should
conclude the main sections of his two most important works with an
affirmation of the material progress of production."

The essential point—a point made clear in Stanley's own essay
on Sorel and in the final pages of Sorel's text—is that it is not so
much the idea of *progress* Sorel detests but, rather, the *idea* of progress. The distinction is, I believe, a vital one. We cannot entirely
place Sorel among that group of alienated nineteenth- and early
twentieth-century thinkers—Tocqueville, Burckhardt, Max Weber,
among others—whose distrust of the idea of progress was rooted in
their distrust of modernism, and especially modern materialism. For
Sorel there *was* progress to be seen in material production, and,
properly understood, progress could serve as an incitement to the
revolutionary action that Sorel adored. What Sorel detested about
the idea of progress—the idea that had made its way down from the
seventeenth and eighteenth centuries, that had implicated not merely
bourgeois philosophers but also socialists, including Marx himself
(see p. 193)—was its overtones of naturalness, normality, and necessity. The author of *Reflections on Violence*, the philosopher of
myths, of elites, and of revolutionary *acts*, could hardly be expected,
as Professor Stanley concludes, to have accepted this aspect of the

idea of progress; not even in the form in which he had found it in Marx, there united, as we know, with a millennialist conviction of the imminence of redemptive revolution.

The "illusion" of progress would appear to be for Sorel an illusion only when the idea of progress is separated from the primacy of the act. I think we are justified in adding the word "progress" to what Professor Stanley says, in the final words of his introduction, about virtue. For Sorel, progress, like virtue, "belongs only to those who act." Nothing more, surely, needs to be said to indicate the profound relevance of this book to ongoing movements of thought and action in our own day.

Translator's Introduction

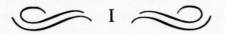

Georges Sorel is known to English and American readers mainly through his *Reflections on Violence* which, aside from one small work,[1] is until now the only one of his dozen books to have been translated. It is not difficult to understand why this is so; the *Reflections* appeared at a time when there was intense interest in the treatment of socialism, and the work's militant stand against rationalism conformed to the temper of the times. Today, the idea of the creative role of violence in social movements is of great interest to students of contemporary events. Even the title of Sorel's work is a bit sensational.

As a consequence of this rather one-sided exposure, English-language readers regard Sorel primarily as an exponent of anarcho-syndicalism and the now famous (or infamous) myth of the general strike. It is true that some of the narrow impressions have been corrected in the course of several recent American works[2] but, how-

---

[1] I refer to Irving Louis Horowitz' translation of *La Décomposition du Marxisme* contained in the former's *Radicalism and the Revolt Against Reason* (New York: Humanities Press, 1961). *Reflections on Violence* was published in 1950 by the Free Press with an introduction by Edward Shils. It was translated from *Réflexions sur la violence* in 1920 by T. E. Hulme with three appendixes by J. Roth. Hulme's introduction is available in his *Speculations* (New York: Harvest Books, n.d.), pp. 249 ff.

[2] Most of the works on Sorel in English were written after 1950. The best of the lot, Horowitz, *op. cit.*, was published in 1961. See also Richard Humphrey, *Georges Sorel, Prophet Without Honor, A Study in Anti-Intellectualism* (Cambridge: Harvard, 1951); James Meisel, *The Genesis of Georges Sorel* (Ann Arbor, Michigan, 1953); C. Michael Curtis, *Three Against the Republic* (Princeton University Press, 1959); H. Stuart Hughes, *Consciousness and Society* (New York: Vintage ed., 1961), chaps. 3, 5; Scott Harrison Lyttle, "Georges Sorel: Apostle of Fanaticism," in *Modern France: Problems of the Third and Fourth Republics* (Princeton, N.J., 1951), pp. 264–290. See also the introductory essays by Shils to the *Reflections*. Neal Wood, "Some Reflections on Sorel and Machiavelli," in *Political Science*

ever competent, these treatments correct the misunderstandings or superficial impressions of Sorel only with the greatest difficulty. Even in France, many of Sorel's own lesser-known works are relatively unread, and a considerable amount of oversimplified thinking about him remains. Jean-Paul Sartre, for example, recently dismissed Sorel's writings as "fascist utterances,"[3] a statement that, despite any particle of truth it may contain, is equivalent to condemning the *Communist Manifesto* as Bolshevik propaganda. Sorel's writings, however offensive they may be to us, must be studied on their own merits.

Interpreting Sorel is not an easy thing to do. He is a poor writer. His organization is bad; one idea is thrown on top of another helter-skelter, and Sorel thought it desirable to keep his writings difficult; the reader has to work in order to understand him. But the translators believe that the presentation in English of another of his important works is an excellent way to facilitate study of this important thinker. This particular work, published originally in 1908 as *Les Illusions du progrès*, was selected for a number of reasons. The idea of progress is of great interest to contemporary scholars and it is partly for this reason that the *Illusions of Progress* along with the *Reflections* is considered Sorel's most interesting and influential work.[4] This is why it is the one work that should be read by students and scholars of the history of the idea of progress, as well as of Sorel's ideas.

Quarterly, LXXXIII, March 1968, pp. 76–91, is a correction of James Burnham, *The Machiavellians, Defenders of Freedom* (Chicago: Regnery ed., 1963; first published in 1943).

[3] In his introduction to *The Wretched of the Earth* by Franz Fannon (New York, 1968), p. 14. More important is Sartre's admission that Fannon's writings owe a great deal to Sorel's notion of the creative role of violence. I find it hard to understand why Sartre finds Sorel more "fascist" than Fannon who emphasizes hatred and race more than Sorel does.

[4] Sorel had a profound influence on Camus. See *The Rebel* (New York: Vintage ed., 1956), p. 194. Camus speaks only of the *Illusions of Progress*. See also John Bowle, *Politics and Opinion in the Nineteenth Century* (New York: Oxford, 1967 ed.), p. 403, and H. Stuart Hughes, *Consciousness and Society*, p. 162. Among Sorel's other works are *Contribution à l'étude profane de la Bible* (1889); *Le Procès de Socrate* (1889); *La Ruine du monde antique* (1898); *Introduction à l'économie moderne* (1903); *Le Système historique de Renan* (1906); *La Décomposition du Marxisme, Réflexions sur la Violence*, and this work, *Les Illusions du Progrès*, all of which were published in 1908 at the height of Sorel's syndicalist period and are the only works translated into English; *La Révolution dreyfusienne* (1909); *Matériaux d'une théorie du prolétariat* (1919); *De l'utilité du pragmatisme* (1921); *D'Aristote à Marx* (1935).

The work, however, is more than academic. Because of almost two hundred years of expansion, continuous westward migration, and an almost exclusively liberal rationalist tradition of political thought, the idea of progress has a particular magic for Americans. Rare indeed is the politician who does not invoke the great "progress" we have made and even rarer the State of the Union address or convention keynote speech that does not invoke progress as one of the great purposes in American life. America in fact might be said to be one of the few industrialized nations in the Occident whose citizens are still ardent believers in the idea that the use of human reason produces human betterment or that every new discovery improves the lot of mankind: though the splitting of the atom may end the human race, it will still provide abundant sources of cheap electric power.[5]

Far from American shores, Sorel wrote *The Illusions of Progress* at a time in European history when there was not only a general disenchantment with the ideas that led Gustave Eiffel to build the tallest monument in Europe, but with the very concept of rationality itself. The new studies in psychology, plus a sense that fantastic opulence was devoid of any taste or refinement, produced an awareness of decadence and immorality. Reason and science had not emancipated man; they had enslaved and debased him. In Sorel's own case this awareness was confirmed by his observations of the very forces that he at first regarded as being the saviors of European civilization. The liberals and socialists had disillusioned him by their disgraceful behavior during the Dreyfus affair, and it was this disaffection that led to Sorel's opposition to the mainstream of French radicalism. To Sorel, the Dreyfusards were not really interested in socialist reconstruction. He observed[6] that many of them had motives of personal ambition in supporting the beleaguered French officer. Sorel thought that the radicals, far from being interested in reforming the order of things, merely wanted a portion of that same order for themselves. They wanted power, not a more virtuous society; or at least they confused personal success with the success of the social revolution, when in fact their achievements consisted primarily in strengthening the existing order.

---

[5] For a good example of the modern American view of progress, see George Gallup, *The Miracle Ahead* (New York: Harper, 1965).

[6] Sorel, *La Révolution dreyfusienne* (1909).

Consequently, Sorel spent a good portion of his intellectual career waging a two-front war against the agents of European capitalism and those of parliamentary socialism. Part of the difficulty, as Sorel saw it, was that both capitalism and reform socialism shared the same liberal rationalist assumptions that many of the European intellectuals began to question at the turn of the century. At the base of these assumptions, according to Sorel, lay the idea of progress.

It is particularly interesting that someone with Sorel's background should call the idea of progress into question. Born into a middle-class French family in 1847, Sorel was educated at France's prestigious *Ecole Polytechnique* and later he went to work as a government engineer. Engineering was not his first love, however, and he retired early in 1892. It was only after his retirement that he did most of his writing. To whatever degree his personal experience led him to a disenchantment with existing institutions, Sorel certainly did not allow a genuine respect for scientific progress to obscure his skepticism of an idea that went far beyond technical sophistication. Sorel knew that the idea of progress arose and flourished in a technological age, but he was aware that the idea spread far beyond the more efficient construction of highways or the multiplication of more efficient means of production. For he rightly thought that the idea of progress was a kind of guiding ideology or myth (in the pejorative sense) of the age—an ideology that had far-reaching political consequences.

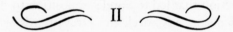

II

In order to explain Sorel's view of the idea of progress, we should compare the idea of simple improvement or technological sophistication with the idea of progress in modern times. In order to do this it might be fruitful to leave Sorel and to discuss briefly three works that maintain that Sorel's understanding of the idea of progress—the modern understanding—actually was held in antiquity. Following this discussion, an analysis of what is meant by "ideology" will be attempted so that we can discuss how Sorel views the "ideology of progress."

The late Professor Ludwig Edelstein contended that the Greeks and Romans had an idea of progress which Edelstein defined with Arthur O. Lovejoy as "a tendency inherent in nature or in man to pass through a regular sequence of stages of development in past, present, and future, the later stages being—with perhaps occasional retardation—superior to the earlier."[7]

If this general definition of progress is what one might call "developmental improvement," it is easy to establish that some of the ancients did believe in progress. It is certainly not true, as one scholar has asserted, that the "ancients looked upon change with dread because it was identified with calamity."[8] To take one noteworthy example, Aristotle regarded the development of the polis as change, and this change was regarded as natural and good; that is, that the polis was both better and in one sense more "natural" than earlier and more primitive forms of political organization. If this kind of thinking is what Mr. Edelstein regards as progress, then the Greeks most certainly believed in it.

But it is fair to say that the modern idea of progress is more than the natural tendency toward developmental improvement (which is the essence of the Lovejoy-Edelstein definition). For in Sorel's time, and even today, the idea of progress was both a law of historical development, a philosophy of history, and as a consequence also a political philosophy. It combined a descriptive analysis of history with a philosophical position that this development was right and good, and this position was used, as we shall see, for political purposes.

Now, the Lovejoy definition is vague enough to entail the possibility of the modern formulation being included in it. It is broad

---

[7] Edelstein, *The Idea of Progress in Classical Antiquity* (Baltimore: Johns Hopkins, 1968), p. xi, cites the definition of Arthur O. Lovejoy and George Boas, *Primitivism and Related Ideas in Antiquity, A Documentary History of Primitivism and Related Ideas* (Baltimore, 1935), I, 6. For other works on the idea of progress, see J. B. Bury, *The Idea of Progress* (New York: Dover ed., 1955); Charles Frankel, *The Faith of Reason: The Idea of Progress in the French Enlightenment* (New York, 1948); John Baillie, *The Belief in Progress: A Reevaluation* (London, 1953); Frederick J. Teggart, *Theory and Processes of History* (Berkeley and Los Angeles, 1962) and *The Idea of Progress: A Collection of Readings* (Berkeley, 1949); Ernest Lee Tuveson, *Millennium and Utopia* (New York: Harper, 1964); R. V. Sampson, *Progress in the Age of Reason* (London, 1956). Robert A. Nisbet, *Social Change and History: Aspects of the Western Theory of Development* (New York: Oxford University Press, 1969).

[8] J. Salwyn Schapiro, *Condorcet and the Rise of Liberalism* (New York).

enough to include historical, philosophical, and political analysis. But Edelstein makes it quite clear at the beginning of the work that "the definition of progress with which the historian begins cannot be that of the philosopher."[9] Thus any example of recognizing piecemeal improvement in any one field is taken by Edelstein to mean a concept of progress. To be sure, he implies that the criterion for improvement can be either piecemeal or total: "The criterion of improvement can be physical survival, the increase in material riches, or even novelty itself, moral advance, intellectual improvement, or greater happiness. Improvement can be looked for in all sectors of life or in a few alone."[10] But it is quite clear from all of his examples that piecemeal progress was the only kind of improvement that the ancients regarded as possible; it virtually excluded the all-encompassing total view of improvement characteristic of the modern view of progress.

In order to understand the modern viewpoint more completely, it is profitable to examine briefly the view of another author who asserts that the ancients went beyond a piecemeal view of progress and approached the modern view. In *The Open Society and Its Enemies*, Professor Karl Popper says that Aristotle's teleological view constituted part of the roots of the Hegelian school of modern progressivism. By this Popper means that Aristotle's "progressivism" was based on the Stagirite's notion of ends or final causes. The cause of anything is also the end toward which the movement aims, and this aim is good. The essence of anything that develops is identical with the purpose or end toward which it develops.[11] Aristotle uses biological analogies: the teleology of the boy is manhood; if we switch and extend this biological analysis to the political arena, we can say that the end toward which the village develops is the most natural and the highest form of organization: the polis.

Popper says that the doctrine of ends or final causes leads to the "historicist" idea of a historical fate or inescapable destiny which can be used to justify all kinds of horrible institutions such as slavery[12] because they are inevitable. It is true that this "historicist" view that events are inevitable (and to a limited extent predictable)

---

9 Edelstein, *The Idea of Progress in Antiquity*, pp. xxix–xxx.

10 *Ibid.*, p. xxix.

11 Karl Popper, *The Open Society and Its Enemies* (New York: Harper paper ed., 1962), II, 5.

12 *Ibid.*, pp. 7–8.

is essential to the modern view of progress. But it is doubtful that Aristotle's doctrine of final causes was as deterministic as Popper implies. Determinism is historical, and even Popper is constrained to admit that Aristotle was not interested in historical trends and made no *direct* contribution to historicism.[13] Determinism aside, Aristotle did not see the growth of the city as being synonymous with either moral or technological growth. Technology had reached perfection in some areas and stood in need of further coordination in others.[14] Furthermore, the growth of the political institutions of the city did not *necessarily* entail a corresponding improvement in morality. Thus Aristotle took care to draw the distinction between the "good man" on the one hand and the "good citizen" on the other; that is, that the good man and the good citizen were identical only in the best city.[15] Theorists of progress, on the other hand, tend to regard moral, technical, and political development as an interrelated whole.

Indeed, the separation of morality from what we call "history" today is one of the distinguishing characteristics of ancient times, assuming that the ancients had a theory of history at all. It is left to Eric A. Havelock in his *The Liberal Temper in Greek Politics*[16] to put forth the view that the Sophistic idea that virtue can be taught possessed the essential qualities of the modern identification of history and virtue. Havelock starts his thesis with the example of the myth of Prometheus, in which fire was stolen from the hearth of Zeus for the benefit of man.[17] But there is no evidence that this theory is like the modern one. For one thing, as has been pointed out,

---

[13] *Ibid.*, p. 7.

[14] Edelstein claims that the "perfection" envisaged by Aristotle is perfection in all fields (p. 127), but earlier on he says that Aristotle recognizes that some arts have reached a stage of excellence not to be surpassed, whereas the art of money-making is limitless since acquisition knows no limits. But Edelstein seems to ignore an important matter here. Aristotle distinguishes between sound and unsound forms of acquisition, i.e., acquisition based on selfish desire for gain and the sound type of acquisition which is concerned with *economics*, the art of household management, which is limited by the natural needs of the household. The importance of this distinction with regard to modern progress will become apparent. Modern progress prefers limitless acquisition and indefinite improvement, whereas Aristotle prefers natural limits. Also, the very notion of the kind of natural end in Aristotle differs from the eschatological visions of Marxist progressives. (For the modern view of limitless acquisition, see Locke's *Second Treatise on Civil Government*, §§ 31, 37, 50; cf. *Politics*, 1258.)

[15] *Politics*, 1276*b*.

[16] Yale University Press, New Haven, 1957, chap. 3.

[17] *Ibid.*, pp. 52 f.

Prometheus' myth reveals no infinite progress, which is more characteristic of modernity. Prometheus' punishment turns progress into a great illusion, a false hope which is ultimately destroyed. More important, the Sophistic viewpoint that virtue can be taught does not itself prove progress in the modern sense. Havelock maintains that Protagoreanism rationalizes an age of social progress.[18] And it does this in rather the same way that Pericles extols Athens in the Funeral Oration.[19] But again, little indeed can be said about progress in antiquity beyond a vague sense of technical improvement; it lacks a sense of history. As Leo Strauss persuasively argues, "Liberalism implies a philosophy of history. 'History' does not mean in this context a kind of inquiry or the outcome of an inquiry but rather the object of an inquiry or a 'dimension of reality.' Since the Greek word from which 'history' is derived does not have the latter meaning, philological discipline would prevent one from ascribing to any Greek thinker a philosophy of history at least before one has laid the proper foundation for such an ascription."[20] As he points out, there is no evidence from the Greek sources that the Sophists or any other school possessed what we would call a philosophy of history—a philosophy that is peculiar to the modern idea of progress. And the Platonic dialogues, it may be assumed, would have gone out of their way to record such views if they had occurred, since progress is so easily attacked and is so antithetical to the Platonic view of ultimate reality as unchanging.

Finally, even if it can be said that ancient historians themselves had a philosophy of history, that philosophy if it was at all progressive was so only in the larger context of a cyclical view of history such as is found in Polybius. It remains to ask, however, just what the modern philosophy of history is. In order to do this let us say what it is not. We can do this if we return to Professor Edelstein's book to help us to enumerate the half dozen characteristics that clearly differentiate modern progress from the notions of improvement or "development" which occur in antiquity.

Instead of focusing on the Sophists, Edelstein turns his attention to Seneca, who is singled out as giving a clearer and more compre-

---

[18] *Ibid.*, p. 176.
[19] *Peloponnesian War*, II, 43.
[20] Leo Strauss, "The Liberalism of Classical Political Philosophy," in *The Review of Metaphysics*, XII (1959), p. 400.

hensive view of progress than any other ancient thinker and one that, as a consequence, is closest to the view of progress held in the nineteenth century. In Seneca, the door to the future is opened. Mental acumen and study will bring forth new and presently unknown discoveries. Progress has not only led to the present but will be extended into the future. According to Edelstein, this will be so not only in the field of science but in all fields of human activity.[21]

Edelstein asserts that by linking all branches of human activity together, Seneca came closer to the modern theory of progress than anyone else.[22] Now, it is true that for modern progressives, progress is not, as we have repeatedly said, a piecemeal process but takes place in all fields, intellectual, moral, political, technical; it extends to liberty of thought as well as to the development of virtue; to science as well as to the eradication of superstition and prejudice. In this way Seneca embodies the first two principles of modern progress.

1. Progress today is multifaceted; each field of human endeavor is looked upon as a member of a team of horses; each animal is held in harness with the others and all advance in the same direction, down the same road. To Edelstein, though not as much to Bury,[23] Seneca fulfilled this view.

2. Most of the thinkers of the past did not speculate on the future as much as comment on the development of the present, but Seneca looked to future development, which is definitely characteristic of the modern view.[24]

There are four other qualities that neither Seneca nor other ancients mentioned in their idea on development.

3. Despite his forward-looking perspective, Seneca and most of the other ancients (including Lucretius and the atomists) were rec-

---

[21] Edelstein, *Progress in Antiquity*, pp. 175–176.

[22] *Ibid.*, pp. 180, 175.

[23] J. B. Bury, *The Idea of Progress* (Dover ed., 1955), pp. 13–15. For Bury the value of natural science in Seneca was confined to a few chosen individuals and not mankind at large. The latter constitutes the modern view.

[24] *Ibid.*, p. 15. Cf. Edelstein, p. 170. Bury and Edelstein agree. (Seneca, *Naturales Quaestiones*, VII, 25, 4–5). Edelstein would have us believe that even Plato flirted with indefinite future progress. Thus he says (p. 108) that in the *Laws* Plato asserts that "not everything can have been debased at the end of the previous civilization." But Edelstein concentrates here on the various arts, whereas the central import of the passage cited is that morally speaking men were "manlier, simpler and by consequence more self-controlled and more righteous generally" before the deluge (*Laws*, 679b).

onciled to the annihilation of the world.[25] Though annihilation was viewed by them as virtually certain, in modern progressive thinking annihilation is open to question. Optimism pervades modern progressivism, not only about the future but about all things human.

4. Not only are modern progressives open to doubt on annihilation, but as a consequence they are open to the idea of "indefinite perfectibility,"[26] an optimism that is shared by no known ancient.

5. Though Seneca views annihilation as an eventual certainty and holds that all the great accomplishments of man will be abolished, a new civilization will arise on the ashes of the old one. In this respect, insofar as he has any historical theory at all, Seneca's view is cyclical: civilizations rise and fall, and this viewpoint is almost universal in ancient thought. All advances in civilization are preludes to a subsequent decline or ultimate end. What little independent identity the idea of "history" had at all, it had in the form of a wheel that, in one or another respect, returned to the same place in the order of things. Modern progressivism is a different approach. The latter depicts history as a line—occasionally broken to be sure—destined to rise in an upward direction of indefinite perfectibility. This linear rather than cyclical concept of history is perhaps the most important single attribute of the contemporary view of progress.

6. In addition to all the above characteristics, modern progressivism has an aura of religious certainty about it. In ancient times history meant the possibility of chaos or tragedy, and this was accompanied by a feeling of resignation against the idea of *Moira*, roughly translated as "fate," which possessed a certain mysterious, unknown quality.[27] The modern view of progressive history, on the other

---

25 *Naturales Quaestiones*, III, 30, 1. Edelstein, p. 173. Bury, *op. cit.*, p. 15, says that Seneca's belief in the "corruption of the race is uncompromising."

26 The expression is Condorcet's in *Outlines of an Historical View of the Progress of the Human Mind*, 10th epoch. The anonymous translation is from the London edition of 1795, p. 346.

27 "*Moira*, it is true, was a moral power; but no one had to pretend that she was exclusively benevolent, or that she had any respect for the parochial interests of mankind. Further—and this is the most important point—she was not credited with foresight, purpose, design; these belong to man and to the humanized Gods. *Moira* is the blind, automatic force which leaves their subordinate purposes and wills free play within their own legitimate spheres . . ." (F. M. Cornford, *From Religion to Philosophy* [New York: Harper ed., 1957] pp. 20–21). Moira is antithetical to progress because it leads to a sense of resignation about a fixed order in the universe (Bury, p. 19). See also William Chase Greene, *Moira: Fate, Good and Evil in Greek*

hand, sees future progress as not only inevitable but, to a limited extent, predictable on the basis of rational calculation of existing data. It is this character of inevitability which contributes most strongly to the modern views of historical determinism and sees social science as a science of prediction.[28] Events had always been characterized by some form of necessity, but only modernity has made this necessity into a virtue.

The idea of progress had its origin in the seventeenth century and matured in the age of Enlightenment. Perhaps no better summaries of the idea of progress are found than in the concluding paragraphs of the *Outline of the Historical View of the Progress of the Human Mind* by the archetypal proponent of the modern idea of progress, the Marquis de Condorcet. In this work, Condorcet puts forth all six of the concepts that make it a new idea in the eighteenth century (though not originating with Condorcet) and an idea that characterizes the following age. (1) Progress occurs in all fields; (2) is projected into the future; (3) rejects inevitable annihilation and the

---

Thought (New York: Harper ed. 1963). Recent scholarship has tried to show that the idea of progress dates back to the millenarian and chiliastic thinkers of the Middle Ages. Certainly Augustine and the church fathers, with their severely pessimistic view of earthly human nature, were not progressive thinkers. In placing the good city in heaven, St. Augustine and the church fathers stand in marked contrast to the millenarian sects who placed the good city on earth. Literature on modern revolution makes frequent reference to the apocalyptic battle between good and evil in chiliastic literature, the result being the establishment of the heavenly city on earth. (See Ernest Lee Tuveson, *Millennium and Utopia* [New York: Harper ed., 1964] and Norman Cohn, *The Pursuit of the Millennium* [New York: Harper ed., 1961]. The view according to these writers is that the medieval chiliasts, inheriting many of the concepts found in the *Book of Revelation* and in Jewish apocalyptic ideas, regarded the world as moving toward a final battle which would result in a New Jerusalem.) Yet even Tuveson admits that these sects fell into disfavor for a thousand years after the death of Constantine (p. 14), while Hanna Arendt notes that hysteria should not be confused with a theory of history, that no revolution is made in the name of Christian teachings until the modern age (*On Revolution* [New York: Viking, 1963] p. 19). Sorel notes the number of Jewish members of Marxist movements; he notes, however, that they are not members of these movements for ethnic reasons but because of their station in life as independent intellectuals. Those who view Marx as "the last of the Hebrew prophets" must contend with the secular and rationalist element which permeates the modern view of history and stands in marked contrast with religious revelation. (Cf. Edmund Wilson, *To the Finland Station* [New York: Anchor ed., 1940], chap. 5.)

[28] Democritus could explain prerecognition of the future through a radically materialist view of the universe, but this universe had no design (F. M. Cornford, *Principium Sapientiae* [Harper ed., 1965], p. 130). Democritus had little influence (Bury, p. 15).

pessimism that goes with it; (4) renders civilization indefinitely perfectible; (5) has a linear view of history; (6) regards the future as having certain inevitable patterns which are calculable.

Condorcet sloughs off the prospect of an apocalyptic end of the world as:

. . . impossible to pronounce on either side [and] which can only be realized in an epoch when the human species will *necessarily* have a degree of knowledge of which our shortsighted understanding can scarcely form an idea . . . By supposing it actually to take place there would result from it nothing alarming either to the happiness of the human race or of its *indefinite perfectibility* if we consider that prior to this period the progress of reason will have walked hand in hand with that of the sciences; that the absurd prejudices of superstition will have ceased to infuse into morality a harshness that corrupts and degrades instead of purifying and exalting it.[29]

Now, this statement does more than describe what we would call "development." It means more than the sophistication of the arts and sciences. By joining a vast number of human activities together and asserting that moral improvement will result from this union, Condorcet depicts the attitude of nearly perfect optimism without which the modern theory of progress would not have arisen. Since progress now means improvement in all fields, the history of all human activity—of mankind itself—is the history of progress. At this point "history" and "progress" become virtually synonymous; so Condorcet opens the future to a definite improvement in all fields, and this improvement is associated with knowledge or "enlightenment." This ever-expanding enlightenment becomes part of the historical process itself; further, this enlightenment not only should take place but, because history is linear, it *will* take place. Progress is both a pattern of development perceived through historical observation and a law

---

[29] Condorcet, *Progress of the Human Mind*, 10th epoch, London ed., 1795, p. 346 (italics added). Charles Frankel, in defending Condorcet's view of progress, asserts that the notion of indefinite perfectibility merely implies that man can never assume that we have reached the limit of human hopes. "The principle of the indefinite perfectibility of man is simply the denial that there are any absolutes which the human mind can safely affirm. It is not a prediction about the future; it is a statement of a policy . . ." (*The Case for Modern Man* [Boston: Beacon, 1959], p. 104). But Frankel ignores Condorcet's assertion that "the human species will *necessarily* have a clearer knowledge" and that this in turn will result in releasing man "from the dominion of chance." (See the final statement from Condorcet below and n. 30.)

of human inevitability. It is this law of inevitable progress which produces the most extraordinary optimism. Here is Condorcet's concluding paragraph, written shortly before he was driven to suicide by the Terror:

How admirably calculated is this view of the human race, emancipated from chains, *released alike from the dominion of chance*, as well as from the enemies of progress, and advancing with firm and *inevitable* step in the paths of truth, to console the philosopher lamenting his errors, the flagrant acts of injustice, the crimes with which the earth is still polluted! It is the contemplation of this prospect that rewards him for all his effort to assist the progress of reason and the establishment of liberty. He dares to regard these efforts as part of the eternal chain of the destiny of mankind; and in this persuasion he finds true delight of virtue, the pleasure of having performed a durable service which no vicissitude will ever destroy. This sentiment is the *asylum* into which he *retires*, and to which the memory of his prosecutors cannot follow him: he unites himself in imagination with man restored to his rights, delivered from oppression, and proceeding with rapid strides in the paths of happiness; he forgets his own misfortunes while his thoughts are thus employed; he lives no longer to adversity, calumny, and malice, but becomes the associate of those wiser and more fortunate beings whose enviable condition he so earnestly contributed to produce.[30]

It is this attribution of an independent character and dignity to history which converted it from a method of inquiry to an object that had such revolutionary consequences. Despite Sorel's contention that the Enlightenment ignored historical necessity, the idea of linear development and advancement in all fields gave "history" a power and coherence it had never attained before. By coming together in all fields progress meant the history of humanity; by becoming linear this advancement was made infinitely good. By becoming infinitely good it strengthened history itself and thereby enabled "history" to become a source of political legitimacy. As long as history was cyclical in nature it could not be used to legitimize a regime. Cycles meant not only improvement but a subsequent decline and fall. Therefore one could not use "history" to justify a regime if the history of that regime would result in ultimate disaster. That is why the ancients found it impossible to justify their best regimes as historical products. Plato's *Republic* as well as Aristotle's ideal state in

---

[30] *Ibid.*, pp. 371–372 (*italics added*).

The Politics are not historical products; they are in fact specifically anti-historical because history means imperfection and tragedy. The etymology of the word "Utopia" as a "city of nowhere" underscores the character of the *Republic* whose discussion of "history" ensues only before and after the *Republic* itself is discussed.[31] It is "reason" or at least "reasonableness" which justifies the best regime, and this reason never becomes identified with "history." Condorcet and the *philosophes*, by identifying history with the progress of enlightenment, make reason itself into a historical product.

As a consequence of the idea of progress, then, it was no longer merely reason that served to justify regimes, but "history" itself. In order more fully to understand the concept of legitimacy, we should note that it is that quality or qualities which lend credibility to and secure obedience for a government or regime and its institutions. This concept depends of course on our criteria of legitimacy and morality. Utilitarians, for example, view a regime as "legitimate" if it strives for the maximum of social pleasures. Whatever the school of thought, however, theories of political legitimacy are usually accompanied by what one writer has called the quality of "beneficence";[32] of producing certain benefits which other regimes do not do as well, whether it be order, security, pleasures, reason, or what not. But the quality of beneficence could not be attributed to "history" until "history" became an object as well as a method of study, and until this object became devoid of any concept of ultimate decline and fall—that is, of a cyclical nature. When this cyclical aspect of history was removed, and when modernity viewed history as a universally progressive phenomenon, "history" as such assumed the character of an independent object and became possessed of a quality of infinite beneficence for the first time. It was at this point that the

---

[31] By "history" is meant here the affairs of men placed in a sequential order, not the modern view. Cf. *Republic*, 367e–374e in which the rise of the luxurious state is described; 543a–575. Despite Sorel's oft-repeated contention that the men of the Enlightenment were "ahistorical" and had no appreciation of necessity, it is probably true in this case that it took an ahistorical man to produce a historicist. If Condorcet was not historicist, the failure of the French Revolution was the event which sparked a reliance on historical determinism as a thing far greater than the wills of individual men but whose apparent thoughts worked to a higher unity and realization. It was this resolution of opposites which led Marx as well as Hegel to the camp of the progressives.

[32] Bertrand de Jouvenel, *On Power* (Boston: Beacon), p. 25. The author separates beneficence from force and legitimacy as the common elements in stable power. But he says they cannot be isolated except analytically.

idea of history came increasingly to dominate political discourse: if a government is an actual entity, it is viewed as a historical event and as such the "product" of historical development; if "history" is beneficent, then so is the regime. As a product of "history," it becomes the best possible regime, while the best regime (as opposed to the best possible regime) becomes the *end* of the historical process. But the difference between the best possible regime and the best regime (e.g., Plato's Cretan city of the *Laws* versus the *Republic*) is obscured, with the virtual disappearance of the latter. The best regime, in ancient times, assumed the qualities of definition. Plato admitted that the Republic might never be attained in the world of becoming (i.e., history), which is why the most brilliant of the theorists on progress, Karl Marx, could proclaim himself an anti-Utopian.[33] As long as a regime could distinguish between the good man and the good citizen, as long as history was viewed at most as a story, a story of disaster and tragedy, a certain plurality in human affairs was axiomatic. History meant chaos and this meant a complicated clash of motives and events. But when the idea of "history" became linear and was coupled with indefinite improvement, tragedy was replaced by a series of minor setbacks on the path to perfection. Heroes were replaced by "reason" or "world historical individuals"[34] who became great, not through great deeds but by their ability to grasp historical necessity. Fate, which had the character of great mystery, was replaced by "history," a history in which everything is either explained or explainable. Tragedy could be explained as a reasonable (necessary) part of the greater plan of historical fulfillment.[35]

In the world in which tragedy becomes rational and in which everything can be explained, truth assumes a broad unitary charac-

---

[33] *Communist Manifesto,* III, 3: "The significance of Critical Utopian Socialism and Communism bears an inverse relation to historical development. In proportion as the modern class struggle develops and takes definite shape, this fantastic standing apart from the contest, these fantastic attacks on it, lose all practical value and all theoretical justification. Therefore, although the originators of these systems were, in many respects, revolutionary, their disciples have, in every case, formed mere reactionary sects. They hold fast by the original views of their masters, in opposition to the progressive historical development of the proletariat." For a defense of Utopianism, see Andrew Hacker, "In Defense of Utopia," in *Ethics,* 65 (Jan. 1955), pp. 135–138.
[34] The expression is Hegel's in *The Philosophy of History,* trans. J. Sibree (New York: Dover, 1956), p. 29.
[35] There are numerous critiques of what is known as historicism. See Karl Popper, *The Poverty of Historicism* (New York: Harper ed., 1964). For a natural law

ter. By becoming historical it becomes part of a broad continuum which obscures the difference between what is and what ought to be, by making both part of the same line extending between past and future. If perfection is possible in this world, events can attain the same unity which had heretofore been characteristic only of Utopias that had in ancient times been explicitly ahistorical. Now, instead of Plato's unitary city, history itself provides man with a sense of oneness with other men and with events themselves.

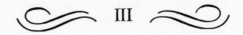

III

The unitary advance which the linear notion of progress was to make so important in the century following the French Revolution was to extend far beyond society and morality and reach into the province of thought itself. If history was viewed as an extension of all fields of human activity, not the least of which was the "progress of the human mind" itself, the exalted place that "enlightenment" originally had in Condorcet's theory of progress was to give way to the notion that knowledge itself is just another factor in historical progress. For what is "thought" but another human activity that can be "explained" historically? At this point philosophy, which had always meant love of wisdom, began to be simply another pattern of human behavior. The use of prudence which was the way political philosophy confronted corporeal reality gave way to a science of historical prediction; and political philosophy, which had heretofore been a method of inquiry about why we should obey, was transformed into a study of the historical origins and background of ideas. This development is credited to Condorcet's near-contemporary Destutt de Tracy, who in his *Eléments d'Idéologie* (1801–1815) calls for a "science of ideas."

The importance of this development should be noted primarily

---

analysis, see Leo Strauss, *Natural Right and History* (Chicago, 1953), Chap. I. For an existentialist view, see Albert Camus, *The Rebel*, trans. Anthony Bower (New York: Vintage ed., 1957), Pt. III. See also Karl Jaspers, *The Origin and Goal of History* (New Haven: Yale, 1953); Sir Isaiah Berlin, *Historical Inevitability* (London and New York: Oxford University Press, 1954).

for those who do not understand the fundamental character of the change of thinking which converted philosophy into what is called "ideology": the significance of explaining all thought in terms of its historical background had the effect of minimizing the importance of philosophy altogether; that is, of denuding it of any intrinsic value and replacing it with explanations of its place in "history." Thus the liberal idea of, say, limited government was not discussed on the basis of the merits of limiting sovereignty, but was viewed instead as a rationalization or justification of certain social interests—in this case of a dominant capitalist class preventing factory legislation, etc. This tendency is found most prominently in the thought of Karl Marx, who asserted even before he wrote the *Communist Manifesto* that ideas were the products of material relations.[36]

It is easy to see, under these circumstances, that the idea of history itself becomes the only viable basis of political legitimacy. If, as in the writings of Marx, all ideas except one's own are placed on the same plane as social classes or conventions, they become as ephemeral as any social phenomena; they pass into nonexistence, just as so much social data changes with those historical preconditions that are proclaimed to have brought them into being. Thus an idea is "true" only if it is close to actual "historical conditions." If it is not proximate to the historical conditions, it is "false consciousness." For this reason Marx was quite consistent in maintaining the truth of capitalism as compared to feudalism insofar as the former represented a more "advanced" stage of historical development; but that the idea of capitalism in a sense became "false consciousness" when confronted with socialism, while the latter would become false after giving way to communism. Under this approach to ideas, thought loses any permanent quality which distinguishes it from society itself.[37]

---

[36] See *The German Ideology* (New York: International Publishers, 1947). "The production of ideas, of conceptions, of consciousness, is at first directly interwoven with the material activity and the material intercourse of men . . . the *direct* efflux of their material behavior" (pp. 13–14; *italics added*). The importance of the word "direct" is not to be underestimated.

[37] "We set out from real, active men, and on the basis of their real life processes we demonstrate the development of ideological reflexes and echoes of this life process. The *phantoms* formed in the human brain are also, *necessarily*, sublimates of their material life process, which is empirically verifiable and bound to material premises. Morality, religion, metaphysics, all the rest of ideology and their corresponding forms of consciousness, thus no longer retain the semblance of

But the notion of ideology, particularly that which is found in Marxism, is further complicated by the appreciation of competing ideas within the same historical periods. Thus capitalism is the ideology of the dominant class, whereas the proletariat whose ideology should be socialism manifests "false consciousness" if it accepts the capitalist argument. Even the temporary efficacy of ideas is weakened when the progress of history is not only used to explain ideas, but is turned against them. For if ideas are only excuses for interests and conscious rationalizations for exploitation, then the idea is not only made temporary but is thrust aside; the idea becomes a mask to be ripped off, if the true face of the proponents is to be discovered.[38] Ideas are changed from being temporary explanations to false consciousness and from false consciousness into unconscious falsehood.[39]

The profound misunderstanding that has arisen with the contemporary use of the term "ideology" should be viewed in this context.

---

independence. They have no history, no development . . ." (*ibid.*, p. 14). By "no longer" Marx does not mean that they did once possess independence, but rather that in contradistinction to German idealist philosophy, ideas in his materialist view "no longer" retain independence. In short "Life is not determined by consciousness but consciousness by life" (p. 15).

38 Hanna Arendt says that even during the French Revolution, the elevation of hypocrisy from a minor sin to a major crime had the effect of doing away with the classical distinction of one's *persona* or legal mask, a word originally developed from theatrical masks into the concept of a "legal personality" or a "right and duty bearing person." "Without his *persona* there would be an individual without rights and duties." See *On Revolution* (New York: Viking, 1965 ed.), pp. 102–103.

39 George Lichtheim says that Marx's vision was that in a rational order, thought determines action. "Men will be free when they are able to produce their own circumstances. Historical materialism is valid only until it has brought about its dialectical negation. . . ." The "mature consciousness which comprehends the necessity of 'prehistory' will not be an ideological one" (*The Concept of Ideology and Other Essays* [New York: Vintage, 1967], p. 21). As a consequence Marx believed that there were some permanent truths which rise above changing social circumstances. "The concept of ideology illumines the historical circumstance that men are not in possession of the true consciousness which—if they had it—would enable them to understand the totality of the world and their own place in it" (*ibid.*, p. 22). It is true that Marx regarded his own ideas as having some measure of transcendent truth; but Lichtheim admits that Marx refused to recognize the dilemma of asserting all thought as determined on the one hand and some ideas rising above being determined on the other. Lichtheim cites Engels' letter to Mehring of July 14, 1893, in which the former says, "Ideology is a process accomplished by the so-called thinker consciously, it is true, but with a false consciousness. The real motive forces impelling him remain unknown to him; else it simply would not be an ideological process" (Marx, Engels, *Selected Correspondence*

An "ideology" is not simply a political idea such as "capitalism" or "socialism," but is rather a justification or rationalization for a particular group in society. In this respect Marx could not have viewed an ideology as merely a political idea. Rather it is a *product* of history; as such, only the idea (socialism) which is closest to historical reality is legitimate, and since history progresses, each succeeding idea is more legitimate. Under these conditions, only the progress of history itself can become the ultimate legitimizing idea and the study of ideas becomes historical. But if ideas are studied historically, then the study of ideology is really not a study but a method. Here then *ideology* as such must be differentiated from the ideological *method* which is the actual process of unmasking or explaining the "real" or historical basis of political philosophy and all other thought.[40]

[Moscow, 1953], p. 541; Lichtheim, p. 15). Thus Marx, according to Lichtheim, held that the difference between "objective" and "ideological" thinking is in the ability "to comprehend the particular determinations which condition each successive phase of human activity" (Lichtheim, p. 20). But the young Marx would not have gone along with this Engels formulation. (See nn. 36 and 37 above.) Lichtheim recognizes Marx's own ambiguity on the question of ideology, i.e., that he retained enough Hegelian idealism and Enlightenment rationalism to take ideas seriously. The consequence of the theory of ideology as being the end of all independent thought was a possibility never squarely faced by Marx; even Engels says that we will be subject to necessity even when we do understand its laws, and it is reasonable to include thought in this process of necessity. "Freedom does not consist in the dream of independence from natural laws, but in the knowledge of those laws, and in the possibility of making them work towards definite ends. This holds good in relation both to the laws of external nature and to those which govern the bodily and mental existence of men themselves—two classes of laws which we can separate from each other at most only in thought but not in reality. Freedom of the will therefore means nothing but the capacity to make decisions with knowledge of the subject. Therefore the *freer* a man's judgment is in relation to a definite question, the greater is the *necessity* with which the content of this judgment will be determined" (*Anti-Düring: Herr Eugen Düring's Revolution in Science* [Moscow: Foreign Languages Publishing House, 1959], p. 157; italics are Engels'). This was written prior to Marx's death. (See the following note.)

[40] For the logical conclusion of Marx's historical materialist analysis of ideas, see Karl Mannheim, *Ideology and Utopia*. Mannheim faces the consequences of Marx's theory of ideas, which sees its culmination in what Mannheim calls the sociology of knowledge. Like Marx, Mannheim sees the perfected ideological method—the sociology of knowledge—as gradually transforming "the Utopian element" in man's thinking into thought which is more and more coterminous with historical reality and thus losing its function of opposition. "But the complete elimination of reality-transcending elements from our world would lead us to a 'matter of factness' which ultimately would lead to the decay of the human will. . . . The disappearance of utopia brings about a static state of affairs in which man himself becomes no more than a mere thing. We would be faced then with the greatest

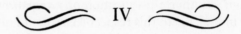

Since the imprimatur of historical progress is the one legitimizing concept that the proponents of the concept of ideology can accept (at least if they are consistent), it was only a matter of time before the idea of progress itself would be brought under the microscope of the *ideological method*. The rather interesting quality of Georges Sorel's *The Illusions of Progress* is that the ideological method, a consequence of the idea of progress, is itself used against the idea of progress and with it the whole idea of historical inevitability.

As Sorel pictures it, however, progress is an ideology which is not part of Marxism, but a bourgeois creation. His purpose in writing the book is to oppose the bourgeoisie by demolishing "this super-structure of conventional lies and to destroy the prestige still accorded to the 'metaphysics' of the men who vulgarize the vulgarization of the eighteenth century."[41]

Methodologically, the concept of ideology has many difficulties. Not the least of these is determining the exact relationship that ideas have to the material conditions out of which they (allegedly) arise. For example, do these conditions "cause" ideas to arise purely and simply; or do ideas arise independently and then become taken over and "used" by particular interests or institutions?[42] Sorel seems to opt for the latter explanation. This is an important part of Sorel's thinking, for it allows him to attribute to ideas themselves a causative influence—an independence—which might raise eyebrows in more orthodox Marxian circles. Thus Sorel is able to say that the concept

---

paradox imaginable, namely, that man, who has achieved the highest degree of rational mastery of existence, left without any ideals, becomes a mere creature of impulses. Thus, after a long, tortuous, but heroic, development, just at the highest stage of awareness, when history is ceasing to be blind fate, and is becoming more and more man's own creation, with the relinquishment of utopias, man would lose his will to shape history and therewith his ability to understand it" (*Ideology and Utopia, An Introduction to the Sociology of Knowledge*, trans. Louis Wirth and Edward Shils [New York: Harvest Books ed., n.d., originally published in 1936], p. 262).

41 See below, p. 152.

42 For an elaboration of the problems which the ideological method poses, and the ramifications which this has for a science of knowledge, see Robert Merton, *Social Theory and Social Structure* (Glencoe: Free Press, 1957 ed.), pp. 460 f.

of progress could be traced back, not to material conditions but to a purely literary conflict between ancient and modern writers; or that the Voltairian spirit also disappeared as the result of a literary revolution and not on the day that the bourgeoisie somehow "decided" that its interests necessitated a return to the church. The latter explanation Sorel rejects as an "ideological and highly superficial explanation."[43]

Furthermore, Sorel maintains that the creator of an idea is as free as an artist working with new materials, but that ideas, once formed, establish links with other current ideas and thereby become part of the predominant doctrine of a given period. This period will find in that doctrine certain meanings and interpretations that may be quite different from the initial intention of the author. Similarly, other classes in other periods may take yet another meaning from the idea. Primary importance is granted to what others see as only secondary; where some see only literature, others see philosophy. Thus, the same idea is upheld in radically varying ways according to the social position (class) of the people upholding it. This is as true for the doctrine of progress (which changes form as it is adopted by different periods: it becomes more deterministic in the nineteenth century) as it is for Marxism, which is looked upon by parliamentary socialists with far less seriousness than by the founders of the doctrine.

There is a definite importance to Sorel's attributing a certain independence to moral ideas. Sorel was a moralist; this is the single most outstanding trait of the man, and no explication of his ideas is possible until it is emphasized that the fundamental and underlying principle behind most of his writing was a genuine despair at the moral decadence of modern Europe. Moral rebirth is possible only under conditions that lie outside the idea of progress and the social institutions that foster the idea. Thus it is imperative that Sorel not regard morality as simply the product of historical forces but rather grant it some autonomy. He maintains, therefore, that the lowering of the moral level of Europe was not due to the persecution of the Jansenists but that it was the other way around.[44]

Sorel's use of the Marxian theory of ideology recalls to mind his

---

[43] See below, p. 9.
[44] See below, p. 10.

notion of *diremptions*: "to examine certain parts of a condition or event without taking into account all of the ties which connect them to the whole, to determine in some manner the character of their activity by isolating them."[45] The difference between Sorel's use of ideology and Marx's is that Marx views ideas as necessarily part of a social whole, much as a physician regards parts of the body, while Sorel views ideology as a method without necessarily relating it either to the whole movement in human society—the totality out of which it arises. The difference between Sorel's diremptive method and Marx's theories is that for the latter the theory of ideology (as well as his other ideas) is viewed as part of a total system, a world view (*weltanschauung*). Ideology must be viewed in the context of this total system. For Sorel, it was desirable to extract certain parts of the system and merely "use" them for the purposes of greater understanding of phenomena. It was therefore not necessary to accept the total system, and obviously Sorel does not accept all aspects of Marxism.

But Sorel still takes care to dissociate Marx from his more simplistic followers and to assert that Marxist ideological methods are devoid of simplified notions and vulgar determinism. In this way, Sorel avoids the pitfalls of ideology and the ideological method. By dissociating Marx from vulgar historicism, he can employ constructively one of the aspects of the total theory without having to accept the total theory itself.

Sorel sees Marx's followers as putting forth a far more unitary system than Marx himself,[46] though he says later that Marxism does indeed share many of the characteristics of the unitary progressive view of the world, which the bourgeoisie first put forth in the notion of progress. The idea of progress has fostered a false sense of social

---

45 *Reflections on Violence* (New York: Collier ed., 1961), p. 259. The editor of this volume, Edward Shils, thinks that Sorel may have coined the word "diremption" as no English equivalent can be found.

46 Lichtheim agrees with this judgment but for different reasons than Sorel. He sees Marx as retaining enough Hegelian idealism that a certain dualism remains in his system between Marx's ideas—pure knowledge—and ideology. (See n. 39 above.) However, he also recognizes that this theory looks to the unity of mankind, an attribute of progressivism. (See *The Concept of Ideology*, p. 22.) But it was left to the positivists to bring the concept of unity to its logical conclusion. It was no longer an ideal but actually existed. Thus Marx was right in asserting that the utopian successors of St. Simon such as Auguste Comte were reactionary. This was true, however, because of their positivism, as much as their utopianism.

unity in society, and this unity has gone a long way in contributing to social decadence. Sorel's purpose is therefore to use the ideological *method* (unmasking) to break down an ideology (progress). Sorel rarely faces the fact that the ideological method sprang forth from the very ideology he is trying to destroy. He admits it only covertly by playing down Marx's progressivism. Anyway, by using the diremptive method, the concept of ideology can be separated from the idea of progress; the ideological method is independent (diremptive) from the total system that he is trying to destroy.

In fact the whole purpose in Sorel's writing on progress is to separate the idea from other ideas and to break the idea itself down into its component parts rather than to build up a unified structure or system. As T. E. Hulme wrote some years ago in the introduction to his translation of *Reflections on Violence*, Sorel saw modern democracy as inheriting most of the ideas of progress which were originally put forth in the seventeenth and eighteenth centuries. As Hulme notes, modern democracy, in seeing itself as the product of undifferentiated progress in society, fails to distinguish between democracy and progress. Similarly, Sorel's fight against the "radicals" of parliamentary socialism was that they were part of the same movement: they too saw no difference between democracy, socialism, and the working-class movement.[47] The idea of progress, in welding all these notions into an interrelated totality, has sapped them of their vitality and moral efficacy. This totality regards itself as possessing moral force; it is actually devoid of morality. It produces only smugness and helps to obscure the truth that contemporary society is not part of the natural order of things.

Sorel's purpose in the *Illusions of Progress*, and in much of his other writings, is to show that moral superiority has long ago been separated from political progressivism (assuming they were ever joined) and has attached itself to the socialism of independent producers.[48] In order to keep this superiority intact, the new men of virtue must retain full independence from all the ideas and institutions which are associated with the idea of progress—an idea whose very purpose is to obscure these distinctions and the social conflict which would result from their being made. This is another reason

---

[47] T. E. Hulme *Speculations* (Harvest Books ed., n.d.), pp. 249 ff.
[48] This is the basic theme of the *Reflections on Violence*.

why Sorel does not regard Marx, a theorist of class conflict and strife, as a progressive thinker.

Sorel tries to demonstrate that progress embraces the various institutions of bourgeois society, and it enables these institutions to encompass and thereby to dominate all of the various disparate elements of society into an apparent unity. Rather than representing the natural order of things, progress is in reality part of the ideology of the modern institutions of domination.

The first aspect of this domination has been the quality of *continuity*. Sorel accepts Tocqueville's version of the French Revolution as having, in reality, strengthened rather than weakened the institutions that grew up in the ancien régime. The ancien régime, bourgeois liberal democracy, and the modern "welfare state" of parliamentary socialism are all different manifestations of the growing power of the institutions of the modern state. Both liberal democracy and parliamentary socialism strengthen the state.

The continuity leads to the second aspect of domination: the elite of one era has survived and strengthened itself in another. Being the ideology of the "victors" of an epoch, the idea of progress serves to mask the interests of the dominant class which inherits power. Democracy itself masks its opposite for, as Sorel says, "nothing is more aristocratic than democracy." Thus parliamentary socialists are compared to officials whom Napoleon made into a nobility and who labored to strengthen the state bequeathed by the ancien régime.[49] Parliamentary socialism strengthens the state machinery and the economic powers of the state through an elite of intellectual and political professionals, civil servants, hangers on, etc.

In Sorel, the two concepts of elitism and the power of the state go hand in hand. As long as the workers accept the idea of unity in the progressive state, the latter is legitimized, and true moral rebirth is impossible because the domination of the old elite is preserved. Furthermore, the ruling oligarchy by flattery and progressive rhetoric encourages mediocrity in the masses and saps them of their virtue—the simple fighting vigor characteristic of the early Greeks and Romans.[50]

---

49 *Ibid.*, pp. 275–276; see also p. 94 where he discusses Tocqueville's view of the conservatism of the French Revolution.

50 What is called "consensus" in American political science and politics is anticipated by Sorel in his discussion of parliamentary socialists who must have working-

Associated with the idea of continuity in the elite domination of the state is Sorel's third concept of domination; that is, that the idea of progress is essentially a conservative force in society. Instead of emphasizing its revolutionary implications, Sorel depicts the idea of progress as legitimizing each strengthening of the state. But since the state keeps the same characteristics throughout these changes, progress really legitimizes the status quo. *Plus ça change, plus c'est la même chose.* Sorel's case might have been bolstered if he had further examined the lives of the proponents of progress. Often they are quite as conservative as Turgot whose "boldness" is responsible for the rise of the third estate but who could remain a loyal servant of the French monarchy—that enlightened despotism which Tocqueville viewed as the real origin of the French Revolution—and who could approve of the hanging of a number of rioters. Condorcet, Turgot's less able successor, could proclaim, "I am a Royalist" only shortly before his more evangelical wife urged him into becoming a moderate liberal (Girondin). The postrevolutionary progressives, St. Simon and Comte (and indirectly Hegel), were even more conservative, being sometime supporters of their respective contemporary regimes.[51]

But Sorel is aware that the idea of progress can produce not only conservatism but a certain political "quietism." Why act at all if progress makes change somehow "inevitable" anyway? Thus Sorel criticizes Marx for the excessiveness of his Hegelian biases, which produce a kind of passivity in the socialist movement itself. Marx's materialist revision of Hegelian dialectics constitutes the Marxian version of progress. Thus American socialists have greeted the success of trusts with enthusiasm because, according to these socialists, trusts represent the final stages of capitalism before its deliverance to socialism. This rationalist construction of history was, to Sorel, a falsehood. (It is interesting to note that a decade after Sorel's

---

class, middle-class, and upper-class constituents. Only in this way can they obtain influence (*Reflections*, p. 120). See also *La Ruine du Monde Antique:Conception matérialiste de l'histoire* (Paris, 3d ed., 1933) for the classic concept of virtue as seen by Sorel.

[51] For a lively and sympathetic portrait of the great progressive thinkers, see Frank E. Manuel, *The Prophets of Paris* (New York: Harper ed., 1965). See especially pp. 15, 45, 58, and 111 for the moderation and even conservatism of Turgot, Condorcet, and St. Simon. For Comte's emphasis on order, see pp. 274–286. For Hegel's practiced conservatism, see his attack on the "English Reform Bill" in Carl Frederich, ed., *The Philosophy of Hegel* (New York: Modern Library, p. 540).

death the German Marxists could proclaim *Nach Hitler uns!*—after Hitler, us—in which German Marxists actually lent support to the Nazi movement in expectation that it too was a "stage of development.")[52]

The kind of passive mentality produced by the idea of progress is one of the bases of Sorel's criticism of the radical movement. Progress is a total "law" of human development as well as an ideology; as such it is a rationalistic construction of the human mind which imposes a false sense of unity in society itself. The reason for this is that it is usually rationalistic and positivistic in its base of formulation, and both rationalism and positivism confine themselves to what is at hand. What is shown to the observer is what is true and what is true is what is shown. This circular unity of thought prevents action because the latter depends on breaking out of what is already given; on striking out in new directions. Action is possible only if a judgment is made that is adverse to the system. However, if all judgments are made on the level of historical analysis and all events legitimized as historically necessary, everything is permissible, including conservatism. Here, as one modern philosopher has said, all action and thought become "one-dimensional."[53] No distinction is made between what is and what ought to be.

Sorel's criticism of modern social scientists can be seen in this light. Rationalist progressives want to see logical development patterns in everything. As such, "development" is often seen as part of a total scheme of things. All of society is looked upon as being swept along in the progress of events. Modern social scientists, regarded by Sorel as handmaidens of the bourgeoisie, earn their living by placing very different things on the same plane from the love of logical simplicity; sexual morality, for example, is reduced to the equitable relations between contracting parties and the family code to the regulation of debts.[54] Thus, throughout his works, Sorel directs barbs at the es-

---

[52] For an excellent portrait of the actual conservatism not to say quietism of the German Social Democracy, see J. P. Nettl, *Rosa Luxemburg* (London: Oxford University Press, 1966), Vol. II passim. (See also n. 40 above.) Rosa Luxemburg's quarrel with Kautsky, the great theorist of Marxism who proved conservative in actual practice, is detailed.

[53] The expression is Herbert Marcuse's, *One Dimensional Man* (Boston: Beacon, 1964). Marcuse's Hegelianism obscures his appreciation of the connection between progress and the one-dimensionality of existence, but he seems to suspect it. See especially, pp. 188–189.

[54] *Reflections*, p. 147.

teemed professors of social science or the "learned sociologists," the "little science," etc.

But whereas the social scientists see primarily a progressive unity, Sorel says that reality is manifested more in chaotic struggle. Rather than viewing the entire world as representing some stage of what is today called "development,"[55] Sorel sees history as a sea of decline *(décadence)* punctuated by occasional moments of historical greatness. Only at exceptional periods of human history have manifestations of greatness *(grandeur)* occurred, and it is quite obvious that Sorel does not regard his contemporary Europe as manifesting any characteristic of "greatness." Greatness occurs only at those rare times when, through heroic acts of human will, men have "forced" history. Sorel's syndicalism, as well as his occasional flirtations with Leninism and fascism, must be regarded as an attempt to find some movement or individual which would personify the new elements of greatness. For example, Lenin is able like Marx himself to combine action with thought. But it should be noted that, unlike Lenin, Sorel from a distance attached great importance to the Soviet workers' councils, which possessed many of the same characteristics that Sorel saw in the French syndicates.[56] These institutions Sorel saw as alternatives to the harbinger of modern decadence, the modern state. They represented a total revolution or a sweeping aside of the state itself, and they represented the embodiment of a new vital-

---

[55] The literature of modern political science, particularly in the fields of comparative government and sociology, seems to inherit many of the progressive conceptions. The "functional" theorists seem particularly interesting in this respect. See, for example, Gabrial A. Almond and G. Bingham Powell, Jr., *Comparative Politics: A Developmental Approach* (Boston: Little Brown, 1966). "The independent nation has become a nearly universal phenomenon. The past several decades have seen a national explosion on the continents of Asia and Africa. This has produced an extraordinary confusion of cultures, and mixtures of archaic and modern institutional forms. In some way this confusion must be brought to order, and the capacity to explain and predict must be reaffirmed" (pp. 214–215). The authors claim that they "will not repeat the naiveté of Enlightenment theorists regarding the evolutionary progression in political systems" (215). But the authors' concluding paragraph poses "the ultimate question of the Enlightenment. Can man employ reason to understand, shape, and develop his own institutions. . . . ? The modern political scientist can no longer afford to be the disillusioned child of the Enlightenment, but must become its sober trustee" (pp. 331–332). The authors agree that ethical judgments on the system are important although they ignore them. However Seymour Martin Lipset, *Political Man* (Garden City: Doubleday, 1959) reveals a great concern for democracy.

[56] See the appendix to the *Reflections* entitled "In Defense of Lenin."

ity–Bergson's *élan vital*–a life force which sustained itself through incessant struggle.[57]

The reason for this is that these institutions placed themselves outside of the old order. They have effectively destroyed the false principle of unity and replaced it with a principle of struggle. The same principle of struggle Sorel saw as embodied in the moral fiber of great regimes: of ancient pre-Socratic Greece, of the early Roman Republic, of early Christianity, and of the Napoleonic armies. These periods were not corrupted by the sophistry of false philosophy. Rather their virtue was brought forth by the necessity of action and it is through action itself more than any other activity that "man discovers his own best qualities: courage, patience, disregard of death, devotion to glory, and the good of his fellows, in one word: his virtue."[58]

It follows, ironically enough, then, that Sorel juxtaposes the false unity of the modern progressives, which legitimizes the parasitic life of the ruling classes by obscuring all struggle, to the Homeric virtues of the early ancients whose unity was solidified by the action of constant struggle with enemy cities. The closest equivalent of the latter is the modern class war.

The ideology of progress and democracy, once free of Hegelian idealism, leads to the separation of thought from action. In order to reunite action with human thought, a radically different type of thinking is necessary. The unity of thought and action is brought about, not through a new rational ideology, but through myth. It is characteristic of myth–as opposed to other types of thinking–that it obscures distinctions; that is because it is similar to a tale told to children and is incapable of separation of fact from fantasy. In his revolutionary myth of the general strike, then, Sorel sees a modern version which has some of the heroic qualities of Homeric myths. But he emphasizes both the vagueness and the psychological nature of the myth which he defines as a group of images, which by intuition

---

[57] See Irving Louis Horowitz, *Radicalism and the Revolt Against Reason*, for an analysis of Bergson's influence on Sorel.

[58] Georges Sorel, "Essai sur la philosophie de Proudhon," in *Revue Philosophique*, XXXIII (1892), XXXIV (1892), cited in James H. Meisel, *The Genesis of Georges Sorel* (Ann Arbor, 1951), p. 96. See also Neal Wood, "Some Reflections on Sorel and Machiavelli," in *Political Science Quarterly*, LXXXIII, no. 1, March 1968, pp. 79–80.

alone and before any considered analysis has been made, is "capable of evoking, as an undivided whole, the mass of sentiments which correspond to different manifestations of war taken by socialism against modern society." All logicality and rationality have been set aside and replaced by what we would likely call "impulses." "It is the myth in its entirety which is alone important."[59]

To Sorel, myths cannot be interpreted as being similar to ideology. Ideology is essentially a pejorative term. Sorel views it as a defense mechanism which, once exposed, is destined to fall by being revealed as false consciousness when it becomes surpassed by historical events. But Sorel's myth is the answer to the problem of ideology. The myth is indestructible because by virtue of its own vagueness and its own nonrational composition it can change and refine itself in accordance with practical experience. Ideologies are most likely to be surpassed, precisely because their rational characteristics give them a fixed quality which myths do not possess. It is for this reason that Sorel shares Marx's hostility to Utopias and cites Marx in saying that he who draws a blueprint for the future is a reactionary.

But we may raise the interesting question here of whether Sorel, despite his departures from the Marxian notion of ideology, is not contributing further to the denigration of philosophy. Instead of speaking of a rebirth of philosophy and of reason apart from "history," he offers us myths which become further integrated into practical experience and which constitute not "true reason" but impulse. It is Sorel's view of mythology that stands at the core of the accusations leveled against him as a "fascist." As I have stated at the outset of this introduction, such accusations are fruitless: both fascism and Sorel must stand on their own merits, and little can be accomplished by associating one with the other.

The kind of regime actually envisioned by Sorel at the time in which he wrote the *Illusions of Progress* (1908) is a regime of producers bound together in their place of work. In the context of their place of work, Sorel respects the idea of a purely technical and economic progress. It is during periods of economic progress, not times of stagnation and decline, that transformations to the new order of things should occur. It is during these times that people best ap-

---

[59] *Reflections*, pp. 126–127.

preciate the artistic basis of technology on the factory floor. Then the productive arts would become infused with the same qualities of mystery and myth which political and religious movements possessed in earlier times. In this same vein, Sorel calls production "the most mysterious form of human activity."[60]

Sorel has an extremely pragmatic view of the world. He insists that by accepting the idea of the general strike, although we know it is a myth, we are proceeding exactly as a physicist does who has complete confidence in his science, although the future will look upon it as antiquated. "It is we who really possess the scientific spirit, while our critics have lost touch with modern science."[61]

Sorel's equation of science and art—the "social poetry" of the general strike—is justified by the idea that both dislike reproducing accepted types and being dominated by the external standards artificially imposed by liberal rationalists. The progressives of liberal rationalism are not really progressives. Constant dynamic improvement in a workshop or in society is only possible if the models of production or of society imposed from above by bureaucratic or scientific "experts" in the social and managerial sciences are thrown aside in favor of the new mythology. "Constant improvement in quality and quantity will be thus assured in a workshop of this kind."[62] It is interesting that a thinker who sets out to debunk the modern idea of progress should conclude the main sections of his two most important works with an affirmation of the material progress of production. It is this constant innovation in the field of production or in everyday experience, carried on *within* the regime of producers, that constitutes Sorel's version of progress. In this sense, Sorel's idea of true progress is almost as necessary to his perspective as the general idea of progress was necessary to the *philosophes*. In one way, Sorel represents the idea of progress run amuck. Much of his work—even after the syndicalist period of his writings—consists in the anguished protests of a progressive who has been betrayed and who places the blame on the men of his time rather than on "history," on the lack of sufficient will to control one's environment and not on "unfavorable social conditions." Sorel's desire to control this environment is certainly an idea he shares with modern liberal-

---

[60] *Ibid.*, p. 148, and *Illusions* below, p. 156.
[61] *Ibid.*, p. 150.
[62] *Ibid.*, p. 242, and *Illusions* below, p. 156.

ism. The trouble with the latter, according to Sorel, is that it has lost its will to do so. Sorel would give the social movement a revived moral basis by showing that the liberal idea of progress is really not identical with virtue; virtue belongs only to those who act.

J. S.

Riverside, California

Preface to the First French Edition

In describing the illusions of progress, I have sought to follow the advice Marx gave to all who, in studying the history of ideas, would like to delve into the most basic sources attainable by a knowledge founded on reason.

The indifference professional historians have so generally shown for Marxian historical methods must be explained for the most part by the tastes of the public, whose patronage assures them fame, academic honors, and fortune. The public, more "enlightened" than studious, detests nothing so much as efforts that upset its habitual tranquility. These people like to read and improve their minds, but on the condition that this endeavor will not cause any great strain. They demand that their authors serve them up precise distinctions, easily applied principles, and dissertations of at least seeming clarity. It is of little consequence to them that these Cartesian qualities are found only in utterly superficial historical works, for this reading public contents itself with superficiality precisely because of these Cartesian qualities.

When we proceed to an analysis that probes history the least bit in depth, we perceive that things present an impossible complexity, that the intellect is unable to analyze or describe them without producing insoluble contradictions. It is better that reality remain protected by a vagueness that philosophy will respect if it wishes to avoid the pitfalls of charlatanism, lies, or romanticism. One of the great advantages of the Marxist method (when it is well understood) is that it respects this fundamental mystery, which a shallow approach to history claims to clarify.

Unfortunately, the Marxist methods are more often talked about than truly known. They have almost always been defined in expressions difficult to understand. We know of a scant few examples of their actual application. Ten years ago the Italian professor Antonio Labriola, who made very laudable efforts to introduce Marxist

ideas into Italian university culture, announced that he would forthwith publish historical studies conducted according to the principles
he championed. He did not wish, he said, "to imitate the instructor
who taught swimming from the shore by means of the definition of
swimming."[1] He died without fulfilling his promise.

It seems to me the commentators on Marx were on the wrong
path when they believed they had found the classic expression of
their master's doctrine in the preface he wrote in 1859 for the
Critique of Political Economy. This renowned text does not aim to
furnish the rules for studying a particular period in history. It deals
rather with the succession of civilizations; thus, the word "class" is
not even mentioned. The phrases that describe the role of economics
are extremely obscure, partially symbolic, and, consequently, very
difficult to interpret. Thus we need not be astonished that many
liberties have been taken with this preface, which so many men
cite without ever having studied it seriously.

Enrico Ferri, who is not only the leader of the Italian Socialist
Party, but who claims to be a philosopher and a scholar, has told us
that Marx sums up and completes with his economic determinism
the "two one-sided and therefore incomplete, although positive and
scientific, explanations" that had previously been given of history:
Montesquieu, Buckle, and Metschnikoff had proposed an environ-
mental determinism, whereas the ethnologists had proposed an an-
thropological determinism. Here is Ferri's formulation of the new
doctrine: "Economic conditions, which are the result of ethnic
energies and aptitudes acting in a given natural environment, are
the determining basis of every moral, legal, and political manifestation of human life, both individual and social."[2] This remarkable
jumble, composed of nonsense, absurdities, and misconceptions,[3]
constitutes one of the main works of that science Italian politicians
call "positive science." The author was so pleased with his explanation of Marxism that, several years later, he felt the urge to boast

---

[1] Antonio Labriola, *Essais sur la conception matérialiste de l'histoire* ("Essays on
the Materialist Conception of History"), 1st ed., p. 272.
[2] Enrico Ferri, *Socialisme et science positive* ("Socialism and Positive Science"),
p. 152.
[3] It is somewhat absurd to say that individual life is determined by the causes
that are set forth here and that are not in the least individual. When Marx had
occasion to speak of economics as a foundation on which ideologies rest, he used
terms (*Basis* and *Grundlage*) that effectively ruled out the idea that this foundation
was active.

of having discovered these wonderful things all by himself, whereas in letters that were not yet known Engels gave a much broader interpretation to historical materialism than had been given for many years.[4]

I do not wish to appear to be comparing Enrico Ferri and Antonio Labriola, but it does not seem to me that the latter succeeded in extracting from Marx rules capable of guiding historians. He was able to give only a general idea of Marxist conceptions by combining several paraphrases of the 1859 preface with several ideas drawn from other writings. At the time when Labriola was publishing his *Essays on the Materialist Conception of History*, no one had yet made the observation that great precautions must be taken in combining the diverse theses of Marx: according to the questions with which he dealt, Marx considered history under varied aspects, so that there are several Marxian historical systems. And there is no better way of betraying Marxism than by wishing to combine statements that have value only when they are placed in the particular system in which they figure.

It is from the *Communist Manifesto* that I will take the text that, in my opinion, best applies to the type of research undertaken here: "Does it require deep insight to understand that man's ideas, concrete observations, and abstract conceptions (*Vorstellungen, Anschauungen und Begriffe*)—in a word, man's consciousness (*Bewusstsein*)—changes (*sich aendert*) with every change in the conditions of his material existence, in his social relations, and in his life in society (*Lebensverhaeltnissen, gesellschaftlichen Beziehungen, gesellshaftlichen Dasein*)? What else does the history of ideas (*Ideen*) prove, if not that intellectual activity changes (*sich ungestaltet*) as material activity changes? The ruling ideas (*herrschenden Ideen*) of each age have ever been the ideas of its ruling class."[5]

The theory of progress was accepted as a dogma at the time in history when the bourgeoisie was the dominating class, and it thus should be regarded as a bourgeois doctrine. Consequently, the

---

[4] Enrico Ferri, *Evolution économique et évolution sociale* ("Social and Economic Development"), p. 27. Lecture given in Paris, January 19, 1900.

[5] *Communist Manifesto*, p. 51. Whatever the merit of this translation, it is nevertheless necessary to recall the German expressions that have a technical meaning (originating from the Hegelian school) which are not easily translated.

Marxist historian should find out how this doctrine depends on the conditions under which the formation, rise, and triumph of the bourgeoisie are observed. Only when we examine this whole great social adventure can we truly understand the place the idea of progress occupies in the philosophy of history.

This conception of the history of social classes provides a great contrast to ideas almost universally accepted today. Everyone readily agrees that a great diversity exists in our societies, that professions, levels of wealth, and family traditions produce vast differences in the ways of thinking of our contemporaries. Many observers have shown this in great detail. Proudhon could even write, without, however, accepting the Marxist notion of class,[6] that a great modern nation contains a "representation of every stage of human development"; that primitive times are represented by "a multitude of poor and ignorant, whose misery produces unceasing crime"; that a second stage of civilization can be observed in a "middle class composed of laborers, artisans, and shopkeepers"; and that an "elite, formed by magistrates, civil servants, teachers, writers, and artists, marks the most advanced stage of the species." And yet, after having so strongly pointed out the contradictions present in the world, he is unable to abandon the notion of a general will. He says, "ask these various interests, these semibarbarian instincts, these ingrained habits, and these lofty aspirations what their intimate thoughts are. Classify all the views in accordance with the natural progression of groups; then you will divine a general formulation, which (while embracing contrary terms), expressing the general tendency and being the will of no one, will comprise the social contract and the law."

It seems to me that, in thus posing the problem of the general will in a perfectly clear way, Proudhon reduces to an absurdity the unitary dogma that democracy constantly opposes to the doctrine of the class struggle. Indeed, it would be utterly impossible to proceed

---

[6] From this fact some very great difficulties result in Proudhon's interpretation; the reader expects to see the Marxian doctrine of classes appear at any moment and is disappointed. I believe Proudhon was prevented from following Marx's path because of his moral preoccupations: he regarded conjugal fidelity as being the most important element of ethics. He did not see that this fidelity was, generally speaking, dependent on class conditions. As he was, above all, a great moralist, he had to conclude from this independence that all ideologies are formations of the mind, on which the existence of classes exercises only a secondary influence.

to construct the synthesis he asks for. When the historian speaks of a general tendency, he does not deduce it from its constituent elements but constructs it by means of the results revealed in the course of history. Proudhon himself seems to agree that it happens in this manner, for he wrote immediately after the passage quoted above: "It is thus that general civilization evolved, under the guise of conflicts, revolutions, and wars, unbeknownst to the legislators and statesmen."[7] The synthesis thus came about outside of the realm of reasoned thought.

We can easily understand that social movements presuppose an enormous number of negotiations. The accounts of contemporaries allow recognition of many calculations of prudence, many compromises, and many arbitrations imposed on the parties by groups capable of exercising a decisive action. The historian could not pretend to follow these moves in all their detail. Moreover, the philosopher or statesman could not detect them before they revealed themselves through their results.

What the historian strives the most to know and what, besides, is the easiest to know is the ideology of the victors. It depends on all the historical adventures just discussed. It depends in different ways on the instincts, habits, and aspirations of the dominant class. It also has many connections with the social conditions of the other social classes. The ties that can be observed between the prevailing ideology and all its points of connection cannot be completely defined; as a result, to speak of historical determinism is nothing but charlatanism and puerility. The most we can hope to do is shed a little light on the paths historians ought to follow to direct their course toward the source of things.

Democracy looks upon Marxist ideas with horror, because democracy is always seeking unity. Having inherited the ancien régime's admiration for the state, it thinks that the role of the historian is limited to explaining governmental actions by means of ideas predominating in the ruling classes.

We can even say that democracy has perfected the unitary theory. In times past, it was thought that in a perfectly functioning monarchy no discordant voice had the right to be raised against the

---

[7] Pierre-Joseph Proudhon, *Philosophie du progrès* ("Philosophy of Progress"), p. 99.

ruling prince. Nowadays it is declared that each citizen has willed (at least by indirect means) everything that is demanded of him. Therefore, acts of government are supposed to reflect the general will, in which each one of us is thought to participate. This general will is possible because the thoughts of men are, in each period of history, submerged by certain ideas that exist in the pure state in the minds of those who are perfectly enlightened—free of traditional prejudices and disinterested enough to obey the voice of reason. Before these ideas, which no one has and in which everyone is supposed to share, the real causes of human acts are obscured—causes that can be grasped, at least in general, in the social classes. To consider dominant ideas without considering social classes constitutes something as fantastic as was the idea of an abstract man, of whom Joseph de Maistre declared that he had never met an example, and for whom, nevertheless, the legislators of the revolution claimed to have made their laws. We know now that this abstract man was not a completely imaginary figure. He had been invented in the theories of natural law in order to replace the man of the third estate. Just as historical criticism has reestablished real people, it should likewise reestablish real ideas; that is, it should return to the consideration of social class.

Democracy is succeeding in throwing minds into a state of confusion, preventing many intelligent people from seeing things as they really are, because democracy is served by apologists who are clever in the art of beclouding questions. This is due to cunning language, smooth sophistry, and a great array of scientific declamations. It is above all of democratic times that it can be said that humanity is governed by the magical power of impressive words rather than by ideas, by slogans rather than by reason, and by dogmas whose origins no one thinks of looking into rather than by doctrines founded on observation.

It is my opinion that it would be well to submit one of these charlatan dogmas (that is, the idea of progress) to an analysis conducted according to that method which alone is able to guarantee us against all deception; that is, an analysis founded on a historical investigation of the relationships among the classes. Having in this way formulated several observations (which I consider worthwhile) on bourgeois ideology, I have taken the liberty to submit them to the public. More than once, I have played truant; whenever

I have found the opportunity of clarifying the origin, meaning, or value of a modern idea, I have believed myself justified in digressing on that point. Several of these digressions will most surely be forgiven me without difficulty, because they could inspire more than one intellect gifted with curiosity to make new and more profound applications of Marxist methods. I intend actually to show, rather than merely to inform, how it is possible to work toward a goal of greater truth.

I first published these studies on progress in the *Mouvement socialiste* (August–December, 1906). I was then able to perceive that my lack of respect for the great men whom the university praises was capable of offending many readers. In reexamining my text carefully and in some places entirely rewriting it, I might have modified the tone of my discussion if I had been trying to please a frivolous public. Instead, I have preserved the tone I originally adopted, not to imitate the harshness of Marx's polemics anymore than to attract attention by intemperance of language, but because I have found upon reflection that, of all the illusions that the bourgeoisie seeks to instill, the most absurd is the cult it seeks to impose on us—the cult of lay saints who are definitely not very praiseworthy.

Among the writers who claim to be the official representatives of French democracy, there are not a few admirers of Auguste Comte. What they admire above all else in him is the man who wanted to restore respect in France by means of his *neofetishist* religion. Few people nowadays are naive enough to assume that prayers, sacraments, and positivist sermons are able to have a great influence on people, but every effort is made to develop veneration for the more or less renowned men whom democracy has adopted as its heroes. Many hope that if the masses come to accept the cult of these so-called representatives of mankind, they will perhaps also have some respect for the orators who make a profession of disseminating the cult—all the more so as there is not such a great gap between the new saints and their priests. Thus, it is their own interests that our democrats pursue when they cultivate the glories of the eighteenth century with so much solicitude. Reestablishing historical truth, therefore, is not only a question of conscience but also a question of immediate practical interest.

January 1908

Preface to the Second French Edition

In this second edition, I have made many improvements of detail. I hope I have succeeded in making perfectly clear, theses that seemed to present difficulties to some people. I have added an appendix on the notions of greatness and decline, which, in my opinion, have been excessively neglected by our contemporaries.

July 1910

Contents

xlix

Contents

First Ideologies of Progress

I. *The dispute between the ancients and the moderns. The question of good models in religion and literature. The society people against Boileau. The triumph of good language technicians.*

II. *Morals at the end of the seventeenth century. The philosophy of Fontenelle. The political origin of the ideas on nature. Pascal versus superficial rationalism. Cartesianism and society people.*

III. *The idea of a pedagogy of humanity. The popularizers. Condorcet conceives of popular education on an aristocratic model; his illusions with regard to the results of education.*

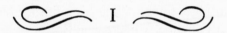 I

Historians have traced back the question of the doctrine of progress to the dispute between the ancient and modern writers, which caused so much furor at the end of the seventeenth century. It might seem very odd to us today that such a purely literary conflict could produce such consequences, for nowadays we would hardly be willing to admit that artistic progress can exist at all.

Nothing appears stranger to us today than the manifestations of bad taste on the part of men like Perrault, who systematically ranked his contemporaries above the great men of antiquity or the Renaissance—who preferred Lebrun to Raphael, for example. At first sight we might be led to believe that he was acting only in the silly role of official cultural overseer. Indeed, Perrault's first treatise, read to the *Académie* in 1687, was called *The Century of Louis the Great.* Brunetière very justly said of it: "It must be admitted that Boileau, when *he* praised the prince, used another style and that, lacking an

independent mind (to which no one then had pretensions), a surer
taste, inspired by the ancients perhaps, had at least preserved *him*
from such platitudes in his adulation."[1]

But the discussion soon took on a more general aspect following
the intervention of Fontenelle; and Perrault, after having revealed
his ideas in verse form, developed in three volumes of prose (1688,
1692, 1697) the reasons the modern writers should be preferable to
the ancients.

In order to understand this matter thoroughly, we should note
that the men of the seventeenth century were very far from having
the pious admiration for their great contemporaries that posterity
has attributed to them. Bossuet himself, whom we are so fond of
representing as the archtype of the period, was not at all appreciated
at his true value, even by the king. His audience thought he made
insufficient display of impressive language, fine rhetoric, and affectation (unlike Fléchier), or rather, that he knew not how to arouse
curiosity sufficiently (unlike Bourdaloue) by those portrayals
sought by every aristocratic society, driven as it is by scandal
mongering.[2]

We might believe that Boileau was a universally respected master
if we limited ourselves to examining his influence on works of the
highest order. La Fontaine, Molière, and Racine owe a great deal to
him, according to Brunetière.[3] But we must not judge a century only
by the personalities who have outlived it, for these are more often in
contradiction with the main trends of the time. They have become
immortals especially because of this contradiction.

We imagine rather readily that Boileau's contemporaries would
have been happy to be liberated by him from the yoke of Chapelain:

---

[1] Ferdinand Brunetière, *Evolution des genres dans l'histoire de la littérature*
("Development of Genres in the History of Literature"), 3d ed., p. 116. I will
make extensive use of Brunetière's works, which seem to me to be the most accurate
guide to knowledge of the classical centuries. Several people have reproached me
for having accepted the testimony of a militant proclerical with too much confidence. But I should point out that, until the end of 1894, Brunetière hardly favored
the church. Victor Giraud said: "Under the combined influence of Schopenhauer,
Darwin, and Comte, he then firmly believed that a strictly positivist morality would
henceforth be sufficient in itself. It might even replace the vanished or lapsed
religions to advantage" (*ibid*, pp. 26–27). I have used only the works Brunetière
completed before his visit to the Vatican.

[2] Ferdinand Brunetière, *Etudes critiques sur l'histoire de la littérature française*
(*Manual of the History of French Literature*, trans. R. Devechet), 6th ser., pp.
205–206.

[3] *Ibid.*, pp. 164–165.

"Until Boileau's *Satires*, which only appeared for the first time in 1665, people yawned over *La Pucelle*, but they hid their yawns. Furthermore, while everyone was yawning over it, they proclaimed that the work was perfectly beautiful."[4] Chapelain had been regarded as being the uncontested master of French letters for so long that many cultivated people were upset at the thought of his being vilified by a little parvenu, and they waited for a favorable opportunity to wage war on the critic. Indeed, Brunetière makes the important observation that Boileau was a representative of bourgeois thought as opposed to "the thinking of the salons and literary cliques."[5] Moreover, it was not without difficulty that Boileau entered the *Académie*, the citadel of Chapelain's friends.[6]

French taste has remained faithful to Boileau's principles. Like him, we value good sense, clarity, and natural language above all else. We dread excesses of imagination, and we appreciate a style that holds to a middle road between studied refinement and popular speech. Foreigners were struck with such a great admiration for this literature that, for a long time, they did their utmost to discipline their genius according to the French rules.[7]

In order to give an exact account of the reasons that provoked the slightly superstitious respect Boileau had for the ancients, we must refer back to the method Le Play advised us to follow in order to create a science that would be able to enlighten men concerned with reforming our contemporary societies.

Le Play had the deepest contempt for all abstract discussions relating to the principles of government. He wanted to undertake inquiries with a view to determining which nations were the prosperous ones and, for each of these nations, what the principles were which assured its greatness in the course of history. He wanted the French to introduce into their own country "those excellent models" —which they were thus to succeed in discovering—for the makeup of the family, the organization of labor, and the political hierarchy. Our minds are constructed in such a way that we reason much more by analogy than by syllogisms. We understand a principle clearly only after having been able to evoke a very clear idea of the

---

[4] Brunetière, *Evolution des genres*, p. 79.
[5] *Ibid.*, p. 92.
[6] H. Rigault, *Histoire de la querelle des anciens et des modernes* ("History of the Dispute Between the Ancients and Moderns"), p. 151.
[7] Brunetière, *Etudes critiques*, 6th ser., pp. 189–190.

system to which we try to give a scholarly definition. Always, we tend to admit that we can benefit by reproducing in our own country things which exist in a foreign country that has recently obtained, for whatever cause, great prestige in the world. This is why we have adopted so many institutions from England, America, and, more recently, Germany.

The men of the Renaissance and the Reformation had already proceeded in this way; they had acquired such a great familiarity with ancient literature that they believed themselves to possess a knowledge based on experience. The former studied Greek customs, and the latter applied themselves to apostolic customs. They asked their contemporaries to follow them in a restoration of the past. Ronsard thought it no more difficult to revive the Hellenic spirit than Calvin did to become a disciple of St. Paul.[8] The defeat of these two attempts proved nothing against the principle, for one could ask if the defeat did not arise from an overzealousness of the reformers. Excellent as models are, they are never anything but models, which must be made use of artfully.

The Jansenists acquired a great popularity, which astonished more than one author but which is explained quite easily when we refer to the above observations. The Jansenists believed in the possibility of returning as far back as St. Augustine, suppressing all of the foolishness and impurity that, in their severe judgment, had been introduced by the savants of the Dark Ages and by courtier casuists. Having been nourished completely by the classical traditions, St. Augustine seemed more accessible than the first disciples of Christ. The immense success of Pascal's *Provinciales* (1656–1657) seemed to prove that the public was disposed to accept such an Augustinian direction. According to Brunetière, La Fontaine and Molière were the only notable writers who completely avoided this influence. This influence was noticeable in the Jesuit Bourdaloue, many of whose sermons could have been signed by Port-Royal.[9]

---

[8] Brunetière, *Etudes critiques*, 4th ser., 3d ed., p. 170.

[9] Brunetière, *Etudes critiques*, pp. 164–165. Sainte-Beuve said that Bourdaloue, in practice, made considerable use of "maxims of penitence reestablished by Port-Royal," and that his sermons fully satisfied the friends of the Jansenists (*Port-Royal*, II, 155–156); elsewhere, speaking of the sermon on the small number of elect, he wrote, "M. de Saint-Cyran was saying exactly that to St. Vincent de Paul, who was, however, apparently shocked, as by a blow to the effectiveness of the sacraments" (p. 190).

Why was an intelligent literary reform unable to succeed at the same time, it seems, that the moral reform had succeeded? In both cases, it was a matter of fighting Spanish and Italian infiltration. French writers had too much admiration for the cavalier Marin, who excelled in affected conversation—"the author of that *Adonis* Chapelain himself had introduced with praises in a memorable preface"—and for Gongora, "whose name had become synonymous with exaggeration and obfuscation."[10] Boileau wanted to impose naturalness and good sense on his contemporaries who had been deluded by the aforesaid models; he proposed to them the "excellent models" offered by ancient literature. It could be said that Boileau adopted an idea of Ronsard's and that he was of the same thinking as the "reformers" of the Pléiade, whom he nevertheless judged cruelly.[11] He revived the work of his predecessors, however, just as Port-Royal revived Calvin, while believing that he was doing something entirely different from these predecessors; he thus made reform acceptable to the French.

All the great writers of the seventeenth century were on Boileau's side when the quarrel between the ancients and moderns broke out, whereas Perrault was an indefatigable defender of the bad authors whom Boileau devastated: Chapelain, Cotin, Saint-Amant. Boileau's aesthetics hampered the mediocre writers, who were used to great liberty of style, far too much to be acceptable to them.[12] It is a bit surprising to find a man as learned as Bayle among the partisans of the moderns; but we must not forget that Bayle lacked taste, that he retained all the faults of the preceding century, and that he was indifferent to the literary value of the books that he read.[13] It is wrong to explain his attitude as hostility towards an aesthetic policy patronized by Louis XIV.[14]

Society people naturally supported the moderns for reasons that still constitute the basis of all of the thinking of men of this type. "These sophisticated judges have an instinctive horror for anything

---

[10] Brunetière, *Evolution des genres*, p. 88.
[11] Brunetière, *Evolution des genres*, pp. 45–46, 104.
[12] Brunetière, *Etudes critiques*, 5th ser., p. 190.
[13] *Ibid.*, pp. 121–132. It is particularly curious that Bayle did not understand the degree to which ribaldry in literature had become unpleasant for his own contemporaries.
[14] H. Rigault, *Histoire de la querelle*, p. 233.

serious. Art is only a diversion for them."[15] Almost all of the women sided with Perrault's party; Boileau's tenth satire was perhaps provoked by the bad humor brought on by their opposition to him. On the other hand, his opponent hailed these lenient judges enthusiastically. According to Brunetière, women had a very adverse influence on our literature in discouraging it from treating the truly grave questions of life with the necessary seriousness.[16]

In distributing these certificates of immortality with such generosity, Perrault could not help but greatly increase the number of his friends. Here is an example of his literary pronouncements:[17]

> How they will be cherished by future races,
> The gallant Sarrazins and the tender Voitures,
> The naive Molières, the Rotrous, the Tristans,
> And a hundred others still—delights of their times!

It is thus not surprising that Perrault had on his side the great literary gazettes and the great mass of men who had pretensions to literary taste. The *Journal de Trévoux* furnishes us with the most valuable information on the tendencies of the times. The Jesuits had no reason to be pleasant to Perrault, whose brother, a Sorbonne professor, had supported Arnauld. Boileau made great efforts to obtain the good graces of the influential Jesuits, but he was unable to win them for his cause.[18] We would suppose, however, that men who profess humanism would favor the ancients, but every time the Jesuits had to take some sort of position in France, they were always on the side of mediocrity, because they were thereby assured of having on their side the greatest number of people. Thus they defended moral mediocrity against the Jansenists. Indeed, the Jesuits have often been criticized for having popularized mediocrity in the realm of religion. Apparently, their highly extolled education has resulted in developing a mediocre character in their students. Their schools, which have been renowned as diploma mills, seek after scientific mediocrity; in the seventeenth century they wished to defend literary mediocrity against Boileau.

---

15 Brunetière, *Evolution des genres*, p. 127.

16 *Ibid.*, p. 128. However, Madame de Sévigné, the Abbess of Fontevrault, Madame de Longueville, and the Princess of Conti were among the defenders of the ancients (H. Rigault, *Histoire de la querelle*, pp. 242–243, 248, 259).

17 H. Rigault, *op. cit.*, p. 146.

18 H. Rigault, *Histoire de la querelle*, pp. 229, 231.

Boileau's defeat was thus complete. "All around him he could see a rebirth of literary affectation, while in the coteries, transformed into salons, the Fontenelles and Lamottes returned to the traditions of the Balzacs and Voitures. Several years later, it would be something else again when the Marquise de Lambert and, after her, Madame de Tencin, would become powerful. The first years of the eighteenth century would recall the first years of the seventeenth."[19] According to Fontenelle, Madame de Tencin, and the Abbé Trublet, Lamotte was one of France's finest geniuses. Here is one example of the philosophico-scientific poetry by Lamotte which Fontenelle admired:[20]

> The substance of this void
> Within this supposed body
> Pours like a fluid;
> It is but a plenum in disguise.

Boileau's revenge was complete, but only in our times and, moreover, not without difficulty, for the Romanticists attacked him violently and even tried to rehabilitate some of his victims. Proudhon, on the contrary, could not contain his admiration for Boileau, seduced as he was "by the integrity of his reason."[21] I believe Boileau's vindication in our time can be explained by causes that are dependent on the style of the literature rather than the content of its thought.

A modern revolution has established a fundamental schism between two groups of writers. One prides itself on having become "good literary craftsmen"; its members have trained themselves by a long apprenticeship and have perfected their style remarkably. The other group has continued to churn out works according to the tastes of the day. Brunetière defines the style of an author very successfully as the "type of control exerted by talent over the material of the art of writing," and he adds: "All of the great literary revolutions are revolutions of language. Here in France a close scrutiny of the history of our literature shows us that it is the lan-

---

[19] Brunetière, *Evolution des genres*, pp. 109–110.

[20] H. Rigault, *Histoire de la querelle*, pp. 161, 336.

[21] Pierre-Joseph Proudhon, *De la Justice dans la Révolution et dans l'Eglise* ("On Justice in the Revolution and in the Church"), III, 390. Proudhon said that Boileau's glory reappears "in proportion as the new generation rids itself of the romanticist mantle" (IV, 125).

guage first and foremost which all the innovators have revolutionized: Ronsard, Malherbe, Boileau, Rousseau, Chateaubriand, and
Victor Hugo."[22] Contemporary language has become all the more
difficult to handle as it has abandoned vague expressions to invoke
specific images.

Our contemporary masters of style are the true successors of
Boileau, who was so long held in scorn. Brunetière says: "In this
bourgeois there is an artist, a remarkable technician, and a scrupu-
lous theorist of his art. . . . If anyone felt the value of form in poetry,
it was Boileau. . . . This throws light on the surprising esteem Boileau
always professed for Voiture. He waited for his own death to proclaim Voiture's puns insipid in his *Satire sur l'Equivoque*; mean-
while, he was grateful to Voiture for at least having fashioned his
works meticulously."[23]

The men who work at their writing with patient labor address
themselves voluntarily to a limited public. The others write for
cabarets and newspapers. There now exist two well-distinguished
publics and two types of literature that hardly ever converge. Presently it is difficult to understand the great esteem of our fathers
for Béranger, who was halfway between Parny and the cabaret
singers. The middle position he occupied no longer corresponds to
any of our present literary habits.[24] Today we want someone to be
either a poet preoccupied with his art or an arranger of vulgar re-
frains for *l'Eldorado*. Béranger's masters of the eighteenth century
are as forgotten as he is because they also were mediocre stylists.

The consequences of this transformation on modern thought

---

22 Brunetière, *Etudes critiques*, 2d ser., 5th ed., p. 269. He believes that the same
reasoning could be used for painting and that, in general, "the greatest revolutions
in the history of art are revolutions in the very material of art"; notably, "it is the
technique and perhaps only the technique that Raphael changed" in passing from
one style to another during his career.

23 Brunetière, *Evolution des genres*, pp. 105–108. It is known that the *Satire sur
l'Equivoque* was published only after Boileau's death.

24 "With regard to style and poetic usage, he is simply a disciple of Voltaire and
Parny. No individual characteristic distinguishes him except, perhaps, overworked
and obscure verse. His pleasantries and jokes are generally derived from two suspect
sources: impiety and obscenity. . . . Béranger is serious, not at all naive, often
strained and tender, but never lightheaded" (Proudhon, *De la Justice*, IV, 171).
According to Renan, Béranger's poetry most often represents the exaggerations
of a schoolboy and remains on the "edge of vulgarity" (*Questions contemporaines*
["Contemporary Questions"], pp. 465, 473).

were quite considerable. The little pamphlets Voltaire wrote against Christianity went out of fashion; little by little we descended from the Encyclopedists to Monsieur Homais and the editors of the *Lanterne*, while the literature devoted to questions of religious history became very serious and almost austere. The immense success of Renan's first works resulted from his knowing how to find the serious tone that is, according to our present ideas, suited to the subject.[25] We tend to believe that the spirit of Voltaire disappeared on the day that the bourgeoisie believed it was necessary for its interests to follow the church blindly. This is an ideological and highly superficial explanation. The Voltairian spirit disappeared when a literary revolution made Voltaire's methods ridiculous. We find few examples as remarkable as this for showing the influence style exercises over thought.

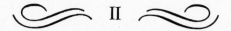

II

The argument between the ancient and modern writers at the end of the seventeenth century had consequences that infinitely surpassed the realm of art. French society, proud of its new conditions of existence and persuaded that it had reached or even surpassed the most famous periods celebrated by historians, thought it no longer had to go and seek models in other countries. It was French society that would henceforth serve as the model to all civilized men; it was French taste alone that would decide the value of intellectual works. In all things, French society meant to revel in the fruits of its own civilization without being criticized by anyone.

At the end of the seventeenth century, the religious questions that had previously impassioned the country left everyone indifferent, to the point where Bossuet and Fénelon preserved from publication important controversial works. Massillon's sermons were concerned only with morality.[26] It has often been thought that the

---

[25] One wonders if Renan was not inspired a great deal by Rousseau, who speaks of Christianity in such a different way from his contemporaries and whose style is so prodigiously refined.

[26] Brunetière, *Etudes critiques*, 5th ser., pp. 162–163. Brunetière calls even this morality a completely lay morality.

persecutions against the Jansenists and the useless quarrels of quietism had an influence on this decline of religious ideas.[27] I do not believe this is a satisfactory explanation.

In the last fifteen years of the seventeenth century, life was very merry. Formerly Jansenism had furnished a means of raising problems of Christian destiny, of combatting the solutions brought forth by the casuists, who preached easy religion, and of justifying an austere discipline.[28] Now, people wanted largely to profit from the well-being permitted by the new era, and, henceforth, Jansenism was found to be quite tiresome. The number of its apologists in good society diminished, and Port-Royal was abandoned to the furor of its enemies. Thus I do not believe that we should attribute the lowering of the moral level to the persecutions against the Jansenists; I believe rather that we may attribute the persecutions against the Jansenists to the lowering of the moral level. There remained, however, several families that preserved the old ways and affected an outdated morality. They were all the more haughty as they were more isolated. In these families, Jansenism remained as an often fanatic protest.

At that time everyone was shocked by the disintegration of feminine morality and also by the indulgence with which good society treated the emancipated women. "Mademoiselle de la Force [who attracted attention as the mistress of the actor, Baron] was on familiar terms with the Princesses of Conti as well as with the Vendômes."[29] In a letter dated November 19, 1696, Dubos said to Bayle that women no longer wanted to have children as their lackeys but rather "the tallest and best-looking young men," and that they no longer had maids but valets.[30]

Boileau had the courage to attack these women, but his satire

---

[27] *Ibid.*, pp. 217–224.

[28] In a word, the moral reforms of Jansenism were not the consequence of its theology; rather, its theology was the consequence of its moral reforms. This appears to me to be Renan's opinion (*Saint Paul*, p. 486; *Nouvelles études d'histoire religieuse* ["New Studies in Religious History"], pp. 472–473). One can understand the importance of this transposition from the point of view of historical materialism.

[29] Brunetière, *Etudes critiques*, 5th ser., p. 210. The king compelled her, however, to live in a convent from 1702 to 1713.

[30] *Ibid.*, pp. 210–211. Dubos indicates that the moral changes had been going on for about ten years. The consumption of brandy had quadrupled, and the passion for gambling had become extraordinary.

caused an enormous scandal. Arnauld, who was in Belgium living with his old ideas, applauded the poet's severity, but his friends warned him that his commendation produced a very bad impression.[31] I suppose that Bossuet passed judgment against Boileau because he sensed the danger of overtly defying the opinion of good society. We know that Bossuet was more than once accused of leniency toward the morals of the great. According to Brunetière, this lenient attitude was due to the fact that Bossuet had only "remained on the fringe of society" and had not lived in it, as Pascal had. "Both in society and in the life of the court, Bossuet always saw only what others let him see or made him see."[32]

It is very remarkable that Bayle preserved from Christianity a pessimistic view of man, so that Brunetière was able to say he had maintained religious morality in the process of de-Christianizing it. According to Bayle, man ought to resist the instincts, an idea that later seemed scandalous. With Fénelon, the idea of the goodness of human nature entered into serious literature.[33] It corresponded so well to the most profound tendencies of the time that an optimistic conception of man soon dominated. We might say that fear of sin, respect for chastity, and pessimism all disappeared at about the same time at the end of the seventeenth century. Thus Christianity vanished from the scene.[34]

This society was not able to do without a philosophy, because it had inherited from preceding generations the habit of reasoning and, in particular, the habit of applying juridical reasoning to all questions. Thus it was that discussions on grace, predestination, and the sacraments could occupy such a preponderant place in French history for half a century. Such a society could not abandon itself to happiness without justifying its conduct; it had to prove that it had the right not to follow the old maxims. For if the society was not able to give this proof, was it not liable to be compared to the son who is in such a hurry to enjoy the paternal inheritance that he

---

[31] H. Rigault, *Histoire de la querelle*, pp. 259–260.
[32] Brunetière, *Etudes critiques*, 6th ser., pp. 202–203. He thinks that "from his ecclesiastical education, Bossuet retained a basic timidity, inexperience, and even clumsiness throughout his life."
[33] Brunetière, *Etudes critiques*, 5th ser., pp. 157–158, 180–181.
[34] On the role of these three concepts, see my *Le Système historique de Renan* ("The Historical System of Renan"; Paris: Marcel Rivière, 1906), pp. 57–61.

devours all resources for the future? Hence, they were very happy
to find able apologists who could solemnly establish that it was all
right to amuse oneself without fear of the consequences:[35] this was
the origin of the doctrine of progress. Fontenelle had the honour of
revealing the possibility of such a philosophy to his contemporaries.

Nobody would have dreamed of disputing the fact that the conditions of life under Louis XIV had become softer for the upper
classes than they had been under the preceding monarch. Henceforth people had the right to ask themselves the following questions:
Could it not be assumed that forces that had produced this improvement of life resulted from the new constitution of societies by a
sequence of events as natural as those found in the physical world? If
these forces continued to operate, would they not have an accelerated momentum in the social world, just as a weight is accelerated
by gravity in the material world? If this is so, why worry about the
fate of new generations, which are destined to have a fate that is
automatically superior to ours? Brunetière has correctly observed
that the idea of the stability of the laws of nature is an element in
the theory of progress.[36] We should determine, however, whether
this idea came from physics or ought to be explained solely by historical reasons. The second hypothesis seems closer to the truth.

The contemporaries of Fontenelle (who popularized the idea of
the stability of the laws of nature) were above all impressed by
seeing to what extent the royal majesty was able to rise above mere
chance in a seemingly definitive way. They were inclined to relate
all social movements to the impetus society received from royal
authority. They, then, must have regarded royal institutions as
being a constant force that added some new amelioration each day
to improvements already acquired. The conception of an acceleration of improvements thus must have seemed to follow in a clear-cut
and necessary way. The law of the acceleration of weights might

---

[35] It is helpful to observe that the need for an apology was all the more obvious
as signs of economic decline were being felt in the same period in which Perrault
wrote *Paralleles* ("Parallels"). The price of land began to decline, and this decline
continued well beyond the reign of Louis XIV (D'Avenel, *Histoire économique
de la propriété, des salaires, des denrées, et de tous les prix en général depuis l'an
1200 jusqu'en l'an 1800* ["Economic History of Property, Salaries, Commodities,
and All General Prices from 1200 to 1800"], I, 387–388).

[36] Brunetière, *Etudes critiques*, 5th ser., pp. 139–240.

conceivably have occurred to Galileo as a consequence of political analogies; in his time, the monarchical power had already become absolute enough for people to see a type of constant force.[37]

According to Brunetière, the idea of progress heavily depended on two important Cartesian theses related to knowledge: knowledge can never be separated from its application, and it is always increasing.[38] It seems, indeed, that we ought immediately to infer limitless progress from such premises as these, but I think it is wrong to attribute to them the scientific scope that a modern writer could give them. In the seventeenth century, they originated from political ideology rather than true science, so that, in measuring their historical importance, we should start by observing the political phenomena.

From the time of Descartes, it was easily seen that the new model of governments, with their concentrated power and their regular administration, were in a position to execute their plans in a most precise way and that they could thus realize a union of theory and practice. Furthermore, the royal power seemed infinite. So many extraordinary changes since the Renaissance had taken place because of the will of the sovereign power, especially in religious matters, that nothing seemed beyond the power of the king. Science could never be lacking to rulers who had affirmed the completeness of their divine right. Science had to grow with the power of those who needed it in order to reign. After the revocation of the Edict of Nantes in 1685, these considerations were much stronger than in Descartes' time. The quarrel between ancients and moderns exploded two years after this great event, which so clearly demonstrated the omnipotence of the crown.

Neither do I agree entirely with Brunetière about the influence of popularization in this matter. According to him, men at the end of the seventeenth century marveled at knowing so many things. Brunetière thought that, instead of occupying themselves with the

---

[37] It is possible that the idea of acceleration, after having gone from politics to physics, forthwith turned around, so the theory of the accelerated fall of bodies contributed to the refinement of the idea of progress. We can observe an analogous phenomenon concerning the hypotheses of evolution; they arose out of the philosophy of history, but they did not make an impression on historians in an imperative way until they took an excursion through the biological sciences.

[38] Brunetière, *Etudes critiques*, 4th ser., p. 122.

care of their consciences as their fathers had done, they preferred science to religion[39] and abandoned Bossuet's point of view for Fontenelle's. In contrast, I consider scientific vulgarization to have had a great, although not direct, influence in the formation of the new philosophy; the taste for popularization helped above all to establish a tight link between the thinking in the salons and Cartesianism. The result was that the literary argument over the ancients and the moderns took on a scope one would not have expected at the beginning—it became a landmark in the history of philosophy. Fontenelle, who was at the same time a literary partisan on the side of the moderns, a very skillful popularizer, and a Cartesian fanatic, could thus strongly influence the development of ideas, a circumstance in peculiar contradiction to his own mediocrity.

In order to understand this question thoroughly we should cast a rapid glance at Cartesianism, looking for the reasons that made it a philosophy of the salons. Here we have a very remarkable example of the adoption of an ideology by a class that has found in it certain formulas to express its class propensities. There are few phenomena more important than such adoptions for the true philosopher who studies such doctrines from the point of view of historical materialism. The creator of a system operates like an artist who interprets everything around him with extreme freedom. If this system has a sufficient number of links with current ideas, it can endure and become the favorite doctrine of a later generation, which will find in it something entirely different from that which pleased its contemporaries. It is on this adoption that the definitive judgment of history rests. Often this judgment upsets the order of values the first followers had attributed to the various parts of the doctrine; it can bring to the fore what they had regarded as secondary.

Descartes' reign began rather late, and Brunetière even says that "the Cartesian influence on the seventeenth century is one of the inventions, one of the errors with which Victor Cousin infested the history of French literature."[40] For a long time, the great theologians did not even seem to have understood what role the Cartesian philosophy would play. They saw that the unbelieving men of the world (who were called *freethinkers*) were not receptive to the arguments

---

[39] Brunetière, *Etudes critiques*, 5th ser., p. 225.
[40] Brunetière, *Etudes critiques*, 5th ser., p. 46.

First Ideologies of Progress

used by the scholastics to prove the existence of God and the immortality of the soul. They thought that the Cartesian explanations would have more success. Bossuet expressed this point of view in his letter of May 21, 1687, to a disciple of Malebranche and in one of May 18, 1689, to Huet.[41] Once the fundamental principles were accepted, the theologians thought that the general body of religion did not present any great difficulties.

It is likely that Pascal wrote the *Pensées* against the Cartesians.[42] He was not a professional theologian and, therefore, had no confidence in scholastic proofs, but he did not appreciate Descartes' theories any more than he did those of the Sorbonne. Rather, Pascal took the vantage point of religious experience, which requires a God who is always present, and he understood that Cartesianism only believed in an absent God. The reasons Bossuet considered sufficient to defeat atheism appeared very weak to Pascal. Bossuet judged everyone like himself, and he failed to see the immense difference between the priest living in the midst of the sacraments, on the one hand, and the laity, on the other.

The pious priest who realizes a religious experience every day is inclined to be convinced by explanations that seem feeble to more worldly men living outside of this experience. Pascal wrote for men who had retained a goodly portion of sixteenth century ways. These new pagans—violent, imperious, and capricious—were not, however, completely shut off from any possibility of returning to Christianity, because they regarded the miracle as a distinct possibility; now, a miracle is a material experience of the divine presence in the world. The miracle strongly attracted Pascal's imagination, but there was no place for it in the Cartesian philosophy, which purported to submit everything to universal mathematics.

Descartes seemed to encourage those who considered experience of miracles impossible. Hence the oft-quoted sentence of Pascal, "I cannot forgive Descartes; he would have liked to have been able to leave God out of his entire philosophy,[43] but he could not resist

---

[41] Sainte-Beuve, *Port-Royal*, V, 367. Brunetière, *ibid.*, p. 47. In his second letter, Bossuet seems to think Descartes followed the church fathers on many points. Brunetière believes this judgment to be fairly accurate (p. 49).

[42] Brunetière, *Etudes critiques*, 4th ser., pp. 144–149.

[43] Philosophy (la philosophie) means physics (la physique); this meaning still exists in England.

having Him snap His fingers in order to set the world in motion. After that, he had nothing more to do with God" (fragment 77 in the Brunschvicg edition).

Sainte-Beuve understood very well that it was by drawing man away from God that eighteenth century philosophy fought against Pascal. According to Sainte-Beuve, it was Buffon who, in creating a science of nature, refuted Pascal most thoroughly.[44] We know that Diderot studied natural history passionately in the hope of rendering God completely useless.[45] Descartes, therefore, is to be thanked for having prepared the way for the Encyclopedists by reducing God to a mere trifle, while Pascal is discredited. Condorcet excelled in the art of making a great genius look ridiculous, all the while showering him with praise. Sainte-Beuve said "Pascal was portrayed as a victim of a sordid superstition; Pascal's vital and tender piety was overshadowed by the emphasis on bizarreness. The repeated discussions of the *amulette* date from Condorcet's comments."[46]

It does not seem to me that present-day admirers of Pascal are always correct in their way of interpreting him. For instance, Brunetière asserts that Pascal tried to reduce the influence of reason.[47] But we must not confuse the scientific use of reason with what is usually called rationalism. Pascal attacked the latter fradulent practice mercilessly, not only because he was a Christian, but also because his mind could not admit pseudo-mathematical reasoning to be used for answering moral questions: "I have spent a long time studying the abstract sciences, and the lack of true communication to be gained from them made me averse to them. When I began to study man, I saw that the abstract sciences are not suited to him and that I was more estranged from my human condition than others who remained ignorant of these sciences" (fragment 144). We must understand that, in Pascal's eyes, the mathematical sciences form a very limited area in the whole field of knowledge and that one exposes oneself to an infinity of errors in trying to imitate mathematical reasoning in moral studies.

Pascal's highly rigorous mind was offended by the fantastic and

---

44 Sainte-Beuve, *Port-Royal*, III, 414.
45 J. Reinach, *Diderot*, p. 170.
46 Sainte-Beuve, *op. cit.*, p. 412.
47 Brunetière, *Etudes critiques*, 5th ser., 147.

often fradulent procedures used by the Cartesians to enable them to give the impression of explaining the whole world. He speaks of the *Principes de la philosophie* with extreme contempt, likening them to the theses of Pico de la Mirandola, *de omni re scibili* (fragment 72); he writes the scornful words, "Descartes is useless and dubious" (fragment 78). Furthermore: "We must say generally, 'it comes about by form and motion,' for that is true. But to say which form and which motion and to assemble the parts of the machine, that is ridiculous. For it is useless, uncertain, and painful. And if it were true, we do not think that all of philosophy is worth one hour of trouble" (fragment 79).

Pascal protests in the name of true science against the pseudo-physics suited only to satisfy the curiosity of those who frequented the fashionable salons. Later, Newton makes the same point; he asks the geometricians not to make hypotheses to explain gravity. We know that this reform raised many objections; even today, some "enlightened" soul never fails to deplore our ignorance of the "causative laws" of celestial mechanics. Pascal did not yet have enough knowledge to say to his contemporaries: The proof that all your pseudo-philosophy is in vain and not worth an hour of trouble is that I have solved all astronomical problems without it.[48] He could not oppose the illusions he believed to be all around him except by protesting as a man of genius. As he wrote only for himself, he did not restrain himself from expressing all the bad humor he felt on seeing the enthusiasm inspired by the elaborate and deceptive Cartesian mechanisms.

It is difficult to know at what conclusions Pascal would have arrived if he had been able to complete his work. His meaning was often unclear, and this has allowed commentators to attribute certain opinions to him which were very likely not his own. I find no

---

[48] At least twice, Newton proclaimed the incompetence of the Cartesian mechanisms in science: "Virium causas et sedes physicas jam non expendo";—"Rationem harum gravitatis proprietarum nondum potui deducere et hypotheses non fingo." He did not dare, however, to deny entirely the interest that considerations about such causes presented. We find proof of this in a letter to Boyle and in another to Bentley (Stallo, *La matière et la physique moderne* ["Matter and Modern Physics"], pp. 31, 34, 35). It was his successors who, provided with an excellent instrument and no longer seeing any interest in Cartesian philosophy, completely freed themselves from it. Côtes was the first to make such a radical declaration, and Euler in his letter of October 18, 1760 ("à une princesse d'Allemagne"; ["To a German Princess"]) still protests against this oversimplification.

great mystery in the famous passage from fragment 233, which is so often regarded as a repudiation of reason: Pascal said to the freethinkers who claimed that they did not know how to arrive at faith, "Follow the way of believers, who begin by doing everything as if they believed—taking holy water, having masses said, etc. Naturally this will make you believe and will also stupefy you [*vous abêtira*]." Pascal contrasts the practices of piety to those of literature. It is very probable that, in order to strengthen this contrast here, he intentionally uses one of the pejorative expressions [*abêtir*] that has always been used by freethinkers to discredit piety. The freethinker answers him: "But that is exactly what I fear." "And why?" says Pascal. "What have you to lose? But to show you that this method leads to faith, it does so by weakening the passions, which are your greatest obstacle." Thus it is obviously a question, not of making the freethinker stupid, but of leading him to think dispassionately. Indeed, earlier in his book, Pascal assumed that the freethinker would decide in favor of religion if he could freely appreciate the advantages of the choice proposed to him, but that passions kept him a prisoner of his own bad habits. At the end of the fragment, he talks of the humbleness of Christian life, and here I see a synonym for stupefied thinking [*abêtissement*]: "You will not partake of foul pleasures, delights, or glory." The question would be to know in what measure this devout practice can produce the results Pascal expected. Perhaps it would be truly salutary for men used to living in a society in which one boasted of unbelief. Above all, Pascal was concerned with changing men's associations. In any case, his advice to the freethinker did not imply any contempt for reason.

In the 218th fragment, I cannot see the slightest indication of the indifference with which Pascal supposedly considered the work of his contemporaries to revive the theory of planetary movement. "It is well," he said, "that we do not go thoroughly into the judgments of Copernicus, but this . . . ! It is important for all of life to know whether the soul is mortal or immortal." Pascal thought that society people should better spend their time in reflecting on our destiny beyond death than in expatiating on astronomical problems that exceed their competence.

If we take an overall view, we can see clearly that Pascal was offended by the superficial character of Cartesian ideas. They were infinitely better suited to conversation than to true scientific study.

Why, however, was there such a need for "scientific" conversation? Because as I have said above, men of the seventeenth century were used to analyzing causes. Cartesian science was not so confused with mathematical technique that men of society, having received a good liberal education, could not converse with professionals. Descartes was adept at improvising explanations, whether of known natural facts or of new experiments people submitted to him. A good intellect familiar with Cartesian reasoning could find an answer to anything: this characterized a good philosophy for the habitués of the salons.

There is, it seems to me, a close resemblance between Cartesian physics and the sophistry of the casuists. In both cases, elaborate mechanisms placed between man and reality prevent the mind from exercising its proper functions; ingenious, plausible chimeras are invented. The frivolity of the rationalists of high society was nourished at the ruinous expense of true reason.

All Descartes did in formulating his famous rule of methodical doubt was introduce aristocratic modes of thought to philosophy. Brunetière very correctly notes that writers of noble origins have very little respect for traditions.[49] It seems that this similiarity of Cartesianism and the scepticism so dear to the hearts of men of quality was one of the major reasons for the success of the new philosophy.

People unacquainted with the methods of experimental science are fully satisfied only if someone succeeds in connecting the explanations (in an inoffensive manner) to other principles their common sense accepts with ease. They do not see that such a process involves a great deal of deceit. Taine cites this phrase of Malebranche as characteristic of the Cartesian spirit: "In order to attain truth, it is sufficient to pay attention to the clear ideas that each man finds in himself."[50]

Thus intelligent men did not fail to embrace Cartesianism when it was presented to them. Indeed this philosophy justifies the pretension men of society have always had to speak of things they have not studied with an imperturbable assurance, all because of their "natural enlightenment."

---

[49] Brunetière, *Evolution des genres*, p. 172.
[50] Hypolite Taine, *Ancien Régime*, p. 262; cf. p. 242.

About thirty years after the publication of the *Pensées*, Bossuet discovered the danger for religion of this wordy rationalism (Cartesianism): "Under the pretext that we must admit only what we understand clearly (which is very true with certain limitations) everyone takes the liberty to say: 'I understand this, I don't understand that.' . . . Without regard to tradition, any thought is boldly put forth . . . so long as Father Malebranche will only listen to flatterers or men who, for lack of having perceived the essence of theology, worship only its beautiful expressions. I see no cure for this sickness."[51]

This letter is extremely important, for it shows us a bishop upset by the audacity of men who treated theology as a frivolous subject. These men were more concerned with beauty of language than reason, and they failed to penetrate questions, which they preferred to judge by common sense. In this letter we have a protest against popularization. Everything connected with Cartesianism presents the same quality, which was recognized by Pascal: it is literature that leads to nothing useful and nothing certain. The whole value of this philosophy lies in its elegance of exposition.

By the terms that Bossuet uses, furthermore, we see that this concerns a totally new situation. The author sees that a great battle against the church is being prepared under the name of Cartesian philosophy. At this time, in fact, Fontenelle had just published his famous work on the plurality of worlds; this is the beginning of the true reign of Descartes.

In examining them closely, we easily recognize that the fundamental ideas of Cartesian philosophy correspond perfectly with the state of mind of that time. Cartesianism was resolutely optimistic,[52] a fact which greatly pleased a society desirous of amusing itself freely and irritated by the harshness of Jansenism. Furthermore, there is no Cartesian morality,[53] for Descartes reduced ethics to a rule of propriety prescribing respect for the established usages; since morals had become quite lenient, this was very convenient. Descartes never seemed to have been preoccupied with the meaning of life.[54] As a former student of the Jesuits, he must not have re-

---

[51] Letter of May 21, 1687, in Sainte-Beuve, *Port-Royal*, V, 368.
[52] Brunetière, *Études critiques*, 4th ser., p. 129.
[53] *Ibid.*, p. 125.
[54] *Ibid.*, p. 131.

flected very much on sin, and his disciples were able, like Renan, to suppress it.[55] Sainte-Beuve said that Descartes relegated faith, "like the gods of Epicurus, into some sort of intermediate realm of thought."[56] This suited those who hoped to be freed from the yoke of Christianity.

III

Henceforth, French philosophy was to remain marked by highly typical rationalist characteristics, which would make it very amenable to Parisian intellectual society. The Cartesian physics could be abandoned and even pronounced ridiculous in the following century, but Cartesianism would always remain the prototype of French philosophy, because it was perfectly adapted to the inclinations of an alert aristocracy proud of its ability to reason and anxious to find ways to justify its frivolity.[57]

The doctrine of progress would always be an essential element in the great movement that would continue up to our modern democracy, because this doctrine permits the enjoyment of the good things today in good conscience without worrying about tomorrow's difficulties. It pleased the old, idle aristocratic society; it will always be pleasing to the politicians elevated to power by democracy, who, menaced by possible downfall, wish to make their friends profit from all the advantages to be reaped from the state.

Today, as in the days of Fontenelle, the dominant society demands a "complete science of the world" that will allow it to expound opinions on all things without having to go through any special instruction in them. What is called science in this society is really a way of inventing nature in the tradition of Descartes; it has no relation to the probing in depth of the problems posed by

---

[55] Renan, *Feuilles detachées* ("Isolated Pages"), p. 370.

[56] Sainte-Beuve, *Port-Royal*, III, 422.

[57] Taine observed that the men of the eighteenth century "claim in vain to be followers of Bacon and to reject innate ideas. With another point of departure than the Cartesians, they tread the same path and, like Cartesians, they abandon experience after a little dabbling in it" (*Ancien Régime*, pp. 262–263).

genuine science, which is founded on prosaic reality.[58] The cos-
mological hypotheses of Spencer or Haeckel amuse the *literati*
today just as mythological stories entertained former aristocracies,
and the consequences of the enthusiasm inspired by modern stories
are considerable. Their readers, after having resolved all cosmolog-
ical problems, like to consider themselves capable of resolving all
daily difficulties. From this state of mind comes the stupid confidence in the resolution of "enlightened men," which remains one
of the ideological bases of that excessive attachment to the modern
state.

Today the idea that everything can be submitted to a perfectly
clear analysis is about as strong as it was in Descartes' time. If someone considers making a protest against the illusion of rationalism, he
is immediately accused of being an enemy of democracy. I have
often heard people who pride themselves on working for progress
deplore the teachings of Bergson and point to them as the greatest
danger confronting modern thought.[59]

For our democrats, as well as for the sophisticated Cartesian in-
tellects, progress consists neither in the accumulation of technical
methods nor even of scientific knowledge. Progress is the adornment
of the mind that, free of prejudice, sure of itself, and trusting in the
future, has created a philosophy assuring the happiness of all who
possess the means of living well. Human history is a sort of *teaching*
that shows how to pass from the savage state to aristocratic life. In
1750 Turgot said: "Considered since its origin, mankind appears to
the eyes of the philosopher as an immense entity that, like each individual, has *its childhood and its progressive growth.*"[60] In resum-
ing the unfinished work of Turgot, Condorcet entered still more
into this train of thought; he tries to describe to us the history of the
education of humanity.

From this point of view, the great question that comes into focus

---

[58] Renan wrote several significant lines on this matter: "We would reach a stage
of Babylon in our own time, if the scientific charlatans, upheld by the newspapers
and by the men of society, invaded the faculties, the Institute and the *Collège de
France*. In France, there are certain needs above the whims of these society gentlemen, such as manufacturing explosives, artillery, and the industries dependent on
science. All of these will maintain true science. In Babylon, the dabblers won out"
(*Histoire du peuple d'Israel* ["History of the People of Israel"], III, 179–180). The
seventeenth and eighteenth centuries did not have scientific industries.

[59] There could be more than one comparison made between Pascal and Bergson.

[60] Turgot (Daire Collection), II, 598.

is how to teach men to reason well. From this arises the extraordinary importance attached to logic; Condorcet presents Locke as one of the great benefactors of the human mind: "Finally, Locke seized on the course that would guide" philosophy. His "method soon became that of all philosophers, and in applying it to morals, politics, and economics, they succeeded in making almost as sure a development in these sciences as we find in the natural sciences."[61] Among Condorcet's projects for a mankind regenerated by revolution was his dream of perfecting our "vague and obscure" language. He thought that if men had received an incomplete education, they needed a precise language all the more;[62] hence he intended to reform popular language on the model of the impoverished language then used by high society. He also hoped that a universal scientific language could be created which would succeed in rendering "knowledge of the truth easy and error almost impossible."[63]

These preoccupations were very natural in men whose aim was to provide society people with a digest of knowledge and to transform everything into agreeable conversational subjects. To Condorcet, this vulgarization appeared to be one of the most honored products of the eighteenth century. The length of the passage and the solemn tones he affected well reveal the importance the author attached to the propagation of philosophy: "In Europe, there formed a class of people who were less concerned with a thorough uncovering of the truth than with propagating it. They . . . gloried in destroying popular errors rather than extending the limits of human knowledge—an indirect way of serving the progress of mankind which is neither less perilous nor less useful. Collins and Boling-

---

[61] Marquis Jean-Antoine-Nicolas Caritat de Condorcet, *Tableau historique des progrès de l'esprit humain* ("Outlines of an Historical View of the Progress of the Human Mind"), 9th epoch.
[62] *Ibid.*, 10th epoch.
[63] *Ibid.*, 10th epoch. Taine thought the French language, in becoming impoverished, had become very suitable for saying clearly those things that it could express (*Ancien Régime*, p. 247). This impoverished French became the universal language of the upper classes in Europe, and it was probably this universality of abstract speech that made Condorcet think it would be easy to create a cosmopolitan scientific language. It is evident that a language is all the more apt to be accepted by diverse peoples when it is less proximate to the common things of life. Contrary to Taine's view, I believe the French language lacked clarity in the eighteenth century. It is only with specific terms—the only ones capable of evoking images—that we can express our thoughts accurately without deceiving our readers and ourselves.

broke in England and Bayle, Fontenelle, Voltaire, and Montesquieu
in France and the schools they founded all fought in favor of truth
. . . using all styles of writing from wit to pathos . . . attacking in
religion, administration, custom, and law everything that bore the
character of oppression, harshness, and barbarism . . . finally adopting as a war cry, 'Reason, Tolerance, and Humanity!' "[64]

It would be impossible to herald in more enthusiastic terms the
passage from literature to journalism, from science to the rationalism
of the salons and debating societies, from original research to declamation.

When Condorcet became an important political figure, he judged
that the time had come to have the *people* participate in the progress
of enlightenment. His ideas on public education have considerable
importance for us because, in studying them, we can obtain an accurate picture of the nature of the eighteenth-century notion of
progress. We should understand this notion as it applies to society;
that is, in all its complex and living reality. A short analysis of Condorcet's proposals is, therefore, necessary here.

Condorcet thought it obvious that if one could show the people
how to reason in the same way as those who frequented the salons
of the ancien régime, world happiness was assured. His plan for
secondary education with this end in mind is not regarded by
present-day specialists as a very successful one. Compayré, though
he greatly admires Condorcet's ideas, thinks that the Convention
was misled in following him too closely on this point. The *écoles
centrales* failed because they were "badly defined establishments
where the instruction was too extensive, the curriculum too turgid,
and, it seemed, the student had to teach himself to discuss *de omni
re scibili.*"[65] It seems to me that Compayré did not understand Condorcet's thinking very well.

Condorcet did not want to produce farmers, manufacturers,
engineers, geometricians, and scholars; he wanted to produce "enlightened men."[66] In his report, he revealed that he was inspired by

---

[64] Condorcet, *Tableau historique,* 9th epoch. Note Condorcet's spite against
Buffon, whom he fails to list here.

[65] Condorcet, *Rapport et projet de décret sur l'organisation générale de l'instruction publique* ("Report and Proposal on the General Organization of Public Education"), preface by Compayré, p. xviii.

[66] *Ibid.,* p. 25.

eighteenth-century philosophy when choosing academic subjects. He wished to be "free from all the old chains of authority and custom." This philosophy, "in enlightening the contemporary generation, presages, prepares, and advances the superior reason to which the necessary progress of the human race calls future generations."[67]

We now know what it means to be inspired by eighteenth-century philosophy and to form enlightened men: it is to popularize knowledge in such a way as to put the young republicans in a position to hold an honourable place in a society based on the ideas of the ancien régime; it is to want democracy to model itself on the defunct aristocratic society; it is to place the new masters on the same social level as their predecessors. To obtain these results, it was necessary to give a smattering of all kinds of knowledge; and it was for this reason that the *écoles centrales* were conceived. Condorcet spoke of the classical languages with scorn: Greek and Latin ought no more to serve the men who aspire to shine in a democratic society than they served those who shone forth in the salons of the ancien régime.[68] Here we have the last echoes of the quarrel between the ancients and moderns. It was the latter who had triumphed in Condorcet's world, and our reformer takes his ideas from the past.

Condorcet believed that, as opposed to the old colleges, it would be very easy to obtain much more satisfactory results in the new schools through the use of synoptical tables,[69] of which he speaks in the following terms: "With the aid of a small number of these tables, which can be easily mastered, we will show how men who never rose above the most elementary education will be able to find at will the knowledge of details useful in ordinary life whenever

---

[67] *Ibid.*, p. 29.

[68] Condorcet's reasons are not satisfactory. It is indeed very rare that the true motives behind questions of this kind are stressed. He claims that the "ancients" are full of errors and that eloquence is a danger for those living under a parliamentary regime, although excellent for those who govern themselves directly in general assemblies. Representatives should not succumb to their personal sentiments but should obey only their reason, lest they betray their duties (Condorcet, *Rapport*, pp. 27–28).

[69] Dupont de Nemours produced a table of this type under the title, *Abrégé des principes de l'économie politique* ("Sketch of the Principles of Political Economy"); (*Les Physiocrates* [Daire Collection], pp. 367–385). This example does not give us a very lofty opinion of what can be learned from the procedure Condorcet admired so naively.

they need them; how, also, by using these same devices, elementary instruction can be made easier in all matters in which this instruction is based either on a systematic order of truth or on a series of observations or facts."[70] Indeed, by such a method, it is possible to have students skim through an encyclopedia. And if they have been drilled to speak at random *de omni re scibili*, they can be made capable of writing articles for the newspapers or of giving parliamentary speeches on subjects about which they have scant knowledge.

Thus we arrive at the ultimate in vulgarization. Condorcet's methods are also the methods dunces use for preparing their examinations: what a lovely democratic ideal!

Our author tells us what goal he hoped to attain by means of public schooling. It is worth a short account: "We can teach the entire mass of the people everything each man needs to know for household economy, the administration of his affairs, the free development of his skills and faculties, knowledge and exercise of his legal rights, knowledge of his duties so as to enable him to fulfill them, and the capability of judging his actions and those of others according to his own understanding. No man would be unacquainted with the elevated or delicate sentiments that bring honor to human nature."

Let us interrupt our thoughts here awhile and note that Taine was shocked to see what uniformity the eighteenth century assumed in humanity. "People were considered to be only well-trained puppets and usually trumpets through which an author blares his declarations to the public. Greeks, Romans, medieval knights, Turks, Arabs, Zoroastrians, Peruvians, and Byzantines are all only outlets for tirades. The public makes a success of all peasants, workers, Negroes, Brazilians, Parsees, people of the Malabar Coast who come to harangue the public."[71] As an audience for literature, "it seemed that there were only salons and the *literati*."[72] It was a matter of vulgarizing the manner of expressing "the elevated or delicate sentiments that bring honour to human nature," to such an extent that there would be a version of Madame Geoffrin's salon in the smallest hamlet. Then the world would be transformed according

---

[70] Condorcet, *Tableau historique*, 10th epoch.
[71] Taine, *Ancien Régime*, pp. 258–259.
[72] *Ibid.*, p. 261.

to the model novels and tragedies have created to the applause of a frivolous literary public.

We will now continue our description of the benefits of elementary instruction. "We should not be blindly dependent on those to whom we must entrust the care of our business or the exercise of our rights; we should be in a position of choosing and overseeing them." But contemporary experience shows that the vulgarization of knowledge does not make the people capable of choosing and supervising their so-called representatives, and it is hardly paradoxical to assert that, the more we march with the wave of democracy, the less efficient this supervision will be.

The newspapers manufacture political opinion just as they manufacture a style, a literary reputation, or the commercial value of a drug. Democracy has systematized certain methods that existed before it came into prominence, but it has invented nothing. In this, as in all aspects of democracy, we find the ideological heritage of the eighteenth century. The similarity between the current press and the world of the old salons does not occur to us because we are shocked by the grossness of our contemporary newspapers and because we view the past a little too much through legend. Basically, there is not much difference in ability between our great modern journalists and the Encyclopedists. As for their customs, unfortunately, they resemble each other in an astonishing way. In both the current press and the salons, one finds satisfaction with superficial reasoning, a great show of noble sentiments, and an admiration for science.[73] There is no reason to expect that the opinions of the modern press should be any better in quality than those manufactured by the philosophical salons.

We are not saying much when we assert that education is not useful to the proletariat, since it has as its object the popular participation in the reasoning methods taken over by the bourgeoisie from the aristocracy. I suppose that our great pedagogues agree with me and that it is precisely for this reason that they corrupt the primary schools with so many of their old ideas. Condorcet hoped that education would abolish all illusions having a magical quality.

---

[73] In order to judge Diderot fairly, he should not be compared to Montesquieu, Buffon, or Rousseau, but to the great concoctors of modern articles. Brunetière said, "He wrote on all subjects indiscriminately, with the same aplomb, without guide rules or choice, order, standards, and at full speed" (*Evolution des genres*, p. 153).

He said that people "should no longer be duped by the popular errors that torment a life with superstitious fears or illusory hopes. They should defend themselves against prejudice with the sole force of reason, and they should withstand the allures of charlatans who set traps for their fortune, health, liberty of opinion, or conscience under the pretext of enriching, curing, or saving them."

In these last words, Condorcet is obviously alluding to Cagliostro, Mesmer, and the *Illuminées* who had such great success at the end of the eighteenth century. Up to the present time, such charlatans have not had a notable influence on the people, but this may be because the people hardly know them. Indeed, it is very doubtful that the type of education they are given could preserve them from these follies. The most genuine scholars of our times have been dupes of the spiritualists, and yet we cannot deny that Crookes and Richet know the scientific method! No one could foresee what could be produced by an adept vulgarization of occultism by the popular press.[74] We should not forget that Benoit Malon was adept at these extravagances, and he was not far from joining them to "integral socialism," which would not have lost much in this mixture.[75] The ease with which all the inventors of new remedies find a large clientele in the bourgeoisie shows that the most absurd beliefs can obtain some credit if only they assume a scientific appearance.

It would seem that Condorcet was a better prophet with regard to Catholicism. Indeed, he alluded to Catholicism in the first lines of his last fragment. It is generally agreed that the development of the primary school is very dangerous for the church. Twenty-five years ago, Renan wrote: "Popular rationalism, as the inevitable result of the progress of public instruction and democratic institutions, causes the churches to become deserted and multiplies purely civil marriages and funerals."[76]

The educational policies of the Third Republic have placed the church in daily conflict with the official representatives of democ-

---

[74] We read in the *Petit Parisien* of March 22, 1910, that "it is not ridiculous to assume in these matters that we are approaching some important discoveries."

[75] It is valuable to recall here a perfectly justified evaluation of the "great man" by Gabriel Deville in 1896: "He made the future of all the pedantic terms and forbidding words that, with any luck, one usually only comes across once in a decade. He discovered America several times with an always new, vainglorious satisfaction, and he sprinkled the whole with extraordinary Latin. The result was the confection of a socialism good at the very most for freemasons and spiritualists" (*Principes socialistes* ["Socialist Principles"], p. xxv).

[76] Renan, *Marc-Aurèle* ("Marcus Aurelius"), p. 641.

racy. The church took up the cause of its teaching orders, whose interests were endangered by lay teaching. The church conducted violent campaigns in the hope of abrogating laws republicans regard as unassailable. Not a single defeat discouraged the church, and she still hopes to triumph. Clericalism thus remains an enemy of democracy, and the latter tries to usurp the faithful from the church. The republicans have been denounced as "enemies of God"; as a result, academic competition has produced a battle against beliefs. Skepticism has become an essential element of the republican program, since the public schools have been successfully defended only through the use of anti-Catholic propaganda.

The church made this propaganda easy because it entrusted its defense to sacrisity-haunting petit bourgeois, who thought it a good idea to teach the people things educated Christians would find offensive if addressed to their children: the doctrine of providence has sunk to the level of the intelligence of savages, their conception of nature is that of fetishists, and the Miracle has been dishonoured by a charlatanism worthy of drug peddlers. Primary schooling has permitted placing in the hands of the people, books and newspapers that show them that the men of *La Croix* and *Le Pélerin* laugh at them. The clerical press, in its blindness, has given its adversaries an easy way of demonstrating the stupidity, bad faith, and crass ignorance of the writers who call themselves the *friends of God*.

The popularization of scientific knowledge certainly creates serious difficulties for Christianity, which has sometimes excessively connected its theology to the medieval concept of nature. These difficulties have been made particularly acute in France in the wake of the struggle undertaken by the church to preserve its teaching orders. That part of the bourgeoisie which possesses a slightly more elevated culture is much less hostile to the church than are the people, because these bourgeois have not been called upon to equate the Gospel with Pélerin.[77] The priests who address themselves to this group almost always take the precaution of declaring themselves adversaries of the sacristy-haunting petit bourgeois, who conduct political campaigns among the poor classes.

---

[77] Educated Catholics know only the theology which they can find in the seventeenth-century literary works, and, in their eyes, this philosophy does not at all seem unworthy of modern man.

CHAPTER II

The Triumphant Bourgeoisie

I. *Creation of the royal bureaucracy. The growth of a class of bureaucrats. The importance of good administration. The need for tranquility. Fiscal control of the Parlements.*

II. *The nature of the ideology of a class of bureaucrats. The great freedom given to theorists. Entering into the realm of practice in three main aspects.*

III. *Contract theories. The vagueness of Rousseau's book. The reasons for the success of an abstract doctrine. The origins of the ideas of contract and Locke's system. Agreement among the members. The general will. Contradictory interpretations of the* Social Contract.

IV. *The physiocrats. Their administrative ideas. Their theory of property and of foundations. The success of their judicial system after the Revolution.*

V. *The men of letters. Their influence derived from the place ascribed to them by the nobility. Their true role in the aristocracy. The absence of a critical attitude.*

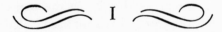

To understand thoroughly the ideas of the eighteenth century, we must start from the fact that France was gradually taken over by a bourgeois oligarchy, which the monarchy had created for its service but which would lead to its ruin.

Cournot, who was so often a very perspicacious philosopher of history, has shown the folly that induced the Bourbons to do away with everything that constricted their absolute power!

"Once the prestige of the monarchy had been destroyed, all the other truly governmental institutions were also dealt a mortal blow, and there remained only an administrative machine, which could be used by any government. In trying to make the monarchy divine or to model it on a more Asiatic than European example, [Louis XIV] made it a symbol that was exposed to the contempt of the people from the moment it ceased to be the object of genuine veneration.[1] He founded, perhaps for all times, an administrative monarchy in France which he only meant to make an instrument of his will; he lost the monarchy although his goal was to strengthen it. In this sense, the reign of Louis XIV contains the seed of the French Revolution."[2]

Usually our democrats reason very differently from Cournot, admiring what he deplored; the only thing they see in the history of France is a long preparation for the rule of their class. They are irritated at seeing institutions endure too long which they would find disagreeable to have to submit to today; they judge the past from the standpoint of apologists of the bourgeois regime. Consequently, they place praise or blame on former statesmen according to whether the latter seem to have been favorable or unfavorable to the future interests of the bourgeoisie; the more a sovereign or a minister was blinded by the interests of the moment and compromised the future of the monarchy, the greater he appears in the eyes of the bourgeoisie.

So Richelieu continues to receive the enthusiastic praise of our contemporary writers. "Great leveler and precursor of democracy, he abolished the intermediate powers obstructing relations between the king and the people by their dangerous ineffectiveness." His

---

[1] In writing this, I believe that Cournot had in mind Alexis de Tocqueville's interesting reflections on the special nature of the submission of the French people to their king; they obeyed out of love rather than coercion (*L'Ancien Régime et la Révolution*, p. 176. [All references will be to this edition, hereafter listed as *L'Ancien Régime*, followed by the page number of the American edition titled "The Old Regime and The French Revolution," New York: Anchor Books, 1955.— *Trans.*]).

[2] Cournot, *Considérations sur la marche des idées et des événements dans les temps modernes* ("Considerations on the Advance of Ideas and Events in Modern Times"), I, 414.

program is summed up in these terms by a Gabriel Hanotaux, one of the most eminent of our contemporary vulgar pedants.[3]

The creators of the administrative monarchy had no idea of the consequences that would ensue from the system they imposed so abruptly on feudal France. In no other case are Renan's words so relevant: "We never know what we are starting."[4] "The first kings who wanted to make their power absolute thought they had only to imitate ecclesiastical institutions; they had before their very eyes an absolutism sanctioned by experience. These princes strove to honor merit rather than position or birth; they perfected education; and they invited all men of talent to their court, no matter what their social origins. They reinstated the prestige of justice and the tribunals; they gave the highest positions, until then reserved for the nobility, to lawyers and clerics. The princes who played this part most skillfully were Henry VII of England, Louis XI of France, and Ferdinand of Spain. Of these 'three magi,' as Bacon calls them, Ferdinand was the cleverest. In Machiavelli's opinion, he was the living prototype of one of these 'princes of the new school' whom Machiavelli's perspicacity led him to recognize as the necessary remedy for that period."[5]

Royal policies did not produce the same consequences everywhere; in France the results were entirely out of the ordinary because power was more systematic and, above all, because there was a sufficient number of functionaries to form the nucleus of an administrative class.

The church, by choosing its dignitaries from the lower classes, had not in the least altered the social structure of Catholic countries, any more than Oriental potentates destroy slavery by transforming their servants into all-powerful viziers. Thus, a few in-

---

[3] G. Hanotaux, *Histoire du cardinal Richelieu*, II, 483. The author is vehemently opposed to the Protestants, whom he must sacrifice to the glory of the great forerunner of the democratic movement. Brunetière explains that Montesquieu's criticism of Richelieu and Louvois is due to Montesquieu's aristocratic prejudices (*Etudes critiques*, 4th ser., p. 246). Could it also be said that Mably was influenced by aristocratic ideas? Yet Mably wrote that "Richelieu had none of the virtues or even the intelligence desirable in those who are at the head of the affairs of a great kingdom" (*Observations sur l'histoire de France* ["Observations on French History"], VIII, chap. 6).

[4] Renan, *Histoire du peuple d'Israël*, IV, 147.

[5] Gervinus, *Introduction à l'histoire du XIXᵉ siecle* ("Introduction to the History of the Nineteenth Century"), pp. 26–27.

dividuals acquired a certain importance by profiting from auspicious circumstance, but these remained isolated instances, and the class structure was not altered at all.

We must not forget that the great aim the church pursued from the time of Pope Gregory VII, in a more or less conscious and always consistent way, was to infuse something of the monastic spirit in the secular clergy. It thus prevented its strength from being dissipated amidst the social groups that lived beside it to subjugate and exploit it as needed. We might say that the royal policies in France had an opposite tendency, that they sought to encourage this diffusion; even when offices did not evolve into transferable privileges like patrimonies, they were largely limited to a class of men who raised their children with an eye towards a career in state service and who found their protectors among current officials. In other words, the royal bureaucracy begat families and clans of civil servants. The more they increased in number, the greater was the solidarity of these groups. This phenomenon exists today in railroad companies, which tend to recruit their personnel from the families of their employees.[6]

When royal authority was established completely and the bureaucrats were thus assured of a more tranquil existence, this whole organization seemed as stable as if a constitution had divided up the avenues of power among a certain number of families. Those families that furnished functionaries to the state possessed a sort of "right to work"; they considered themselves essential to the state and acquired patterns of thinking bound up with their role. The founders of the system had thought they were only creating a hierarchy of able functionaries independent of feudal traditions and naturally submissive and deeply devoted to the king, who had rescued them from obscurity. They hoped to be easily rid of the obstruction to their absolutism on the part of the nobility and the privileged cities. Gradually, however, there developed a new force that hindered them more than the old forces; in an almost automatic way, the royal functionaries came to acquire the wealth, honor, and power of a sovereign class. Royal power was obstructed at every moment by the resistance of people whom the royal court persisted in treating like simple servants but who were in a position to impose their

---

[6] P. Leroy-Beaulieu in the *Débats* ("Debates") of November 28, 1905.

wills on their master. Although the pronouncements of Louis XV were at least as imperious as those of his predecessor, in fact he only rarely resolved to put his acts into conformity with his haughty declarations. In the royal decree of 1766, for example, the king said to the members of the Parlement: "Magistrates are my officers charged with freeing me from the truly royal duty of rendering justice to my subjects, a function that attaches them to my person and that will always recommend them in my eyes. Only in my person does there reside that sovereign power whose peculiar character is the spirit of advice, justice, and reason; it is from me alone that the courts derive their existence and authority; the totality of this authority, which they exercise only in my name, is always embodied in my person. To me alone belongs the legislative power, independent and indivisible. . . . My people is but one with me, and the rights and interests of the nation, which some dare to call an entity separate from the monarchy, are necessarily united with mine and rest solely in my hands." A more complete theory of autocratic power could not be found. In order to give ever more solemnity to its declarations, the government sent the royal speech to all the Parlements;[7] but the following year all was forgotten, and it was the Parlement that triumphed in the Brittany affair, the origin of all this uproar.

It is not very difficult to understand the reasons for the great and paradoxical strength of these courts of justice, the nucleus of the bourgeois oligarchy.

  a. The administration of the ancien régime had as its foundation the need, which everyone felt, to make judicial proceedings penetrate into the various fields of national activity. To oppose the caprices of great lords and the despotism of the contentious clergy, a power arose which assumed the mission of correcting abuses and

---

[7] Rocquain, *L'Esprit révolutionnaire avant la Révolution* ("The Revolutionary Mind Before the Revolution"), p. 257. There had already been a quite similar affirmation of the absolute power of the monarchy in 1759 (p. 217). The Count de Tocqueville judged that "never had the Parlement seen such strong words come from the king's mouth" as those of 1766: "The formidable opposition of the Parlements, seed of future revolutions, would have been broken by absolute power if the monarchy had persevered in a course of firmness" (*Histoire philosophique du règne de Louis XV* ["Philosophical History of the Reign of Louis XV"], II, 445–446). The Count de Tocqueville (father of the author of *Démocratie en Amerique*, ["Democracy in America"]) was a prefect under the Restoration and a peer of France. At that time, the prefectures were not entrusted to such men as occupy them presently! It is my impression that the Count's opinions carried considerable weight.

interfering with the old authorities whenever the latter committed excesses that offended the consciences of educated men. The prestige of the royal functionaries depended especially on the fact that they represented a relatively enlightened and impartial system of justice concerned with the general interest. Practically speaking, however, great complications arose from this situation; the continued mixing of administrative and judicial powers, one of the fundamental elements of the system, shocks our modern sensibilities. Present-day civil servants no longer have the authority that their predecessors derived from their capacity as judges.

In a country that has no political laws, everything depends on the consistency of administrative services; the independence of the functionaries alone is the only guarantee citizens have. Although this independence has been considerably reduced today, and we "enjoy the benefits" of a parliamentary regime, the relative independence of the civil service is still a very important aspect of our national life. Thus, we can understand the immense confusion caused by the measures taken by the government against the leading dignitaries of the administration and against the members of the Parlement of Paris. It was easy enough to scare Louis XV, but there is no doubt that he was not being misled when he was told that the discontent provoked by such measures disturbed the tranquility of France.

It seems to me that there is often insufficient account taken of a very unusual fact in this regard: until the last days of the ancien régime, certain traditions were followed which appear rather absurd to us.[8] For example, Choiseul gained many enemies for having abandoned the principles of Richelieu and Louis XIV and for having attempted to bring France and Austria together; Marie Antoinette was the object of hatred stemming from the anti-Austrian prejudices of the court. Similarly, in order to uphold the principles of the seventeenth century, persecuting Protestants and Jansenists was thought to be necessary, even though the state secretaries were no longer believers. As another example, Tocqueville notes that the

---

[8] Turgot was very impressed by the sort of inertia that compels governments and peoples to reach far beyond the goal that corresponds to their true interests. He believes, for example, that the hatred of Europe against Louis XIV was nearly fatal to our enemies themselves and that Queen Anne, in making peace, saved the rest of Europe even more than France; yet, he observes, "her people accused her of weakness and treason" (Turgot, II, 673).

monarchy, on the very eve of the Revolution, still trembled at the thought of the nobility's recommencing the troubles of the Fronde. Thus, everyone thought in terms of long-standing, outdated social circumstances.[9] It is, therefore, easy to understand why the monarchy feared the idea of disturbing an administrative structure that had given it so much service and that could still help it to overcome particular powers.

b. Men of the eighteenth century loved tranquility above all else, and Louis XV was no exception to this rule. Today, likewise, we see the upper classes sacrifice everything to their tranquility. They are solely concerned with assuring themselves a few days rest. Only in Maupeou's time did Louis XV have enough strength to face up to the storm; after two years of very vehement opposition, interest lagged, and the coup d'etat of 1771, which had suppressed the old judiciary, was forgotten; it was found that these disputes were not worth the trouble they brought into an otherwise gay life;[10] previously, the first to grow weary had been the king.

In 1753, the *Grand Chambre* having been exiled, a substitute chamber was created to replace it, but the *Châtelet* (magistrate) refused to obey the king or execute his orders; "the monarchy is defeated by this force of inertia which opposes it from all sides; it is necessary to deal with the Parlement."[11] The birth of a grandson to the king was used as an excuse to recall the magistrates, and the drastic action was taken of abandoning the bishops whom the court had, until then, upheld; for, indeed, it was the religious issue that had brought on the conflict. In 1756 the king reverted to his former policy; there were new difficulties and resignations of members of the Parlement. Then, Damien's assassination attempt took place the following year, and the quarrels were forgotten for awhile. They recommenced, however, in 1759; hardships of war led the government to act with prudence, and the Jesuits were the victims of the

---

9 Alexis de Tocqueville, *L'Ancien Régime* [p. 143 in the American edition of 1955, Anchor Books].

10 Rocquain, *L'Esprit Révolutionnaire*, p. 309. Rousseau claimed that, in 1753, the disputes provoked by the introduction of Italian opera diverted attention from the conflict that then existed between Parlement and the clergy. Publication of his *Lettre sur la musique française* ("Letter on French Music") was supposedly a great political event. "It is unbelievable to read that this article perhaps prevented a revolution" (*Confessions*, VIII). Apart from Rousseau's usual exaggeration, we have here an accurate observation of the temper of the time.

11 Count de Tocqueville, *Histoire philosophique*, II, 121–123.

reconciliation (decree of 1761 and 1762, edict of 1764). I have already said that the session of Parlement of 1766 produced no lasting results.

During all these conflicts, the more arrogant the ruling powers became, the more they lost prestige. The ceremony of the seating of the king, during the session of the Parlement, was deeply humiliating for these august magistrates who commanded such great respect. The king treated them almost like children being scolded by a schoolteacher; the greater the humiliation, the more the public applauded the vehement protests that usually followed these ceremonies. "It is dangerous for a weak government," says the Count de Tocqueville, "to make a show of force that it cannot uphold."[12] Perhaps there is even more danger in trying to humiliate those whom the nation reveres and who emerge with greater stature from the trials they are made to undergo.

One could say that, at that time, the fundamental article of French laws was that the government must stop before the least resistance brought by the bourgeois oligarchy, for such was the common practice.

c. The families that furnished dignitaries to the principal Parlements became rich, and they could withstand quite substantial losses when their pride was at stake. Exile from the Parlements was burdensome and awkward but was endured for the sake of honor; several times, groups of magistrates threatened to resign and even did so. These are actions that we no longer easily understand. Undoubtedly, one could point out many weaknesses and even certain acts of cowardice on the part of these men of law—absolute independence could only have been exceptional—but it is out of unusual and striking deeds, not ordinary ones, that ideologies are usually born.

In a great many instances, the opposition of the Parlement concerned fiscal measures. Modern authors often ask by what mandate this opposition was justified, but it seems to me that no one was in a better position than the most prominent men of the third estate to defend the taxpayers' interests. There was no need of an explicit mandate for that; the economic title fully justified their protests.

And yet it sometimes happened that the magistrates' interests

---

[12] Count de Tocqueville, *Histoire philosophique,* II, 446.

were in opposition to those of the country as a whole. This was especially apparent under the reign of Louis XVI when Turgot sought to apply the ideas of the physiocrats and to make reforms for the benefit of production. At this time was shown the insufficiency of the control over the judiciary, which, representing the interests of an urban oligarchy, was unwilling to see its privileges reduced.

Turgot advised Louis XVI not to restore the Parlements that had been suppressed by Louis XV, but only he and Marshall de Muy were of this opinion in the cabinet. He proposed the establishment of an elected assembly that would discuss the distribution of taxes among the provinces, decide the large-scale public works to be undertaken, and grant subsidies to local authorities for calamities or projects in the general interest too costly for their budgets.

Turgot wanted the various elective assemblies to represent a very restricted bourgeois oligarchy; the royal assembly would have been formed of delegates to the provincial assemblies and the latter of delegates to the district assemblies, which would be appointed by the town councils. The latter would be composed of only a few people: in the country, the heads of families having a net income of 600 pounds in land; and in the cities, those who possessed land worth at least 15,000 pounds.[13] Several votes would be given to citizens having several times the minimum wealth, and those who had less could join together to name delegates in proportion to the right of their group. A system of representation of interests very similar to that which Turgot conceived is functioning in our associations for agricultural improvement, formed by the law of June 21, 1865. The delegate from a local city to the district assembly would have a vote proportional to the importance of his commune. Account would no longer be taken of the historical distinction between orders; nobles, however, would not participate in deliberations concerning the distribution of taxes from which they were exempt. "The first principle," said Turgot, "is that one be involved only in what concerns him and in the administration of his property."[14]

---

13 The difference was based on economics; houses are not productive forces. Their owners are "townsmen" and not true "citizens" like rural proprietors; an urban family does not have a stake in society. Turgot estimated that there were no more than a hundred persons in Paris who possessed the minimum fixed by him (Turgot, II, 528–530). We will see farther on at the end of chapter 2 exactly what the term "citizen" signified to Turgot.

14 Turgot, II, 527.

It is evident that this governing body was modeled after an industrial association. It was truly the epitome of all the ideas that could be developed by enlightened statesmen who wanted to bring about the conquest of the state by the productive bourgeoisie.

 II

The ideology of the eighteenth century is the one best suited to the life situation of a class of royal assistants. Thus, I differ completely from Taine, who assumes as the basis of this ideology the life of an "aristocracy idled by an overpowering monarchy—well-born and well-bred people who, cut off from action, fell back on conversation and spent their leisure time tasting all of the serious and refined pleasures of the mind."[15] The English aristocracy, so deeply involved in the management of important interests, who did not let themselves be duped by theorists, he contrasts with the French aristocracy, who, because they were removed from reality, "lightheartedly, boldly, walked in the steps of the philosophers."[16] He is struck by the fact that the boldest doctrines of the eighteenth century were imported from England; that they had not succeeded in taking firm root in their native land; and that, instead, they prevailed in France, the country of beautiful language.[17]

A "class of clerks" cannot construct its ideology on the same model as that of a "class of masters"; the former does not attend as much to its own affairs as to those of others. Its ideology tends to take the form of opinions given by jurists, historians, or scientists on problems put to them. In order to facilitate this exercise, it is necessary to submit everything to scholarly analysis. That is how the habit developed in France of making all opinion depend on abstract ideas, general theories, and philosophical doctrines. These methods of reasoning hardly suit men who take charge of their own affairs themselves and who are consequently used to subordinating their behavior to particular conditions they perceive through personal experience.

---

[15] Taine, *Ancien Régime*, p. 241.
[16] *Ibid.*, pp. 363–365.
[17] *Ibid.*, pp. 330–331.

It seems likely that a fact that had made such an impression on Sumner Maine is related to this phenomenon: everyday language enters much more into English legislation than into any other.[18] Since, in France the parliamentary assemblies themselves write the laws without much help from professional jurists, the wording is becoming far more vernacular; from this, innumerable misunderstandings develop between parliament and the tribunals, who do not speak the same language.[19]

When the special conditions long imposed on French literature are considered, the mode of expression that Montesquieu adopted in the *Spirit of the Laws* is understood easily: "He spoke like an oracle," said Taine, "enigmatically and by maxims; every time he touched on matters about France or his own times, he trod as if on hot coals."[20] Not that Montesquieu would have been in danger for being more daring, but I think this abstract style seemed to him more worthy of his nature and his public. His style was imitated by writers like Benjamin Constant and Tocqueville, who had nothing to fear in the nineteenth century but thought they should appear remote from prosaic concerns.[21]

Civil servants always fear arousing the irritability of their superiors; consequently, they incline toward subjects that are remote from reality, so as to not appear to be infringing on ground reserved for their superiors. We know the church has generally shown a great tolerance for scholastic, rhetorical, and poetic theses, whose bases do not seem to have had a direct relation to questions that have concerned the church. G. Boissier has shown us professors of the sixth century giving their students purely pagan composition subjects, seemingly unaware that Christianity had been the state religion for two hundred years.[22] Contemporary papists are often at a loss to explain why the Holy See protected the humanists of the Renais-

---

18 Sir Henry Sumner Maine, *Etudes sur l'histoire du droit* ("Studies in the History of Law"), p. 386. The result is a high degree of verbosity in English laws and a lack of the precision in philosophical language found on the continent.

19 Parliamentary language in France is a jumble of common expressions and misused judicial terms.

20 Taine, *Ancien Régime*, p. 278.

21 Laboulaye notes this in his edition of Montesquieu, III, xix–xx. If it were not a question of literary discipline, it would be difficult to understand why England is not mentioned by name in chapter 27 of Book XIX, on English customs; this surprised Laboulaye.

22 G. Boissier, *Le Fin du paganisme* ("The End of Paganism"), I, 216.

sance,[23] for these favorites of the Roman court were often clearly nonbelievers, but modern writers often see lofty philosophical doctrines where men of the sixteenth century saw only literature.

The monarchy followed more or less the path of the church; it was not alarmed to see its bureaucrats construct theories on natural law, enthusiastically praise republican virtues, or propose to their contemporaries that they abandon all traditional institutions to go live in a utopian city. Books that we regard as bold socialist manifestos appeared in other days more inoffensive the more they were removed from reality. It could have been dangerous to criticize the abuses of the salt tax, but it was not so to praise communism.

It has often been pointed out that the abstract theories in the *Social Contract* did not provoke the severity of the Parlement in the least, although the latter condemned *Emile* because of inferences of a practical nature attributed to it in religious matters. The oligarchy of Geneva regarded the *Social Contract* as a seditious satire[24] that sought to arouse protest against the ruling council by the mass of voters; that is why this book, like *Emile*, was burned by the Geneva magistrates.

Eighteenth-century bishops denounced the audacity of the innovators from time to time, but repression was always rather feeble and usually more apparent than real.[25] The authorities would ban a book, but they would permit it to be sold. The *Encyclopedia* was printed in Paris after its legal suppression: the administration asked only that the ten volumes appearing in 1765 be distributed without too much noise. All of the authors who composed declamations against society found protectors among the magistrates charged with keeping a close eye on them. From 1750 to 1763, Malesherbes was constantly occupied with watching over the fate of the "forerunners of the Revolution" in order to prevent them from committing indiscretions and to soften the application of measures ordered against them.[26]

---

[23] Baudrillart, *L'Eglise catholique, la Renaissance, le protestantisme* ("The Catholic Church, the Renaissance, and Protestantism"), pp. 67–102.

[24] *Correspondance inédite de Condorcet et de Turgot* ("Unpublished Correspondence of Condorcet and Turgot"), ed. Ch. Henry, p. 146.

[25] Repression often became severe when influential persons thought that they had personal reasons to complain of the writers.

[26] See the whole chapter on the publishing industry under Malesherbes in Brunetière's *Etudes critiques*, 2d ser.

Modern historians have been shocked that Fréron, the enemy of the philosophers, was much less well treated than the latter. Malesherbes assigned him friends of the Encyclopedists as censors of his work. In 1754, Malesherbes suppressed his newspaper because it had criticized d'Alembert's reception speech at the *Académie Française*; he permitted abuses against Fréron but forbade him from naming his adversaries when he answered them.[27] Malesherbes' behavior is easily explained when one looks at it from what must have been his point of view, that is, viewing the philosophy of the eighteenth century as a simple exercise in rhetoric for the amusement of society people.

This unusual manner of writing continued until the eve of the Revolution. The second edition of the *Histoire Philosophique des deux Indes*, which appeared in 1780, brought persecution upon Raynal, but we must add that this happened after the fall of Necker. Raynal was suspected of having collaborated with the disgraced minister on the latter's dissertation concerning the provincial assemblies.[28] During the Revolution, Raynal displayed such unrevolutionary sentiments that it seems impossible that he took seriously the declamations Diderot inserted in this edition. For example, on the matter of the Ceylonese law punishing the king by death for violation of the constitution, we see this stupid remark: "The law is nothing but a blade that cuts down indiscriminately all heads and that strikes what rises above the horizontal plane on which it moves."

During the Revolution, this literature changed its significance. Then, simple schoolboy paradoxes were taken seriously, fairy tales took on a realistic meaning,[29] and the distinction the old society had made between theory and practice was abolished. Literature passed from one class to another—from an oligarchy down to the masses. Generally speaking, common people understand nothing of literary wiles: when they are told about making "a cord for the last of the kings out of the entrails of priests," they literally believe that Diderot wanted to convince enlightened men about the necessity

---

[27] Fréron had no right to tolerance because he did not belong to good society. He was detained at Vincennes for "having let it be said of a painter that his landscapes looked as if they had been painted with burned sugar." Grimm heartily approved of this official severity (Brunetière, *Etudes critiques*, 2d ser., p. 304).

[28] Rocquain, *L'Esprit Révolutionnaire*, p. 389.

[29] Cf. André Lichtenberger, *Le Socialisme et la Révolution française* ("Socialism and the French Revolution"), p. 221.

of disemboweling curés and strangling rulers in order to assure the happiness of man.

Since we live in a country ruled by parliamentary institutions, it seems remarkable to us that propositions can be made which are not intended to become a party platform and which, consequently, are not realizable. Often we must stretch our imagination to understand the meaning of the abstract literature of which our predecessors were so fond. This by no means signifies, however, that their practices have completely disappeared, for parliamentary socialism would not recruit so many adherents among the wealthy class if Jaurès' revolutionary harangues were taken seriously in those rich bourgeois circles that seek to imitate the inanities of the old aristocracy.

This great outpouring of abstractions followed a period of resounding quarrels about dogma, and it preceded a period completely preoccupied with practical solutions. Positivists would not fail to find in this an application of their famous law of the three phases.[30] In their view the highest discipline is sociology, and before the Revolution the French reasoned exclusively on this basis; it could be said, then, that a positivist era had arrived after the eras of theology and metaphysics. This evolution can be explained very simply without calling upon profound considerations. When the decay of the monarchy permitted the third estate to take courage and view reforms as possible, the third estate no longer limited itself exclusively to the realm of scholarly dissertation.

Bachaumont's continuator says that the Encyclopedists perfected metaphysics, dissipated the fuzziness in which theology had enveloped it, and destroyed fanaticism and superstition; that economists were then occupied with morals and practical politics with the aim of making men happy; and that "times of trouble and oppressions have given birth to 'patriots' who, returning to the source of laws and of the constitution of governments, have delineated the reciprocal obligations of subjects and sovereigns and established the

---

[30] *Translators' note:* This "law" of Auguste Comte describes man as passing through three stages of historical development: (1) a primitive stage characterized by subjectivism, fetishism; (2) an abstract, critical, and metaphysical stage; and (3) the organic stage of positivism and science. See Roger Solteau, *French Political Thought in the Nineteenth Century* (New York: Nelson, 1959), p. 211. Also Frank E. Manuel, *The Prophets of Paris* (New York: Harper Books, 1965), pp. 277–278.

great principles of administration."[31] Maupeou's reforms occasioned this last transformation; then, the government was indeed discredited, and political upheaval was believed imminent. Several years later, when even greater hopes were becoming possible under the ministry of Turgot, there appeared a literature destined to make the masses understand social science in the way the philosophy of that time had formed it. In 1775 the *Catéchisme du Citoyen* popularized the doctrines of Montesquieu and Rousseau, which, according to the same chronicler, "had been submerged in complicated metaphysics."[32] From this it can be seen how ideological development was the consequence of the history of the French monarchy.

Now we will examine in detail the ideology of the class with which we are concerned; we will single out several sources of this ideology.

A first factor depends on the condition of existence of the whole third estate, the reservoir that furnished the men of the intellectual oligarchy, who were auxiliaries of the monarchy and were destined to supplant it. The third estate was closely bound up with the economy that produced the wealth in a society of merchants and manufacturers. Thanks to the ideas of this category, theories hostile to trade guilds, to the feudal regime, and to arbitrary administration take on a major importance. At this time, many ideas imported from England were very successful because they were associated with these ideas of commercial production; they contributed notably towards introducing principles of liberty.

The second source of the ideology of the third estate is connected with the administrative and judicial functions entrusted to the bourgeois oligarchy. Here, we do not find many liberal tendencies; rather we see a strengthening, regulating, and extending of the power of the state, which the oligarchy more and more regarded as its property, from the time when the prestige of the aristocracy started to diminish. The greater this power, the more important the state functionaries would be.

The third source is caused by the need for imitation that led the bourgeoisie to ape the aristocracy; the third estate was not satisfied

---

[31] Rocquain, *L'Esprit révolutionnaire*, p. 298. Accounts of the eighteenth century need to be amended. That is why I have borrowed so much from Rocquain, who has already done the job so skillfully. I have found this method more accurate than direct recourse to memoirs. I thought that my readers would have more confidence in a selection made by a member of the Institute than in my own work.

[32] Rocquain, *ibid.*, p. 332.

with wealth and power; it demanded status. Taine was so struck by the importance of this phenomenon that he believed the entire ideology of the eighteenth century derived from the customs of the nobility. He did not see that it is necessary to consider, not what the nobles thought, but what the bourgeois, who desired aristocratic elegance, thought. Clearly there was more than a nuance between these problems.

If Taine had been more careful in studying the conditions under which the ideas of the eighteenth century were formed, he would not have found the situation he describes here so paradoxical: "An aristocracy imbued with humanitarian and radical maxims, courtiers hostile to the court, privileged men who help to undermine privileges. We see this strange spectacle in the testimony of the time. . . . High and low, in meetings and in public places, among the privileged, we encounter only malcontents and reformers."[33] Actually the nobility in this period no longer had an ideology of its own; it borrowed subjects for discourse from the third estate and amused itself with projects for social reform, which it considered on a par with accounts of marvelous voyages made in the land of milk and honey.

Two neologisms deeply impressed Taine and should have put him on the path to a solution. The word *energy*, "formerly ridiculous, became fashionable and turned up everywhere." That the origin of this term was found in the language of the common people cannot be questioned. A formidable word, "citizen," imported by Rousseau, entered into everyday language, and, conclusively, women took hold of it like the latest fashion."[34] In signing his books "citizen of Geneva" Rousseau probably wanted to point out to his French readers that he belonged to the upper class of Genevans and, thus being qualified to occupy the highest offices,[35] he *stood*, in his coun-

---

[33] Taine, *Ancien Régime*, pp. 388–389.
[34] Taine, *Ancien Régime*, p. 386. The word "energy" is found in a letter of 1779 and the word "citizen" in a letter of 1762.
[35] There were five classes in Geneva: "citizens" who were eligible electors; ineligible "bourgeois," whose children were born in Geneva and became citizens; "residents"; "natives"; and "subjects." According to the *Septième Lettre écrite de la Montagne* ("Seventh Letter from the Mountain"), the General Assembly had never been comprised of more than 1,500 citizens and bourgeois out of a population of 20,000. It has been pointed out that Rousseau displayed passably aristocratic sentiments in not demanding equality of rights for all Genevans (J. Vuy, *Origine des idées politiques de Rousseau* ["The Origin of Rousseau's Political Ideas"], pp. 145–146).

try, as an equal to nobility. Like most of Geneva's citizens, however, he was an artisan, and he lauded the eminent dignity of the artisan with much impassioned conviction. Consequently, I think the word "citizen" should be translated as "a man who has the right to everyone's respect by reason of the productive work from which, by his labor, his country benefits."

In this connection, we should refer to Turgot's dissertation on municipalities. The author calls "a complete citizen: a free tenant farmer, a man who can be given, or rather to whom should be given, the highest freedom of the city; one who possesses real estate whose revenues would suffice to support a family, for the latter is or could be a head of a family when he so desires. He is rightfully what the Romans called *pater familias*. He has a fixed hearth and home, he remains on the land and keeps the foundation of his family there." A little farther on, he speaks of the landowner's "citizen family."[36] The word "citizen," then, has an economic significance corresponding to the living conditions of the third estate.

In the first category of these ideologies are found the theories that base society on the social contract, theories that had such great influence in times past and that seem so difficult to understand today. We must pause here at length in order to take the opportunity to delve into questions that seem to have remained rather obscure.

III

There are many and fairly obvious reasons why doctrines that seemed so simple to our ancestors are so unintelligible to us. Today many studies on primitive societies have been made, and nothing has been found which would permit one to suppose that they were begun by social contracts.[37] On the contrary, we find that magic played a large role everywhere, and enslavement to magic could not be further removed from the spirit of free agreements. Studies made on the Middle Ages have shown that our ideas, customs, and institutions depend enormously on the ancient church government;

---

36 Turgot, II, 513, 528.
37 Henry Sumner Maine, *Essais sur le gouvernement populaire* ("Essays on Popular Government"), pp. 225–226.

the idea of the social contract takes no account of this tradition. Finally, we sense today that the economy binds us in a narrow way to the nation of which we are members due to the accident of birth; thus the physiocrats' idea that when someone acquires a piece of land he "freely and voluntarily forms a society with the sovereign"[38] appears rather ridiculous to us.

Even in referring to the course of ideas in the eighteenth century, however, it is hard for us to understand that contemporaries of Montesquieu could allow themselves to be misled into reducing society to something as simple as Rousseau made it. One could explain their attitudes by saying that we do not, perhaps, understand adequately the *Spirit of the Laws*,[39] that we read it with attitudes that arise from yet unborn historical schools.[40] But there is something more important here. Men of the eighteenth century had the Prussian monarchy before their eyes, and they saw Frederick II as the ideal type of philosopher-sovereign. Their admiration for the conqueror of Sicily should have prepared them to understand the conditions of practical politics. Occasionally we come to wonder if the admirers of the contract theory had not wanted to proceed by the method of complete detachment, as Fourier said later, placing themselves directly outside of every hypothesis that permits reasoning about successive reforms. But this state of mind was formed fairly late, and Taine observes that Rousseau did not reject every historical consideration.[41]

In order to understand this paradox, we must remember that the social contract doctrine was brought ready-made into France under the patronage of Locke's great name. An imported ideology can very well exist alongside facts that would have prevented the ideology from arising spontaneously in the country that adopts it. Rousseau gave it its definite shape by condensing it in a marvelously obscure masterpiece of literary exposition.[42] The Marxist theory of value shows us the importance of obscurity in giving force to a

---

[38] Mercier de la Rivière, "Ordre naturel des sociétés politiques" ("Natural order of Political Societies"), in *Les Physiocrates* (Daire Collection), p. 453.

[39] Brunetière says that the more he read *L'Esprit des lois* ("The Spirit of the Laws") the less he could discern its true purpose (*Etudes critiques*, 4th ser., p. 254).

[40] One wonders mainly whether Montesquieu really created the history of law and the science of comparative government, as Laboulaye believes (Montesquieu, *L'Esprit des lois*, p. ix).

[41] Taine, *Ancien Régime*, p. 306.

[42] The book, wrote Bachaumont, "is enveloped in a scientific obscurity that makes it unintelligible to the ordinary reader" (Rocquain, *L'Esprit révolutionnaire*, p. 235).

doctrine: enlightened people dare not avow that they do not understand reasoning presented in well-turned language by a renowned
writer.

The obscurity of the *Social Contract* is such that Rousseau must
not have seen the incoherencies for which he was reproached later.
There is a very important incoherency that does not seem to have
been noticed much. The fundamental principle of the *Social Contract* is "the total alienation of each member together with all his
rights to the community." This idea recalls the feudal system of
the communes; this alienation is the submission to the "collective
domain"[43] of the city. Society receives all the assets of its members; in fact, the latter are not despoiled; freeholding proprietors
exposed to a thousand dangers are transformed into vassals of a powerful domain. "The right of sovereignty becomes at the same time
real and personal. It puts its possessors in a position of greater de-
pendence and makes of their very power the guarantee of their
fidelity. This is an advantage that does not seem to have been greatly
appreciated by ancient monarchs who, by calling themselves merely
kings of the Persians, Scythians, Macedonians, etc., seemed to have
regarded themselves as leaders of men rather than masters of countries. The more acute rulers of today call themselves kings of France,
Spain, England, etc. In holding the land in this way, they are very
sure of holding the inhabitants."[44] While the physiocrats did their
utmost to reduce the feudal regime to a financial structure,[45] Rousseau strengthened it and could make his thesis acceptable due to the
extreme obscurity of his presentation. Jacobinism was to draw frightful conclusions from the *Social Contract* which would have horrified Rousseau.

Our predecessors were not at all bothered that the system of the
Social Contract had very little to do with reality, because they were
used to a physical science that took great liberties with experience.
They were not even far from admitting that in order to reason on
the true principles of nature one must not linger too long over data
furnished by observation; discovering truths beyond experience was

---

[43] On the feudal character of the old municipal institutions, cf. Luchaire, *Les
Communes françaises* ("The French Communes"), p. 10.

[44] *Contrat social* ("Social Contract"), I, 6 and 9.

[45] In their eyes, the king is no more than a "tutelary power" who has a right to a
part of the net revenue.

the purpose of intelligence. That is why Rousseau did not in the least astonish his contemporaries when, inspired by memorable examples of philosophers, he wrote in his *Discourse on the Origins of Inequality Among Men*: "Let us begin, then, by putting aside all the facts, for they do not bear on the question of natural law. One must not consider the research upon which one could embark on this subject as historical truths, but only as hypothetical and conditioned arguments, more suitable to illuminate the nature of things than to show their true origin, like the research that physiocrats are always undertaking on the formation of the world."

Our predecessors were very apt to make the greatest sacrifices in order to introduce clarity into the first hypotheses that serve to formulate principles. That is one of the main reasons for the success of the atomist theories. Like physics, society can also be simplified, and it can be found to contain an atomistic clarity if national tradition and the genesis of law and the organization of production are disregarded in order to consider nothing but the people who come to the marketplace to exchange their products and who, outside of these accidental meetings, preserve their complete liberty of action. By so idealizing commercial law, social atoms are indeed obtained. In the eighteenth century men had such a high regard for commerce that they were very much inclined to think that natural law, thus arrived at by an abstraction of commercial law, must prevail over the existing law, as the latter was full of traces of historical influences.

Now we are going to discuss the origins of the ideology of the social contract.

Workmen and petty bourgeois of the industrial cities naturally tended to conceive of all civil groups on the model of the associations that they formed among themselves for their pleasure, security, or professional purposes. These fairly mobile associations depended greatly on historical conditions: the artisans of times past had very nomadic habits. Rousseau pointed this out, and sufficient account of the fact has not been taken in interpreting the *Social Contract*. "Of all human conditions, the one most independent from chance and other men is that of the artisan. The artisan depends only on his work; he is as free as the farm laborer is a slave: for the latter depends on his field, whose harvest is at the discretion of others. The enemy, the prince, a powerful neighbor, or legal action can take this field away from him. Through his field, he can be plagued in a thousand ways. But whenever someone tries to plague an artisan, his baggage is soon packed; he takes his tools and moves on."[46] Such a person is not very different from the social atom or the abstract citizen who is the subject of numerous theories.

The theories of the Protestant sects that were not established as state religions[47] furnish a second type of society formed on the temporary agreement of wills. These sects resembled monastic orders much more than churches, and, like monastic orders, they sought to form little states within the state. The first American colonies were established through compacts. On November 11, 1620, the forty-one heads of family who had gone over on the Mayflower submitted themselves to the will of the majority and to the magistrates whom they would elect. These colonies were so much like convents that, for a long time, they expelled people who were not of their faith. The English Puritans had already thought of founding the government of their country on a contract: in 1647, the Levelers presented to the army council a proposed declaration which they wanted every citizen to sign.[48]

Business corporations that issue stocks furnish a third type of group that, with the preceding ones, completes the foundation of the contract doctrine: here again we have the temporary agreement of wills, since any member can withdraw when he so wishes by selling his shares at the stock exchange. The colony of Massachusetts had been organized by a charter on March 4, 1629, under the form of a commercial corporation. When the seat of the administration was transferred to America a few years later, this charter became the law of the colony. Thus a private contract became the foundation of a state.

These practices are sufficient to explain the theory that Locke sets forth in Chapters VII and VIII of his *Second Treatise on Civil Government*. Men who are naturally free, equal, and independent form societies in order to assure their personal security and, above all, their property. The advantages gained are considerable

---

[46] Rousseau, *Emile*, III. Turgot stresses the nomadic character of rural workers in his work on municipalities. They "belonged to no place" (Turgot, II, 511).

[47] A great many members of these sects belonged at the same time to the world of artisans, which was discussed previously.

[48] Jellinek, *La Déclaration des droits de l'homme et du citoyen* ("The Declaration of the Rights of Man, and of the Citizen"), pp. 64–66.

because, henceforth, there are positive laws, judges, and a public force capable of keeping order. The contracting parties abandon their right to act as they please in the defense of their interests, especially the right of punishment. The society, which takes on the responsibility of security, must not overstep the limits of what must be done to remedy the faults found in the state of nature. Thus the government will have only the functions of assuring peace, security, and the obvious public good. The social constitution will do no wrong to those men who do not accept it, who can, if they wish, remain in the state of nature.

Locke's doctrine passed almost completely into the teaching of the physiocrats, who possibly emphasized better the view that political societies are syndicates of landowners and that the government is a "tutelary authority that watches over all, while each one attends to his own business."[49] Montesquieu's *Spirit of the Laws*, on the contrary, does not allow this as a conclusion of historical analysis, but this is what the prominent men of the third estate wished to see as the principle of all further legislation.[50]

Today we are very much inclined to give Montesquieu great credit for not having speculated on the origin of societies,[51] but his contemporaries needed such speculation to justify the views on reforms to be made. The bourgeoisie did not understand that its property titles were awarded by privileges conceded by former sovereigns or by feudal relics, which it regarded as being outside of civil law. It was in this contract mentality that they liquidated the ancien régime several years later, and this liquidation was being prepared for a long time.

Because of his memories as a traveling artisan, Rousseau regarded society in a much more abstract way than did the physiocrats; unlike them, he was not preoccupied with productive forces. He thought in terms of men who are not governed by economic necessities; he found it completely natural, therefore, that society could banish those who refused to accept the profession of faith of the civil religion. This banishment would hardly be a rigorous measure for

---

[49] Dupont de Nemours, "Origine et progrès d'une science nouvelle" ("Origin and Progress of a New Science"), *Les Physiocrates*, p. 347.

[50] Taine says that "Montesquieu remained respected but isolated, and his fame had no influence" (*Ancien Régime*, p. 378). Montesquieu's isolation seems to have been badly explained until now.

[51] Brunetière, *Etudes critiques*, 4th ser., p. 263.

nomadic artisans, and it seemed necessary to him in order to facilitate agreement among citizens.[52]

This question of agreement is the great stumbling block for all social-contract theories.[53] It seems that Rousseau did not much worry about this difficulty because he was a great admirer of old Swiss customs. He found frequent examples in his country of how easy it was to arrive at an agreement between neighbors or within a profession with a view to the common good. The best way to understand Rousseau's way of thinking is to refer to Paul Bureau's book on Norway; the region of the fiords, studied by this French scholar, remains very backward and greatly resembles the old Swiss regions of which Rousseau was so fond.

In Norway groups form effortlessly, and discipline is easily accepted provided that it seems reasonable: "As soon as several men are together in a boat or engaged in some enterprise for work or pleasure, they choose a leader and enact rules. But the men must themselves have enacted this ruling or this law; otherwise they will not accept it."[54] "While very rebellious against all discipline imposed from outside, the young Norwegian obeys only when he has thoroughly understood the reason and the meaning of what he is ordered to do and when he can repeat to himself a similar injunction."[55]

Moreover, Rousseau thinks that man is completely transformed by entering into civil society. "The voice of duty succeeding physical impulse and law succeeding appetite, man who until then considered only himself sees himself forced . . . to consult his reason before heeding his passions."[56] As happens daily with political theorists, Rousseau presents things completely in the reverse of what they are in reality: human nature is not changed by the solemnity of the social contract, but the contract theory presupposes individuals entirely dominated by calculating reflection. This is completely

---

[52] Chuquet thinks that Rousseau was inspired by the ecclesiastical ordinances of Geneva, which punished by banishment those who did not participate in worship. (*J. J. Rousseau*, pp. 145–146). Note that Rousseau does not admit the intervention of authority in the matter of worship.

[53] This is what preoccupies Taine so much (*Ancien Régime*, pp. 306–318).

[54] Paul Bureau, *Le Paysan des fjords de Norvège* ("The Peasant of the Norwegian Fiords"), p. 84.

[55] *Ibid.*, pp. 228–229.

[56] *Contrat social*, I, 8.

logical, since it assumes the hypothesis that, in the principal acts of their lives, citizens are likened to prudent merchants.

What seems particularly paradoxical in Rousseau's doctrine is the hypothesis of the infallible general will. Taine points out that this leads easily to despotism,[57] and Sumner Maine thinks that Rousseau's city reproduces, in a democratic form, the absolutism that certain theorists of the ancien régime had created for the kings of France; thus the principle heritage bequeathed by Rousseau to modern times consists in the idea of an omnipotent democratic state.[58]

Here again, the vagueness of the *Social Contract* was a great factor in the easy acceptance by contemporaries of a concept of public law which was to have such frightful consequences.

The sources of this doctrine can be found in the following way: For a very long time, Protestant communities believed they were inspired by the Holy Ghost and that, as a result, no doubt could be cast on their decisions. Since the Renaissance, there was an excessive admiration for the peoples and laws of classical antiquity. It was thus easily admitted that at the time of their splendor the ancient republics produced acts of reason in their popular assemblies.[59]

Finally, no one in the eighteenth century would have doubted seriously that universal consent was an irrefutable proof in favor of the thesis that mankind had accepted. Everyone knows that in order to form a mean defining the normal state of a meteorological phenomenon observations are often made only during a rather limited time. To know the opinion of mankind on a question it is by no means necessary to interrogate all men;[60] the only precaution to take

---

[57] Taine, *Ancien Régime*, pp. 319–327.

[58] Henry Sumner Maine, *Essais sur le gouvernement populaire*, pp. 225–227. Bossuet, in his *Politique tirée des propres paroles de l'Ecriture Sainte* ("Politics derived from the Words of Scripture"), is very far from these absolutist doctrines.

[59] I think it is useful to cite an important passage from Vico, which I take from Michelet's translation: "The spectacle of the citizens of Athens uniting by an act of legislation in the idea of an interest common to all helped Socrates form ideal or abstract universal types by means of induction, an operation of the mind which gathers the uniform particulars capable of composing a type with respect to their uniformity. Then Plato observed that in these assemblies minds of individuals, each one impassioned by his own interest, reunited in the dispassionate idea of the common utility. . . . This paved the way for the truly divine definition that Aristotle left of the law: 'Will free from passion' " (Michelet, *Oeuvres choisies de Vico* ["Vico's Selected Works"], pp. 601–602).

[60] This thought appears in the *Commonitorium*, a book Rousseau surely knew because it had often been invoked in the polemics of Protestants and Catholics. Vincent de Lerins says that, in order to know the universal opinion of the church (*quod*

is to be careful that the men consulted do not repeat a party line conveyed to them by factions. This is why Rousseau is persuaded that "if, when a sufficiently informed body of people deliberates, the citizens have had no communication among themselves, the general will will always result from the great number of little differences, and the deliberation will always be good."[61]

When the *Social Contract* appeared, no one was much concerned with the difficulties of applying it. Today they seem so considerable that this book is no longer regarded as having any doctrinal value whatever. In 1762 readers wanted to be shown, above all, that the existing regime was condemned to perish; for twenty years, there had been extraordinary unrest in France, and, several times, a revolution was believed imminent. But the unrest always remained limited to a small group of theorists. Probably the latter retained from the *Spirit of the Laws* only the necessity of better respect for legal procedures,[62] but even this was a serious protest for a time when everything was so arbitrary. The *Social Contract* was popular because it exalted the role of reason as being identical with the general will; every salon believed that it possessed the secret of this general will.[63]

When the circle of Rousseau's readers grew, the meaning of his doctrines changed; founded on the hypothesis of a society of self-governing artisans, they were taken literally by the people when the latter were called upon to play an important role in the formation of opinion. In discussions of the history of the eighteenth century, sufficient notice has not always been made that the same thesis could have three profoundly different implications, according to the position of the persons who upheld it.

The contract doctrine, consistent with the major interests of the third estate, was accepted by the upper bourgeoisie as a scholastic method appropriate to bringing legislation around to economic ends that were in keeping with the aspirations of landed property. Brought into the domain of good literature by Rousseau, it became

---

ubique, quod semper, quod ob omnibus creditum est), it is enough to proceed as they did at the Council of Ephesus and refer to the opinions of ten theologians in different parts of the Christian world.

61 *Contrat social*, II, 3.

62 Rocquain, *L'Esprit révolutionnaire*, p. 124.

63 Sumner Maine says that the *Social Contract* served to uphold the argument that the government must subordinate itself to an ever-changing will (*Essays*, p. 224).

a brilliant radical innovation by means of which witty, amusing, and bold conversationalists could denounce the follies of the royal government in the salons of a frivolous aristocracy. But when Rousseau's book fell into the hands of the people, it was distorted into a program of immediate action.

The most contradictory conclusions could be drawn from the *Social Contract*. Siéyès imitated it when he demanded a greater role for the third estate;[64] the Constituent Assembly embraced its axioms. "Chateaubriand maintained that Rousseau, more than any other, condemned the terrorists; Lally said that Rousseau would have died of grief after the second month of the Revolution; Buzot said that he would have shared the fate of the Girondins . . . Duhem said that he was an aristocrat and would have been guillotined." But, on the other hand, the Jacobins discovered in the *Social Contract* the justification for all their upheavals, for they possessed the general will. "The government," they repeated with Jean Jacques, "was the work and the property of the people; the deputies were but servants of the people. But by the people, they meant the club. . . . In the name of Rousseau's doctrines, the Jacobins accused the Assembly of usurpation. The latter was disrespectful to them, and it made sport of the national majesty."[65] The Jacobin clubs reasoned in this way, like the salons in which the *Social Contract* had been so successful; each club, as before it each salon, claimed to express the true "general will," which is always infallible.

Every scholastic formulation of political principles will have the same destiny; after having amused the *literati*, it will end up by furnishing justification to groups whose existence the author had not even suspected.

IV

In the middle of the eighteenth century, economic writings appeared which Taine erred in confusing with the body of political literature; the physiocrats are much less renowned than the *philo-*

64 Sumner Maine, *Essays*, p. 228.
65 Chuquet, *J. J. Rousseau*, pp. 148–151.

sophes—in part, perhaps, because they were concerned with questions of a more practical nature. It is doubtful that they had much influence, but they decidedly represent the second strain of which I spoke above: from them we learn how that segment of the bourgeoisie which was closely involved in the affairs of state interpreted the governing power. In a letter written to J. B. Say in 1815, Dupont de Nemours says that he stood alone at the time of the Revolution with Abeille and Morellet for preserving the tradition of Quesnay, that no chance was lost in the Constituent Assembly to ridicule the theories of the school, but that, in spite of everything, the Assembly often ended up deciding according to these very theories.[66] This observation is very important to us, for it helps us understand the role of these writers. They so well expressed the most widely held and most considered opinions of the administrative class that they must often have believed that the reforms achieved by the Revolution resulted from their reasoned proofs. Actually they were the culmination of a great movement to which the physiocratic theories were attached as a simple ideological accessory.

In Condorcet's opinion, there were only very few men "who embraced their whole doctrine. People were frightened by the generality of their maxims and the inflexibility of their principles. They themselves prejudiced their cause by affecting an abstruse and dogmatic language, by seeming to forget the interests of political liberty for those of commercial liberty, and by presenting some parts of their system which they had not sufficiently refined, in an excessively absolute and imperious way." Their principle success was supposedly due to the condemnations they leveled against fiscal administration and the tariff.[67]

The above is the opinion of an enemy, but it is generally true. The Encyclopedists detested the physiocrats. Grimm accused them of having "a penchant for religion and platitude which is quite contrary to the philosophic spirit."[68] The great success of the Marquis de Mirabeau's books made the fashionable declaimers fear for a moment that the reading public was escaping them. Therefore, they vigorously heralded Galiani's dialogues on the grain trade in order

---

[66] *Les Physiocrates*, p. 410. Alexis de Tocqueville says that the substance of the Revolution is found in these principles (*L'Ancien Régime*, p. 158).

[67] Condorcet, *Tableau historique*, 9th epoch.

[68] Brunetière, *Etudes critiques*, 2d ser., p. 243.

to play a mean trick on the physiocrat partisans of free trade. When Morellet wrote to answer the Neapolitan buffoon with serious arguments, Diderot made every effort to prevent the publication of his answer. He had been given the task of reading this book as a censor; "if the Abbé Morellet's refutation was printed," says Brunetière, "it is not that all possible excuses a police lieutenant could muster in order to suspend the printing were not brought forth."[69]

Necker, who was so bent on making a reputation by flattering the *philosophes*,[70] did not fail to declare himself an enemy of the physiocrats, and he was accused of having advised Turgot's enemies. His book on the grain laws was admired, as Galiani's book had been. Turgot, although he frequented Mme Geoffrin's salon at an early date, never adopted the *philosophes'* ideas.[71]

If, in spite of the intrigues of the salons and the Encyclopedists, who knew so well how to make and break reputations, the physiocrats nevertheless had stature, it is obviously because their ideas roughly corresponded to a very strong current of opinion.

The reproach that Condorcet directs against them about their lack of concern for political liberty is only too well founded; this should not surprise us, since we regard them as having based their doctrines on the tradition of monarchical France. With such a perspective, they could have nothing but scorn for the division and balance of powers.[72] Thus Le Trosne judged that France was in a better position than England, because there reforms did not run the risk of being obstructed by political parties.[73]

At times it seems that the physiocrats employ a Napoleonic language: they speak of the state as an impersonal power which by law is subordinate to the citizens and in reality is their master; it is "the creation and representative of the whole and must make the right of each one bend under the will of the whole." They dream of "a democratic despotism," as Tocqueville saw it: the chosen rulers doing everything without following the impulses of political assemblies,

---

[69] Brunetière, *Etudes critiques*, 2d ser., pp. 247–248. This report of Diderot is full of hypocrisy, as was so often the case at this time in the literature of the *philosophes*.

[70] Rocquain, *L'Esprit révolutionnaire*, p. 358.

[71] Turgot, I, xxxi, xcix–cxi. The intermediary between Necker and the Court was the Marquis de Pezay, soldier and poet, son of a Genevan financier, and a great friend of Maurepas.

[72] Alexis de Tocqueville, *L'Ancien Régime*, p. 159.

[73] *Ibid.*, p. 162.

controlled only by a public reason that has no means of expressing itself.[74]

Turgot proposed to Louis XVI the creation of elected bodies, but he thought that it would be possible to limit them to purely administrative functions. Tocqueville points out that no one could have been more mistaken about the importance of the measure or the spirit of his time. But he adds that this system was realized after the Revolution, when the country was tired of politics.[75] Here again, the physiocrats were forerunners of the empire, but their mistake was in not seeing that, at the expiration of the ancien régime, the country thirsted for liberty.[76]

They had absolute confidence in an enlightened power, which would establish judicial equality, expand education, and govern according to uniform rules. According to Quesnay, "despotism is impossible if the nation is enlightened." His school saw only one effective means of fighting against despotism: "continued general public education concerning natural justice and the natural order."[77] This was an illusion very like that of the utopians who hoped to lead the bourgeoisie into practicing socialism. An educated and well-informed administration was supposed to be the taxpayer's guarantee, just as a humanitarian bourgeoisie is supposedly the proletariat's guarantee in modern utopias. "With the help of this little piece of literary nonsense they meant to remove all political guarantees."[78] We can also ask our official socialists if they truly believe that their nonsense is capable of producing a serious organization of labor.

Unlike Rousseau, the physiocrats did not find their model in the republics of Protestant artisans. Nothing is more revealing for understanding their doctrines and the considerable current of opinion that they represented than this oft-quoted passage from Tocqueville: "Finding nothing around them which seemed to conform to this ideal, they found it in the heart of Asia. I do not exaggerate in af-

---

[74] *Ibid.*, pp. 163–164.
[75] *Ibid.*, pp. 144–145.
[76] Tocqueville believed that everyone was caught up in liberal ideas, even including the physiocrats (*ibid.*, p. 167). This was the result of the struggle between the government and the Parlement.
[77] Natural justice and the natural order are the fundamental tenets of the physiocrats.
[78] Alexis de Tocqueville, *L'Ancien Régime*, p. 160.

firming that not one of them does not fail to praise China grandiloquently in some part of his writings. In reading their books, one is certain to encounter at least that, and, as still very little was known about China, they tell us some fantastic tales about it. This mindless and barbaric government . . . was in their eyes, a perfect model for all nations to copy. . . . They were enraptured at the sight of a country whose absolute but unprejudiced ruler works on the land with his own hands once a year in honor of the utilitarian arts, where a literacy examination must be passed to qualify for all positions, and which has a philosophy as a religion and men of letters as aristocrats."[79]

The judicial ideas of the physiocrats have had a cardinal importance in the history of our institutions. In the eighteenth century, everyone in France, regardless of his school, was in agreement in admitting that property is a social creation. Montesquieu, Mirabeau, Tronchet, Necker, and Mallet du Pan do not differ from Robespierre or Rousseau on this principle.[80]

The physiocrats introduced the Lockean doctrine according to which property is the source of all laws. "Citizens," wrote Turgot in his article on foundations, "have rights, and rights that are sacred to the very heart of society. The citizens exist independently of society and are its necessary elements. They enter society solely in order to put themselves, together with all their rights, under the protection of laws that assure their property and their liberty."[81]

Contrary to the opinion of many modern jurists, they did not think that moral entities could be regarded as being true proprietors. Where no more than one judicial category is seen today they saw two economic categories, and, in their opinion, law had to follow economics. Tocqueville was obviously quite mistaken in believing that he could draw a conclusion about their opinions on all civil affairs from their opinions regarding endowments. "Contracts," he says, "inspire little respect in them; private rights are given no con-

---

[79] Alexis de Tocqueville, *L'Ancien Régime*, pp. 163–164.

[80] André Lichtenberger, *Le Socialisme et la Révolution française*, pp. 182, 185–188. In Book V of *Emile* Rousseau has put forth a theory of property which would later be the inspiration for Lassalle's doctrines: The ruler has no right to touch the property of one or several private individuals, but he can legitimately seize the property of all, as happened in Sparta at the time of Lycurgus. On the other hand, Solon's abolition of debts was an illegal act.

[81] Turgot, II, 308.

sideration. Rather, in their eyes there are no longer any private rights, so to speak, but only a general utility." He marvels that such a revolutionary concept could be so easily accepted by upright men of mild and quiet manners, honest magistrates, and able administrators."[82] In their capacity as honest magistrates, Quesnay's disciples held private law sacred and were ready to defend it against arbitrary rule, but they regarded endowments as belonging to the domain of administrative law. They were struck by the faults of the bodies charged with managing endowments. In their capacity as able administrators, they wanted all the resources destined for public use to be employed in an efficient way. Hence, they did not deem worthy of respect endowments whose general expenses were so often excessive and which were defended by people interested in maintaining long-standing administrative abuses.[83]

Turgot thought that the government had the incontestable right "to dispose of old endowments and to direct their funds to new uses or, better still, suppress them altogether. The public interest is the supreme law and should not be tempered by a superstitious respect for what is called the intention of the original contributors, as if ignorant and limited individuals had the right to bind generations to come to their capricious wills. Nor should it be tempered by fear of offending the alleged privileges of certain groups, as if particular groups had privileges under the state. . . . Particular groups do not exist by themselves or for themselves; they were formed for society, and they should cease to exist at the moment when they cease to be useful."[84] Here the language of the administrator is in perfect harmony with the thinking of the economist, in whose eyes the land should be managed according to the ideas of the living, not the dead. If, as Turgot thought, public needs could be satisfied better with budgetary resources than with endowment funds, the latter were no more than a nuisance.

The administrative procedures of the ancien régime were most often quite cavalier; thus it should not be surprising that the men who had some connection with the administration hardly shared that respect for tradition that appeared in France during the Restoration. "The past," says Tocqueville, "is an object of unbounded

---

[82] Alexis de Tocqueville, *L'Ancien Régime*, p. 159.
[83] Turgot, II, 304.
[84] Turgot, II, 308–309. In the case where the church has interest in endowments, Turgot thought that the state must act in accord with the church.

scorn for economists. . . . There is not one institution, however ancient and well-founded in our history, whose abolition they did not demand if it inconvenienced them or distorted the symmetry of their plans."[85]

The Revolution would soon liquidate the ancien régime, very often by imitating its very practices. But this imitation was full of horrors, because, during the Terror, power fell into the hands of men who were not, in general, completely prepared to accomplish tasks as formidable as those then imposed by government. The most dangerous procedures of the ancien régime were pushed to the greatest excesses. It was necessary to wage a battle against starvation: the price of commodities was fixed, requisitioning to feed the large cities never ceased, men whom oft-crazed opinion denounced as black marketeers were hounded in a thousand ways. In order to maintain the armies, the country was treated like a besieged citadel whose entire resources were at the disposal of the commanding officer. When the civil war complicated the state's difficulties, the property of the rebels was confiscated. Thus circumstances produced an almost total eclipse of judicial ideas, and administration degenerated into police action, which always happens whenever it is entrusted to men who do not feel compelled by force of legal opinion to moderate their entrusted arbitrary power.[86] Financial laws were more than once directed by considerations of police strategy: the rich were strongly suspected of misusing their fortune in order to undermine the republic; thus they were treated as enemies.[87]

When calm began to return, everyone felt the need of obtaining guarantees against the return of such arbitrary measures. Those who acquired national wealth during this period were even more desirous than all the other proprietors of having the inviolability of property proclaimed. Everyone knows how important their interests have been in the course of our history. The return of the Bourbons was impossible so long as the validity of the revolutionary sales was unsure.[88] Thus we can understand how, after the experiences of the Terror, the doctrine of the physiocrats gained an

---

[85] Alexis de Tocqueville, *L'Ancien Régime*, p. 159.

[86] It is this moderation of arbitrary power which gives birth to administrative law, a very fragile creation when traditions are not powerful.

[87] André Lichtenberger, *Le Socialisme et la Révolution*, pp. 255, 258–262.

[88] Fearing the weakening of their validity, jurisprudence has attached an almost religious quality to the revolutionary sales of property.

authority it had heretofore lacked. It seems that the Constitution of the year III was inspired by these ideas, not only in Article 5 of the Declaration of Rights, which defined property, but especially in the Declaration of Duties. Article 8 affirms that all work and all social order depend on the maintenance of property; Article 9 imposes on each citizen the obligation of defending the motherland, liberty, equality, and property.

This was truly the triumph of the physiocrats, a triumph that has long endured and that is due to historical circumstances whose future existence the physiocrats themselves could not foresee.

Historians have not achieved a convincing explanation for the truly paradoxical role played by eighteenth-century men of letters. That is because they have considered society as a whole, instead of examining the relationships of men of letters with each class. Our task is to determine why the third estate listened to them like oracles, although their knowledge did not generally qualify them to give advice to the bourgeoisie. Let us refer here to what I have called the third ideological current of the eighteenth century, a current which depends on imitating aristocratic manners. Members of the newly dominant class had absolute confidence in men whom they regarded as being coddled by the high nobility and the monarchy. They never questioned the causes for this privileged treatment, which astonished, fascinated, and misled them.

Foreign opinion played an important role in our history at that time. When Voltaire departed for Berlin he was still less renowned than Montesquieu and Fontenelle. Upon his arrival in Paris in 1749, Grimm was very surprised to learn that Voltaire was admired less in France than in Germany.[89] Voltaire went "to Potsdam to seek the consecration of glory and popularity which was refused him in his native land."[90] His strategy was excellent, for on his return his reputation was considerably enhanced, in spite of his misadventures at the Prussian court.

[89] Brunetière, *Etudes critiques*, 2d ser., p. 176.
[90] *Ibid.*, 4th ser., p. 322.

We find a choice example of this role played by foreigners in quite an unusual dissertation by Diderot addressed to Spartine, who had consulted him on a play by Palissot. Diderot wrote: "If you can proceed so that it will not be said that with your permission public insults have been twice directed against those of your fellow citizens who are honored in all parts of Europe, whom travelers make it their duty to visit, and whom they consider it an honor to have known when they return to their native country, I believe that you will have acted wisely."[91] French high society was very sensitive to the judgments that foreigners passed on its great men, and the bourgeoisie had an almost superstitious respect for these judgments. It does not seem that this situation is about to disappear: the democratic regime has continued the tradition of the third estate, and each time men of letters so desire, they can still exercise a veritable dictatorship over it. Following the Dreyfus affair, we have seen a refined boudoir entertainer of the Monceau Quarter transformed by a few spectators into an oracle of socialism; it appears that Anatole France was at first very much surprised by this metamorphosis, but he ended up by wondering seriously whether, in telling his little drolleries to the fine ladies and gentlemen of high finance, he had not perhaps solved the puzzle of the social question. If the movement that, for several years, propelled the most intelligent workers toward the public universities had developed as the bourgeoisie had wished, socialism would have fallen into the democratic rut.

Democracy has as its object the disappearance of class feeling and the merging of all citizens in a society containing forces capable of elevating every intelligent individual into a higher social rank from that into which he was born. It would achieve its object if the most energetic workers strived to become like the middle class, were happy to accept its advice, and asked esteemed men for ideas. From that time onward there would be no reason for a democratic structure not to be stable. It could then be shaken only by difficulties caused by the ambition of a few men; it would not be threatened in principle by socialism as it is today. Thus intelligent democrats are right in trying so hard to defend the prestige of men of letters. They seek to direct mass education so as to encourage the maintenance of this prestige; to this end, instead of teaching workers what

[91] *Ibid.*, 2d ser., p. 164.

they need to know to equip themselves for their life as workers, they strive to develop in them a lively curiosity for things found only in the books written to amuse the bourgeoisie.

The success of such teaching depends on the workers' having a humble sense of their current inferiority and regarding the millieu of men of letters with the satisfied admiration of a provincial commoner for the royal court of days past. There must be a great distance between the position of the mass of admirers and that of the makers of reputations. Thus when many of our most refined and most aristocratic writers display so much zeal in praising the benefits of popular education, we ought to admire, not their "love of humble persons," but their great perspicacity in understanding the art of creating a constituency. For several years the public universities were a vast advertisement for reading the books of the *Dreyfusards*, and if the advertisement had not been conducted in such a scandalous manner the results would probably have been more lasting.

In the *Eloge* of Montesquieu, d'Alembert says that "the part of the public that teaches dictates to the part of the public that listens what it must think and say" about the *Spirit of the Laws.* Laboulaye thinks that d'Alembert was speaking of his friends, the *philosophes*, in excessively proud terms and that lettered Frenchmen of the eighteenth century could very well read Montesquieu without recourse to the *philosophes*.[92] This distinction of an *Ecclesia docens* and an *Ecclesia dicens* is still fundamental in our democracies: if, on the one hand, they want to suppress class consciousness, they still fully intend to maintain and, if need be, perfect the "hierarchies of culture."

Now let us see what the position of men of letters was in relation to the aristocracy of the eighteenth century. This is a very important question to resolve, for the interpretation of the literature of the eighteenth century depends on its solution.

There was an old tradition that a court needed skillful orators, who pleased with brilliant conversation and who were capable of shedding luster on the prince who patronized them. These orators also comprised part of the accoutrements of wealth required of rich personages. In the eighteenth century, this tradition had not dis-

---

[92] Montesquieu, *L'Esprit des lois* (Laboulaye edition), III, xxv.

appeared, and every great household had a small court abundantly provided with its exceptional persons.

"Every evening they dine in society and are the adornment and amusement of the salons where they go to talk. Among the houses in which society people dine, there is not one that does not have its house philosopher and a little later its economist or scientist. . . . Their path can be followed from salon to salon, from château to château . . ."[93] Taine believed that the philosophy of that time was "a kind of superior opera in which all the great ideas capable of interesting a thinking person march in procession and collide, sometimes in serious costume, sometimes in a comic disguise . . ."[94] "The most cultivated and outstanding foreigners came one by one to the Baron Holbach's. . . . There one heard [Morellet tells us] the most free, lively, and informative conversation that ever took place. . . . Every possible bold idea in the political and religious realm was brought forward and discussed, pro and con. . . . Often a single person took the floor and proposed his theory, calmly and without being interrupted. At other times, remarkable debates took place, which the rest of the company quietly observed.[95] How could one prevent the nobility, which spends its life talking, from seeking out men who talk so well? It would be just as well to prevent their wives, who go to the theater every evening and playact at home, from enticing famous actors and singers to their homes."[96]

There is still another reason for the importance of the benevolent relations the aristocracy maintained with recognized men of letters. Ever since the invention of printing, authors of satires never ceased to be greatly feared. We know how impudently l'Arétin exploited the terror he inspired. In a letter, he boasts of being able to laugh

---

93 Taine, *Ancien Régime*, p. 333. Custom still authorized the parasitic life of which Marmontel provides such a scandalous example, but second-rate authors had to live in a way that seems highly undignified to us today. Brunetière wrote a terrible sentence on d'Alembert: "It is indeed d'Alembert of whom I am speaking when I say he was housed by a Lespinasse, enamoured of his Guibert or his Mora, and, to top it off, supported, in part, by the king of Prussia and in part by Madame Geoffrin" (*ibid.*, p. 217). On Marmontel, who owed a large part of his fortune to the fact that he was a "robust Limousin," cf. Brunetière, *Etudes critiques*, 6th ser., p. 254.
94 Taine, *Ancien Régime*, p. 333.
95 *Ibid.*, pp. 367–368.
96 *Ibid.*, p. 369. In order to understand clearly the salons of the 18th century, we should remember the role of the influential journals a half century ago; the salons served to inform a public similar to that which later placed its confidence in the *Correspondant* and the *Revue des Deux Mondes*.

at the world thanks to a feather pen and a few leaves of white paper; furthermore, he said that he became rich by the sweat of his writing desk.

The *philosophes* of the eighteenth century were past masters in the art of calumny. When they had the opportunity of exercising their satiric imagination on someone, their work always proved quite superior to their serious writings. For instance, this is obvious in Voltaire. These writers respected nothing and were feared even by the most imperturbable people: a member of the Academy of Inscriptions of whom Malesherbes asked an opinion on Diderot's *Père de famille* begs his correspondent to be discreet, because he does not "wish to have cause for a misunderstanding with people who think that they alone possess all human reason [and whom he] dreads as much as theologians."[97]

Foreign rulers who support or flatter a philosopher do not do it simply out of admiration for his intellect.[98] Frederick regarded Voltaire as an extremely dangerous man whom he had a great interest in controlling, but it was the Empress Catherine above all who then controlled opinion. After the assassination of her husband, she asked the French ambassador if he knew Voltaire and if he could explain the event to him.[99] Voltaire seems to have resisted for awhile, but he soon enlisted in the ranks of admirers of the "Semiramis of the north" to the point of scandalizing Mme de Choiseul and Mme du Deffand. Walpole wrote to the latter: "How does one make amends for a murder? Is it by retaining hired poets, by paying mercenary historians, and by bribing ridiculous philosophers a thousand miles from home? It is base souls like these who sing Caesar's praises and remain silent about his repressions."[100]

---

97 Brunetière, *Etudes critiques*, 2d ser., p. 192.

98 Laboulaye says that "Frederick the Great played a comedy with Voltaire and his friends from which he derived all the benefit"; he could "attempt the most criminal attacks with the complicity of those who controlled public opinion" (Montesquieu, *L'Esprit des lois*, p. xliv). And farther on: "In 1767, Catherine, no less skillful than Frederick at winning over public opinion, fancied that she presented herself to Europe as the apostle of civilization and of new ideas" (p. 1).

99 Desnoiresterres, *Voltaire et Jean-Jacques Rousseau* ("Voltaire and Jean Jacques Rousseau"), p. 371.

100 Desnoiresterres, *op. cit.*, p. 380. We are often tempted to think that Brunetière is only too correct when he says that Rousseau was the only man with any courage of all the celebrated authors of that period. "It is true," he adds, "that they practically made a crime out of this very courage" (*ibid.*, p. 222). Turgot was indignant at seeing Helvétius praise Catherine and Frederick so much (*Correspondance inédite de Condorcet et de Turgot* ["Unpublished Correspondence of Condorcet and Turgot"], p. 147).

But we would have a very incomplete idea of eighteenth-century literature if we limited ourselves to the above considerations. In addition, we must recall the role of the court jesters in the Middle Ages. In the eighteenth century there were veritable clowns in the salons, such as "Galiani, who was a clever dwarf of genius—a kind of Plato or Machiavelli with the zest and mannerisms of a Harlequin. He had an inexhaustible repertory of stories and was an admirable buffoon, a perfect skeptic, believing nothing and having faith in nothing. With his wig in his hand and his legs crossed on the sofa where he is perched, he proves [to the philosophers] by a comic argument that they reason [*raisonnent*] or resound [*résonnent*], if not like blockheads [*cruches*], at least like bells [*cloches*]— in any case, almost as badly as theologians. A witness called it the most brilliant thing in the world; it equaled the best spectacles."[101]

The men in the foreground were not always aware of the ridiculous role they played in high society. The story of the relationship of Frederick the Great and Voltaire has become impossible for us to understand, because our customs are so different from those of the eighteenth century. The pledge the king sent for the great writer to sign during the latter's quarrels with Maupertuis seems incredibly overbearing today; clearly, for Frederick, there was not a great difference between a famous man of letters and a servant.[102]

Much later, after their reconciliation, it is curious to see the tone in which the freethinking sovereign wrote about the furor provoked by the execution of the Chevalier de la Barre: "Philosophy must not encourage such actions, nor must it irreverently criticize judges who had no other choice than to pass judgment as they did." When Voltaire conceived the project of convening at Cleves writers whom he believed were threatened by a reawakening of religious fanaticism, the king made him this ironic recommendation: "They will all be well received, provided that they are moderate and peaceful."[103]

The objection could be made that Voltaire belonged to a rather old-fashioned generation and that he had been raised with the idea

---

[101] Taine, *Ancien Régime*, p. 369.

[102] "I promise V. M. that as long as she will do me the kindness of lodging me in the château, I will write against no one, be it the French government, the ministers, other rulers, or famous men of letters, toward whom I will render the respect due to them. I will not abuse S. M.'s letters, I will conduct myself in a suitable manner as a man of letters who has the honor to be S. M.'s chamberlain and who lives among upright people." The whole of Desnoiresterres' work on Voltaire and Frederick should be read, for it describes out-and-out buffoonery.

[103] Desnoiresterres, *Voltaire et Jean-Jacques Rousseau*, pp. 502–505.

of respect for the great. This would explain certain cowardly deeds of which his contemporaries sometimes were ashamed. But Diderot! He is the archetype of the man of letters of the new system, to such an extent that our present-day bourgeois have placed him in the democratic Hall of Fame. Joseph Reinach uses the most exalted expressions of admiration when he speaks of him. Diderot does not suspect that when Empress Catherine seemed so familiar with him, it is because tradition permitted buffoons much familiarity with the great, in order to sharpen their wits.

Taine came close to recognizing what Diderot's real position was in the salons, but he was restrained by his admiration for this model precursor of the contemporary bourgeoisie.[104] The portrait of Diderot which he has given is very favorable, and he pleads extenuating circumstances in Diderot's favor in the following way: "He is a newcomer, a parvenu in society. In him you see a plebeian, a powerful thinker, an indefatigable worker, and a great artist,[105] whom the circumstances of the time introduced into the world of fashionable dinner parties. There he dominates the conversation, leads the orgy, and, by contagion or wager, he alone makes more shocking statements than all the other guests combined."[106] If Taine had not been restrained by the respect he declared for the eighteenth-century writers, he would have said that Diderot was patronized in high society like a literary clown.

Such a period could no longer appreciate the rules of good sense, moderation in language, and practical wisdom, the code of which Boileau set down in an earlier period. Diderot again must serve as the archetype: Taine says, "Not only did he descend to the very depths of antisocial and antireligious doctrine with all the severity of logic and paradox more impetuously and more noisily than even Holbach himself, but, what is more, he fell into and wallowed in the slime of the century, which was declamation. In his leading

---

104 Perhaps Taine is more representative of the bourgeois tradition than anyone else. That is why his account is of very special value to us. He admires science with as much naiveté as the Encyclopedists, and he has a special affection for the "novelists of moral emancipation," for Stendhal as well as for Diderot.

105 Brunetière thinks that, in the writings of Diderot, "confusion has been too often taken for profundity," and that "beneath an air of independence extending sometimes to cynicism," he has "all the prejudices of a bourgeois or a philistine" (*Evolution des genres*, p. 153).

106 Taine, *Ancien Régime*, p. 349.

novels, he develops at length the double entendre or the lewd scene. In his work, crudeness is not attenuated by cleverness or cushioned by elegance. It is neither subtle nor biting. He does not know how to portray appealing rascals, as does Crébillon the younger."[107]

Reinach is very embarrassed by the moral code of his hero, which "results in the most unbridled return to the state of nature," which plunges "most often into the mire of primitive bestiality," and in which he finds to his great regret "the panegyric of incest, prostitution, and sexual promiscuity." This admirer of the Encyclopedists states sadly that Diderot, who rejects everything outside of the laws of nature, recognizes only two ends in the latter: "the preservation of the individual and the propagation of the species."[108] Thus we can compare Diderot with those bourgeois freethinkers who embraced Darwinism with such enthusiasm because they thought that they discovered a means of justifying their base appetites in the hypothesis of their simian origins.

Now we touch on the essence of the psychology of eighteenth-century men:[109] This boasting of lubricity concerns not only a moral code but also intellectual production. It proves that reflection exercised a very feeble control on their imagination. Thus historians surely are wasting their time by trying to penetrate the thinking of the eighteenth-century *philosophes*; the latter were nothing but idle talkers, peddlers of satire or flattery, and, above all, buffoons of a degenerate aristocracy. What Brunetière says about Diderot applies to almost all of them:[110] "The difficult thing is to know what he thought, and the reason for this will appear plausible to you if I say, as I believe, that he never knew, himself, what he was thinking."[111]

The middle class read the works of the *philosophes* in a different spirit from the nobility; it took seriously what was written by people with such impressive social connections. The more unconventional

---

[107] Taine, *Ancien Régime*, p. 349. Here one cannot help think of Zola, who also lacked elegance and cleverness. That great peddler of trash boasted of "having been the first to give the sexual instinct its true place in the novel. To believe him, sex would become the great preoccupation of mankind" (Guyau, *L'Art du point de vue sociologique* ["A Sociological View of Art"], p. 158).

[108] J. Reinach, *Diderot*, pp. 174–175.

[109] Some time ago, I called attention to this manner of penetrating the secrets of the human soul by examining ideas about sexual relations.

[110] Rousseau, who is unlike any of the other 18th-century *philosophes*, is an exception.

[111] Brunetière, *Evolution des genres.*, p. 154.

an opinion was, the more the middle class admired the genius of such bold and profound thinkers in freeing themselves from the chains of tradition; the more confidence it had in the enlightenment it could acquire by such readings; and the more was it disposed to dare similar attempts. The immeasurable stupidity of Flaubert's bourgeois prototype, Monsieur Homais, is the logical result of this influence of men of letters on the French bourgeoisie. For almost a century, educated people talked nonsense as a result of their incapacity to understand the meaning of books which, coming from a very aristocratic milieu, appeared to have fallen from the sky.

Our predecessors' lack of any critical capacity should not surprise us. It could not be found in the men of letters whose occupations we have just examined. We would not think of seeking it in the aristocrats who busied themselves solely with laughing, slandering, or laying traps for people who displeased them. Experience teaches us that the critical capacity is always lacking in social classes that do not take account of their own conditions of life in their thinking. Thus it was lacking in the bourgeoisie. The history of ancient and medieval writers illustrates this proposition in a remarkable way, and the experience of the nineteenth century furnishes another proof of it.

As Renan saw so well when he wrote in connection with Augustin Thierry, from the day the past was examined by people who wanted to find instructive examples in order to understand the struggles in which their class was engaged, history took on an entirely different aspect: "The ultimate significance of human affairs is only grasped by an ability to understand the present, and the present yields its secret only in proportion to the stake which one takes in it. . . . [In order to interpret the texts of medieval history] it was necessary to have an experience in secular life which neither monastic life nor the untroubled investigations of the paliographer gave. A young man of twenty, cast into a passionate milieu and gifted with the perspicacity attained through familiarity with politics, could at the first attempt call attention to a collection of gaps and erroneous views in the work of these great masters [the Benedictines]."[112]

That is why my friends and I never cease to urge the working

---

[112] Renan, *Essais de morale et de critique* ("Critical and Moral Essays"), pp. 117–118.

class not to allow itself to be pushed into the rut of bourgeois science or philosophy. A great change will take place in the world on the day the proletariat acquires, as did the bourgeoisie after the Revolution, the feeling that it can think according to its own conditions of life. The parliamentary regime revealed to the great historians of the modern bourgeoisie their vocation: "the body of ideas that the Restoration labeled with the term of liberalism was the soul of [Augustin Thierry's] history."[113] This explains the statement that "the golden age of serious studies followed the revolutionary excitement almost immediately."[114] This was due, not only to the fact that the end of the Napoleonic Wars contained many unforeseen teachings, as Renan says,[115] but also to the fact that, around 1820, the bourgeoisie considered itself capable of thinking alone.

As has been said many times, the proletariat possesses a system of institutions that are as much its own as the parliamentary regime belongs to the bourgeoisie. It is the syndicalist movement that can accomplish the intellectual liberation that would rid the working classes of all respect for bourgeois nonsense.

---

[113] *Ibid.*, pp. 115–116.
[114] *Ibid.*, p. 124.
[115] *Ibid.*, p. 116.

CHAPTER III

Science in the Eighteenth Century

I. *Science as an object of curiosity. The* Encyclopedia. *General knowledge necessary for administrators. Discoveries that inspire great hopes.*

II. *Application of mathematics to social questions. Condorcet's illusions. Reasons for the error then made. Perpetuation of a false science of probabilities.*

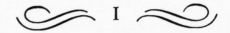

The doctrine of progress would naturally emerge out of the aspirations of a conquering class that had complete confidence in its future, believed itself perfectly prepared to take power, and had great plans for reforms in mind. And yet, we could not fully understand the ideas of this class if we did not render an exact account of the notion it held of science.

At the present time, science is an austere discipline in which each practitioner chooses a narrow field to cultivate painstakingly for his whole life. One can become truly adept in a discipline only by undergoing a long training period, by keeping abreast of latest developments, and by controlling the methods of particular investigations. The division of scientific work into independent groups seems so natural and so fruitful to us that it does not occur to us to ask whether such a social structure could ever have aroused objections. Our predecessors considered this specialization a routine worthy of farmhands, a degradation of the mind, and an outrage to man's noble destiny. "Most of the literary minds of the eighteenth century prided themselves on understanding geometry; scientists, on their side, prided themselves on dabbling in literature."[1]

---

[1] Cournot, *Considérations sur la marche des idées et des événements dans les*

Fontenelle found himself suited to give once again a philosophical formula: he praised the good results that would come from the coordination of the sciences. Brunetière was mistaken in believing that Fontenelle had made a great discovery;[2] he should have left such stupidity to the positivists. The alleged coordination of the sciences is in no way the supreme aim of modern research; it is rather the expression of the customs of the old French society, and it depends above all on the ways of the salons. The great concern in the eighteenth century was to be able to sustain a conversation with the enlightened people whom one encountered in good society. If the coordination of the sciences still fascinates the democratic bourgeoisie, it is because this class has few ideas of its own and has a mania for nourishing itself at the sources of the ancien régime. There are several reasons for our predecessors' conceptions about science, but the principal one is always the inquisitiveness of the upper classes.

a. At the end of the seventeenth century, the world conceived a passion for a whole series of subjects hitherto completely unknown. The honest man (the ideal type of the seventeenth century) of the preceding generation had a rather limited horizon; now, insight into everything was desired.[3] Lemery's chemistry course, published in 1675, had many editions and was translated into several languages. Ladies esteemed du Verney's lessons in anatomy; this scientist, in commending Mademoiselle de Launay to the Duchess du Maine, wrote that she was the "one daughter of France who best knows the human body."[4] At that time, Thomas Diafoirus could invite his fiancée to attend a dissection without appearing ridiculous.[5]

Turgot considered curiosity the great driving force of progress;[6] this view corresponds perfectly with the sentiments of his contemporaries, who were always seeking new knowledge and never consented to limit themselves by the narrow bounds of a scientific specialty. "As a man of the world seeking fame but unpossessed

---

temps modernes ("Considerations on the Advance of Ideas and Events in Modern Times"), II, 54–55. Clairaut, however, could not bear d'Alembert's "seeking to distinguish himself in letters" (Diderot, *Oeuvres complètes* ["Complete Works"], VI, 474).

[2] Brunetière, *Etudes critiques*, 5th ser., pp. 239, 242.

[3] Brunetière, *Etudes critiques*, 5th ser., p. 236.

[4] Brunetière, *ibid.*, 5th ser., pp. 232, 235.

[5] Molière, *Malade imaginaire*, Act II, scene vi.

[6] Turgot, II, 601.

of literary talent, Buffon began by desiring to practice mathematics; then he experimented in physics of the type for which it is best to be a rich man; then, finally, he found his niche in the position of steward of the king's garden while, at the same time, he became a great naturalist and writer. In this double role, he was the most famous as well as the most effective of the popularizers." Cournot points out that the eighteenth century followed Buffon's example, concentrating first on geometry, then finding demonstrations of chemistry and physics more amusing, and finally settling on natural history.[7]

In a commentary on Clairaut in his correspondence with Grimm, Diderot gives this picture of the varieties of curiosity in 1765: "The metaphysicians and poets have had their day; the systematic physicists[8] succeeded them. Systematic physics gave way to experimental physics, the latter to geometry;[9] geometry to natural history and to chemistry, which have been in vogue lately and which share the limelight with affairs of state, commerce, politics, and, above all, the agriculture craze, without anyone's guessing that agriculture will be the science that national frivolity will make fashionable next." Clairaut did not follow the trend; as a result, he fell from favor: formerly, distinguished ladies "wanted to have a geometrician in their retenue," but now, "a geometrician has trouble finding a bookseller to take on his books or a reader to open them."[10]

It was, indeed, a matter of fads being created in salons; thus a science became less interesting as it became more technical. In the *Pensées sur l'interprétation de la nature* (1754), Diderot informs us that, in his opinion, mathematics had arrived at the point where it could advance no further: "I would almost dare to guarantee that before one hundred years are past there will not be three great geometricians in Europe."[11] This statement gives a sure indication that mathematics was already beginning to be closed to amateurs, and Diderot could not conceive of scientific activity outside of that which attracted amateurs.[12]

---

[7] Cournot, *Considérations sur la marche*, p. 55.
[8] This clearly refers to the Cartesians of Fontenelle's time.
[9] Here Diderot places Clairaut and d'Alembert.
[10] Diderot, *Oeuvres complètes*, VI, 474–475.
[11] *Ibid.*, II, 11.
[12] He said that the works of the great 18th-century geometricians, Bernoulli, Euler, Maupertuis, Clairaut, Fontaine, d'Alembert, and Lagrange, "will exist in fu-

Chemistry enjoyed a success that was all the greater because it was still only an apothecary's art. In 1770 Diderot spoke of Rouelle with an enthusiasm that would astonish us if we did not know about Diderot's poor conception of science. Rouelle "wanted to be a poet, philosopher, theologian, politician, and musician"; he was a "great scientist, a profound theorist"; but "he believed in alchemy" and was an "inept and inattentive manipulator."[13]

Physiology attracted Diderot strongly, especially because it was in its infancy; besides, he was content with elementary ideas. Diderot implored the Empress Catherine to have the organization of the human body and, in particular, the organs of reproduction explained to noble young ladies with the aim of sermonizing to them. In a week they would know enough about "the peril and the result of men's advances," about conjugal duty and childbearing; after three or four lessons in anatomy, Diderot's daughter read *Candide* without "anything in this wicked book taxing her little head." The sight of the wax models the teacher used to illustrate the lessons were sufficient to calm her imagination and make her understand the reasons decorum prescribes the covering up of certain parts of the body.[14]

Above all, Diderot proved that he knew the curious and infantile mentality of his contemporaries wonderfully well when he conceived of relating formulas for the arts and crafts to them; he praised his merchandise with such aplomb that many people took him for the creator of scientific technology. The latter, however, originated in a more modest and natural way: it was created by French military engineers and by the professors who taught in the military schools. Joseph Reinach is undoubtedly unaware of this fact, for he writes: "The philosophers endeavored to discover the working classes, to give recognition to the work without which civilization would be

---

ture centuries like the pyramids of Egypt, whose surfaces, covered with hieroglyphics, awake in us a frightening idea of the power and resources of the men who raised them." Perhaps that also means that these works would become unintelligible.

13 Diderot, *Oeuvres complètes*, VI, 405–409. He speaks to us admiringly of a famous experiment on the desalinization of seawater performed in the presence of ambassadors! Under Rouelle's influence, the number of natural-history collections reached two hundred in Paris; we know that this amounted to an accumulation of trivia.

14 Diderot, *Oeuvres choisies*, centenary ed., pp. 326–329. In this curious analysis, Diderot shows all the naiveté of a perfect philistine. Perhaps it would be useful to point out here that the men who, today, profess to be the champions of the secular spirit are, like their renowned predecessor, philistines.

but a dream, and thus to pave the way for the advent of the third estate to liberty and power, a revolution that was simultaneously intellectual, political, and social."[15] In reality, it was a matter of the philosophers' amusing society people.

It seems that the latter found the *Encyclopedia* very interesting; Joseph Reinach gives us as a typical instance an anecdote of Voltaire, which clearly shows the reasons for the success of this compilation; courtiers learned from it the composition of cannon powder, and the ladies learned what the differences are among various rouges. According to the anecdote, "Madame de Pompadour found the correct interpretation: it was as a storehouse of all useful things that the dictionary of science and arts succeeded with the public; leafing through it enabled one to consider himself the most learned person in the realm."[16] Thus it was definitely a science of the boudoir or the salon that Diderot presented; is it really justifiable to call him "the prophet of modern industry"[17] for having amused his contemporaries with the details of old methods of production?

With his plain common sense, Cournot was shocked by the very idea of the *Encyclopedia*: to draw up an inventory of human knowledge in a period of great transformations seemed strange to him. "In order to explain their mistake, we must regard the Encyclopedists and their patrons or partisans, not as scientists, but henceforth as philosophers, or, if you wish, not as friends of science, but as men who are predisposed in favor of philosophy."[18] But we must add that this philosophy consists of a conversation between society people.

We could not completely understand the spirit of the eighteenth century without taking into account the great success obtained by occultism at that time. We should not be surprised to see readers of the *Encyclopedia* fall into this stupid practice; after having exhausted all branches of material knowledge, they were reduced to exploring invisible domains in order to satisfy their curiosity. And did they not, after all, proceed by the experimental method? Was

---

[15] J. Reinach, *Diderot*, p. 43. The author's naive ignorance is clearly apparent in the passage in which he says that his hero foresaw electric telegraphy.
[16] *Ibid.*, pp. 72–74.
[17] *Ibid.*, p. 42.
[18] Cournot, *Considérations*, pp. 56–57.

it not one of those pursuits open to all, which achieve marvelous results when a large number of laymen participate in them?[19]

b. The curiosity of society people was, on the whole, in perfect harmony with the preoccupations of all of the members of the governing oligarchy. In order to be an excellent administrator, it was not in the least necessary to have the knowledge of a specialist. Every day, we see our political assemblies make decisions on questions the technicalities of which completely escape our deputies. And yet, none of them thinks of abstaining when it is a matter of enacting a program of naval construction, railroad building, or customs. For a rather long time after the Revolution, the *Encyclopedia* and similar compilations seem to have helped functionaries grasp a general picture of the things they had to administer. This type of instruction could usually even seem adequate for those who directed industrial establishments; indeed, until a short time ago, factories were directed by merchants, accountants, or former workers, who were much appreciated by capitalists because they showed an inflexibility toward the workers which is hardly ever found in trained engineers.

A great deal of will, notions of cooperation, and several skills formed the assets of the foremen of the large workshops. Around 1830, Ure said that the owners of English spinning mills were not up to date on machinery and relied on their managers, who were less than outstanding.[20] Le Play, who, for a long time, taught metallurgy at the School of Mines and visited all the factories in Europe in order to learn his profession of teacher, stated "that the true elements of the art often remain unknown to the managing shop foremen." "In most cases," he adds, "in order to make effective use of my time, I could only beseech these managers for permission to be put in the workers' schools."[21] It took a long time for students of the industrial schools to be chosen as managers.

Biographers of Turgot tell us that he studied physics, chemistry,

---

[19] Condorcet believed that great progress could be expected in mineralogy, botany, zoology, and meteorology as a result of repeated observations over a huge territory by men who had received a general education (*Tableau historique*, 9th epoch). Occultism has the same conditions; it is a "science" that everyone can cultivate. No science better merits being called democratic than occultism, provided the term "democratic" means "accessible to the greatest number of people."

[20] Ure, *Philosophie des manufactures* ("Philosophy of Industry"), I, 66–67.

[21] Le Play, *La Reforme sociale en France* ("Social Reform in France"), 5th ed., II, 20.

and mathematics "in their relationship to agriculture, manufacturing, and commerce."[22] All of that probably was a very cursory study; in 1765 Diderot calculated that only six months were needed to learn all that is necessary in geometry, if one did not wish to become limited by a rather useless specialty; according to him, "the rest is pure curiosity."[23]

One wonders if Condorcet might have had the idea of historical investigations similar to those in which Le Play later placed so much importance. "What truly comprises the human race—the mass of families who subsist almost entirely from their labor—has been forgotten [by history]; even among the class of men in public professions who act, not for themselves, but for society, whose occupation is to instruct, to govern, to defend, and to ease the burdens of other men, only the leaders have engaged the notice of historians." Condorcet wanted to have good descriptions of Frenchmen like the descriptions of foreign types travelers have made. Unfortunately, usually these travelers have been superficial and ill-prepared.[24]

There is nothing that allows us to suppose that the eighteenth-century philosopher held the nineteenth-century economists' notion that it is possible to penetrate to the root of knowledge of a people by the use of monographs about a few laboring families. It is true that Le Play did not go so far as to justify his method scientifically; he was led to it by an intuition natural in a professor of technology who was unusually enthusiastic about the practical science that he taught and who had many opportunities to learn by contact with workers.

Condorcet's aim was much simpler: "Whether one seeks to render an account of a discovery, an important theory, a new system of laws, or a political revolution, the problem is to concentrate on determining what its effects were for the greatest number of people in each society; for in that consists the real object of philosophy, since all of the intermediary results of these same causes

---

[22] Turgot, I, xxxii. The editor of the *Correspondance inédite de Condorcet et de Turgot*, Charles Henry, notes that Turgot studied mathematics without much success, because his correspondence indicates only an elementary knowledge (pp. xii–xiii).

[23] Diderot, *Oeuvres complètes*, VI, 475.

[24] Condorcet, *Tableau historique*, 9th epoch.

can only be considered as means toward the final result of acting on that portion which truly constitutes the mass of humanity. In arriving at this end . . . men can appreciate *their real title to glory* or enjoy the advances made by their reason with a certain pleasure: it is in that only that the real perfection of the human race can be judged. The idea of relating everything to this last point is dictated by justice and reason."[25] The physiocrats and all of the creators of projects for reform in the eighteenth century believed it was necessary to direct the administration of the state so as to improve the condition of the largest and poorest class;[26] the Saint-Simonians did nothing more than take up this tradition; their only merit was in giving vigorous expression to a wish held by all the former theorists. Condorcet's investigations were meant to enlighten a government motivated by reforming intentions, in order to enable it to see, by means of exact and detailed statistics, the results of the rules it introduced into public administration.[27]

c. Administrators, scientists, and businessmen believed the economy of the country could be rapidly and profoundly changed provided that enlightenment was truly sought according to the encyclopedic methods. At this time several occurrences had a very substantial influence on the public mind from this point of view; I believe the discoveries made in chemistry were particularly decisive.

We should note that there is no field of knowledge that astounds men so much as chemistry. In ancient times, a superstitious veneration surrounded the processes of treating ores, refining metals, and preparing alloys; there are no other fields that lend themselves so easily to trade secrets and special knacks; inventors still obtain easily the confidence of capitalists when they announce new metallurgic processes to them, for there still remains something of alchemy in chemistry in the eyes of the uninformed. Explosive substances and

---

[25] According to Condorcet, every improvement that occurs in the material conditions of life can, indeed, be traced to a political event or to a discovery of pure science.

[26] Turgot, I, lxxii. The editor says that Quesnay's school was the only one to concern itself seriously with this end.

[27] Jaurès comments on Condorcet's text in such grandiloquent terms that one wonders if he understands it: "Democratic and human history is much more difficult than oligarchical history. But when it reaches the roots of social life . . . it will be in order to make justice and joy gradually penetrate into it" (*Histoire socialiste, La Convention* ["Socialist History, the Convention"], p. 1792).

dyestuffs taken from coal mines have exalted the imaginations of our contemporaries far more than the most lofty scientific discoveries.

Lavoisier's experiments revolutionized chemistry at the end of the eighteenth century;[28] they present an impressive example of what the encyclopedic knowledge of a man belonging to the governing oligarchy can accomplish. Lavoisier was a tax farmer when he published his great tracts on chemistry. Because of his work, this science emerged from the domain of the pharmacy dispensary to become completely bourgeois. But I believe the fact that most impressed our predecessors was the introduction of the manufacture of hard porcelain into France.

For a very long time, Europe had been striving to rival China in the manufacture of high-quality pottery; in Saxony, chance had led an alchemist to discover the properties of porcelain clay. This stage was reached a little later in France, but here science intervened; Darcet did a number of experiments on soil and presented them to the Academy of Sciences (1766–1768). As a result, the manufacture of porcelain appeared to be a victory for the scientific method and no longer the result of a happy coincidence.[29] For society people, no other matter cast such luster on chemistry.

Darcet and the other chemists of his time occupied themselves with numerous problems of a practical nature,[30] and we understand how Condorcet could laud the services they rendered to industry and to the cause of efficient administration: "We have seen the chemical arts become enriched with new procedures, purify and simplify the old methods, rid itself of all that tradition had introduced of useless or harmful substances, of ineffectual or imperfect practices; at the same time means have been found of preventing some of the often terrible dangers to which the workers were exposed. Thus the chemical arts have procured us more enjoyment, and more rewards, with much less cost of unfortunate sacrifices and remorse."[31]

---

28 It seems Condorcet did not thoroughly understand the importance of the new ideas asserted by Lavoisier; he seems to have been especially impressed by the introduction of a scientific nomenclature.

29 According to the article "Darcet" in the *Biographie Michaud*.

30 It was Darcet who later invented gelatine, of which the food value engendered so much discussion.

31 Condorcet, *Tableau historique*, 9th epoch. Jaurès finds that, in this sentence, Condorcet reveals himself to be "a great revolutionary [and] thus combines science

Although Condorcet's friends attached a tremendous importance to natural history,[32] Condorcet himself is rather restrained in his views on this subject, perhaps because of his aversion for Buffon. He speaks, however, of a "valuable light [shed] on the cultivation of the vegetables intended for our needs; on the art of feeding, breeding, and preserving farm animals, of perfecting their stock and improving the products derived from them."[33] It is very probable that the first judgment refers to the works of Nicolas de Saussure on wheat and the grapevine and to his articles in the *Encyclopedia*; then we find an allusion to the experiments made by Daubenton to breed sheep that produce fine wool.

In 1766 Daubenton announced that it would be easy to change the native stocks by taking better care of them; at Montbard he got remarkable results on Roussillonnais animals that had Merino blood. Turgot introduced Spanish sheep; in 1786 the great Rambouillet flock was introduced. Society people, administrators, and industrialists were equally interested about this question; the success of these experiments would be evidence of the victory of science over tradition. Under the treaty of Basel in the year III, Spain pledged to release 4,000 ewes and 1,000 rams; this authorization was only utilized in 1798 by an association directed by Girod de l'Ain. Napoleon, exaggerating the ideas of his predecessors, as was his habit, wanted to transform the whole French flock into Merinos.[34] It is evident how much France had conceived a passion for enormous agricultural progress, which science and the government tried to put into effect.

Condorcet next speaks of new means "for preparing and preserving the products of the soil and the foodstuffs furnished to us by animals." We know that, at the end of the eighteenth century, much research was done on food products—research that was not completely successful, but all of which provoked great enthusiasm. In

---

with democracy in his thinking" (Jaurès, *Histoire socialiste, La Convention*, p. 1792). One wonders if "the great democratic leader" understands what he is reading, for this passage contains very little that could refer to the research that later resulted in making work with mercury less dangerous.

[32] Diderot, *Oeuvres complètes*, III, 463. In his view, three fields of knowledge are essential in order to satisfy our needs: mechanics, natural history, and chemistry.

[33] Condorcet, *Tableau historique*, 9th epoch.

[34] According to the article, "Mérinos," in the *Dictionnaire d'Agriculture* ("Dictionary of Agriculture"), by Barral and Sagnier.

1756 the printing office of the Louvre published a dissertation by the academician Tillet, titled "Abstract of experiments made at Trianon on the cause of spoiled wheat," which was sent to the provincial administrators.

A great revolution in the use of wheat took place in this period. Until then, a huge quantity of flour was lost because the groats were given to the livestock; during the drought of 1709, a miller from Senlis apparently took advantage of the groats by reprocessing them through the mill. In the middle of the eighteenth century, the new processes were used in great secret around Paris; in 1760 and 1761, in the presence of the lieutenant general of police, experiments were made by Malisset, who was in charge of the service of "the king's wheat" for supplying Paris; soon, however, science intervened and overshadowed all the work of the artisans. In 1765 the Academy of Sciences gave a prize to Dransy for his dissertation on mills; this engineer constructed the factories of Corbeil, where the new milling process called "economic" was practiced. In 1778 Parmentier published the "Perfect baker, or the complete treatise on the baking and sale of bread," in which he sets forth the advantages of the new method of milling.[35]

We know how brilliant the history of the potato was in the eighteenth century; society people, enlightened administrators, and scientists competed with each other in enthusiasm to such an extent that they ended up by believing that, without themselves, the people would be deprived of this precious food.

In 1761 Turgot sought to popularize the potato in Limoges; in 1765 the Bishop of Castres made it the subject of a decree; Madame d'Egmont urged the King of Sweden to plant Dalecarlia with potatoes;[36] Parmentier's famous dissertation was written in 1778. There is no need to recount the experiments in tillage made at Grenelle, the personal intervention of Louis XIII, and the gastronomic inventions that accompanied this philanthropic campaign.[37]

---

[35] G. Bord, *Le Pacte de famine*, pp. 59–60, 67. This method of milling was supposedly called "economic" because Malisset wanted to place the new system under the protection of Quesnay's school. Until then, the groats were thought to be injurious to health, perhaps as a result of a vague association with spurred rye.

[36] Geoffroy, *Gustave III et la Cour de France* ("Gustave III and the French Court"), I, 246. Taine, *Ancien Régime*, p. 387. The author does not give the date; the Countess d'Egmont died in 1773.

[37] According to the article "Parmentier" in the *Biographie Michaud*, the "gateau de Savoie" is owed to the renowned pharmicist; thus, science even came to the point of perfecting cooking.

After having been the philosophic vegetable,[38] the potato became the patriotic vegetable during the Revolution. Never had the union of science and intellectual power expressed itself with more naiveté.

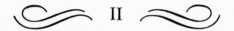

By examining the conditions in which science took shape at that time, we can understand the remarkable ideas on the calculation of probability that enjoyed such a vogue—ideas that John Stuart Mill called "the scandal of mathematics"[39] and that held sway until the middle of the nineteenth century. It is important to examine the question very closely because we are then able to penetrate deeply into the thought of that period.

The approximate regularity of many phenomena has always impressed observers and has led them to suppose that there exists a mathematics of chance. A friend of Galileo had found that with three dice the number eleven can turn up in twenty-seven combinations and the number twelve in only twenty-five; the relationship of recorded cases would be here identical to that of combinations. Buffon had a die thrown into the air 4,040 times and found 2,048 faces; that is about half the throws.[40] There is clearly no reason why one number turns up instead of another; it is thus very strange that the results appear in relationships that are often very close to those shown by combinatory analysis. This is a question of fact that would be no more than a curious paradox if similar regularities were not found in practice which were able to serve as a basis for important applications.

The calculation of premiums in life insurance companies is founded on the extraordinary regularity of human mortality. Artillery men have observed that projectiles fired from firearms are distributed following a law that is always constant (Gauss's Law) and

---

[38] Prejudices against the potato persisted, however, during the first half of the nineteenth century, for in 1847 Marx accused it of having "brought on scrofula" (*The Poverty of Philosophy*, p. 69). The question is discussed at length by Morel in his *Traité des dégénérescences* ("Treatise on Degeneration"), published in 1857.

[39] John Stuart Mill, *System of Logic*, II, 64.

[40] J. Bertrand, *Calcul des probabilités* ("Calculation of Probabilities"), pp. vii, ix.

that applies also to errors in astronomical observations. Quetelet
has even shown that the distribution between the heights of army
conscripts and the mean are subject to the same law. According to
Colonel Journée, the frequency of diverse physical aptitudes in
soldiers can be classified in one table.[41] But it is always necessary to
keep in mind that these chances that obey an order are entirely
exceptional. People who are not much in the habit of observing
things easily believe that there is only one type of chance and that
the calculation of probabilities applies in every case where many
small indeterminate causes come into play. Mathematicians, like
society people, have been duped by this illusion innumerable times.

Society people understand the usefulness of the calculation of
probabilities very differently than do the actuaries who establish the
premiums of insurance companies. The latter base their calculations
on masses of figures in the midst of which all chance disappears; a
company with a large clientele operates in a manner as certain as if
it knew the fate of each one of its clients; thus, in the hands of the
actuary, the calculation of probability leads to a certainty. For
society people, on the other hand, the notion of probability has significance only from the point of view of the gambler: they want
the calculations to tell the individual who deals with a life insurance
company what he has the right to claim in exchange for the sum
he pays into what he considers a sort of open lottery on the chance
of survival.

There is no basis for the establishment of the rate of a life an-
nuity set up in a contract between private individuals; almost invariably the premiums of the large companies are used, but this is
obviously a matter of convenience and not because of a calculation
on probability; for, in such a contract, one cannot count on the
compensations that appear between the advantageous and the disadvantageous chances in the mortality tables.

Likewise, there is no rule of equity for two gamblers who bet on
red and black. What is called a rule of equity is that which would
be adopted by the operator of a roulette game who would be philanthropic enough not to want to win anything; he would give two
times his stake to each lucky player, because in the pattern of an

---

41 Journée, *Tir des fusils de chasse* ("On Shooting Hunting Rifles"), 2d ed., pp.
377–378.

enormous number of plays, there is for him approximately a balance of wins and losses—admitting that the game will have the outcome predicted by combinatory analysis.[42] This measure is considered by society people as being the expression of a natural equity which should apply to all games, even when there are merely individuals playing a few rounds against each other. Mathematicians have obtained this rule of equity from gamblers, and they have not generally examined whether or not it is well-founded.

The great difference between the two points of view that can be adopted on the subject of the phenomena of chance—depending on whether they are considered in relation to a banker or to individuals—was manifested in a most striking way in the course of discussion about inoculation in the eighteenth century. Daniel Bernoulli wanted to prove that this practice should be encouraged because its popularization would result in a prolongation of the average life expectancy, in spite of the danger it presented. D'Alembert contested the validity of such an argument, and he gave the following example: how many people would accept undergoing an operation that would kill one patient in five and prolong the average life by thirty years? D'Alembert put himself in the place of the individual, while Bernoulli reasoned as would a king who treats his subjects like animals in a herd; in order to make the calculation entirely satisfactory, it would have even been well to calculate the value of the herd in the hypothesis of the inoculation and in that of the status quo.[43]

Geometricians in the eighteenth century sought a means of rendering calculation even more applicable to questions posed by individual cases. Laplace wanted to *demonstrate* that the game regulated according to the so-called rule of equity is disadvantageous; that it is well not to put one's stake on a single risk; and that there is an advantage in being insured, although the insurer benefits by the operation. To this end he used a theory given by Daniel Bernoulli, a theory that is not easily defended but that was very successful because it is based on an estimation that is, so to speak,

---

[42] In fact the banker would still win, because gamblers go through stages of enthusiasm and discouragement.

[43] Diderot says that in Sparta, d'Alembert's conditions would have been accepted, (*Oeuvres complètes*, IX, 211).
and that he observes that in certain battles a fifth of the fighting force was killed

universal for *people who consume without producing*; for the producer, everything is thought of in terms of a value on a balance
sheet and meant to bring out a cost price; on the other hand, the
consumer's only concern is in estimating the ease with which he
is able to put his hand on some cash. The variations of the amounts
used must be estimated by relative rather than absolute value; this
is Daniel Bernoulli's principle.[44]

Nowadays economic changes have alienated us from ideas that
seemed excellent to our predecessors. J. Bertrand is surprised that
Buffon adopted the doctrine of "moral hope," but that position was
completely natural for this great lord, whereas no one admits to
it today.[45] Since, to begin with, the notion of probability has no
mathematical significance for the individual who operates at random,
its combination with the calculation of relative values constitutes a
compounding of nonsense or a redoubling of the subservience of
science to the modes of thinking familiar to society people!

Condorcet introduced an idea into science which is even stranger
yet: that of applying the calculation of probability to judgments.
He was so proud of his work that he proposed that the Convention
introduce his theories into secondary education. In the *Tableau historique* he lauds the immense benefits to be derived from his researches:

"These applications have taught us to ascertain the various degrees
of certainty that we can hope to attain: the probability according
to which we can adopt an opinion while making it the basis of our
thinking without violating the rules of reason,[46] and the rules of our
conduct without being remiss toward prudence or offending justice. They show the advantages and the disadvantages of different
types of elections and the diverse modes of taking decisions by a
majority of voices."[47]

---

[44] This principle leads to the measurement of moral values by a logarithmic
formula, which Fechner has recently proposed to be applied to the sensations.

[45] Laplace, *Théorie analytique des probabilités* ("Analytical Theory of Probabilities"), pp. 441–447. J. Bertrand, *Calcul des probabilités*, pp. 66–67.

[46] The idea of calculating the likelihood of a solution has long persisted in the
thinking of geometricians; it is a probability of individual wagering and consequently an absurd notion, originating with society people. Laplace calculated that one
could bet a million to one that the relative error made about the mass of Saturn did
not exceed a fiftieth; since then, the error has been shown to be greater (J. Bertrand,
Calcul des probabilités, p. 305).

[47] Condorcet, *Tableau historique*, 9th epoch. I do not go into the predictions of
the 10th epoch.

In particular, he investigated how the tribunals should be organized so that their sentences would be as fair as could reasonably be
desired: they should be composed of sixty-five members, pronounc-
ing judgments with a majority of nine votes in order that the probability of error be not more than that of the danger entailed when
one embarks to cross the channel between Dover and Calais in good
weather; this probability being 1 to 144,768.[48]

Madame de Staël, who gives us the opinion of the salons after the
Revolution, has no doubts about the merit of this new science; she
praises Condorcet's admirable discoveries and predicts, following his example, many remarkable applications of probability calculation in government: "There is no reason why, one day, we might
not reach a point of setting up tables that would contain the solution
to all political questions, according to statistical knowledge and the
positive facts that would be compiled in each country. It might
be stated that, in order to govern a particular population, it is
necessary to require a certain sacrifice of individual liberty: thus
certain laws and certain governments suit a particular empire. For a
particular wealth and particular size of country, a certain degree
of power is necessary in the executive: thus a certain amount of
authority is necessary in one country and would be tyrannical in
another. A certain balance is necessary among the powers to enable
them to protect each other: thus, a certain constitution is inadequate
and another is inevitably despotic."[49] And all this would be founded
on the calculation of probability, which "presents a morally infallible result" when "it is applied to a very great number of chances."[50]

Nowadays all these lovely ideas appear perfectly ridiculous to
geometricians. J. Bertrand even wonders how Condorcet's book
could have been accepted: "None of his principles is acceptable,
none of his conclusions comes near to the truth. . . . Laplace rejected
Condorcet's results; Poisson did not accept Laplace's; neither one
nor the other could submit to calculation something that essentially
escaped it." Nevertheless, some fine minds have found it very difficult to free themselves from a tradition that held such assurance.
"In the discussion of laws on juries, Arago invoked Laplace's au-

---

48 J. Bertrand, *Probabilités*, p. xlvi.
49 De Staël, *De la littérature considérée dans ses rapports avec les institutions
sociales* ("Literature Considered in Accordance with Social Institutions") in the
Oeuvres complètes (1820 ed.), IV, 522–523.
50 *Ibid.*, p. 520.

thority. He said that judiciary error could be diminished in the proportion of five to seven. A deputy dared to express doubt and Arago
treated him harshly. When he spoke in the name of science, it was
not for the uninformed to contradict him!"[51] The prudent Cournot
himself proposed a method for calculating the professional value of
judges.[52]

Condorcet's observations must have appeared less fallacious in
another age, because they could pass for an effort attempted in order
to perfect the old system of law. The latter seemed to be based in
part on mathematical axioms: the tribunals called on to pronounce
capital punishment without appeal had to be composed of seven
judges and hand down a condemnation with a majority of two
votes.[53] The rules of legal evidence also contained something that
brought probability to mind, in such a way that Voltaire—who
knew all that the *literati* and society people knew about penal law—
wrote that the Parlement of Toulouse had the absurd habit of adding
quarters and eighths of evidence in order to arrive at certainty.[54]
In the Calas affair, experience had shown that the procedures of
the old system of justice did not offer the desired guarantees; much
talk was heard then about the English jury, comprised of twelve
citizens who must reach a unanimous decision in order to condemn.
It was, therefore, natural enough for people to wonder if it might
not be possible to improve criminal justice substantially by fixing a
sufficient number of judges (or jury members) and by requiring
a rather large majority for condemnation. Given the ideas of that
time on science, it was natural for mathematicians to be asked for
suggestions if not a solution.

Although scientists of that time almost invariably spoke of probability as if it were a question of estimating the chances to which
an individual is exposed, it is not impossible to find at times a rather
reasonable significance in their theories by transforming them
slightly with a view to passing from individual cases to masses and
to the compensations they entail.

---

51 J. Bertrand, *Probabilités*, pp. 319–320.
52 *Ibid.*, p. 325.
53 These rules are still used by our war tribunals.
54 A letter of March 22, 1763, reported by Athanese Cocquerel in *Jean Calas et
sa famille* ("Jean Calas and his Family"); 2d ed., p. 169. This author appears, moreover, to be remarkably unaware of the criminal laws of the ancien régime.

Enlightened men of the eighteenth century always put themselves in the position of a learned oligarchy that governs in the name of reason. The masters were supposed to have a great deal of initiative, enlightenment, and thought, and the agents of their power were passive beings, working blindly and acting by rote.[55] The mistakes committed by these menials approximate those that are frequently seen in a purely mechanical activity, resembling phenomena of chance, able to be compared to "risks" every director of a business enterprise must take into account in his predictions. By thus putting matters of justice on a commercial plane, it was as easy to reason about the errors of the magistrature as about any material difficulty.

It was admitted without further inquiry that the calculation of probabilities should be applied to these moral mishaps, because it was believed that all mishaps can be covered by insurance. It would not have been too difficult to observe that the scope of insurance is more extensive than that of the calculation of probabilities. Maritime insurance contracted for in time of war is naturally not subject to combinatory analysis! But in the eighteenth century, science had such prestige that people did not think of regarding it, as they do today, as a product of the intelligence, capable of only limited application.

Condorcet compares a judicial error to a shipwreck; here is what that means: for the sake of the prosperity of the country, it is important that there be frequent communications with England; public opinion is of the mind that the advantages of this commerce are worth a few accidents resulting from circumstances outside anyone's control. Likewise, the advantages of order produced by criminal justice are worth tolerating the death of a few innocents. If one likens the people to a herd, all of whose accidents are placed on the same plane, it would be completely natural to compare the death of an innocent to that of a trader perishing in the course of crossing the channel.

This manner of visualizing justice has become foreign to us because we no longer have the same conception of the state as did

---

[55] We will see farther on (Chap. IV, sec. 1) with what scorn Condorcet speaks of Perronet and his engineers. In one of his letters he calls the tax farmers, who were opposed to his method of measuring barrels, "rabble." This so-called rabble seems to include Lavoisier, among others. *Correspondance inédite de Condorcet et de Turgot*, pp. 273–274.

our predecessors. In the eyes of our contemporaries, the *jus gladii* is no longer a threat directed almost uniquely against those half-human beings against whom magistrates of old had sought to defend society by frightful punishments. A profound change has taken place in ideas since the Terror caused so many esteemed people to mount the scaffold; penal justice has become something too noble for it to be henceforth possible to compare it to a business enterprise: it is above the realm of accounts of profits and losses.

At times our reason revolts against decisions made by an administration that is solely occupied with material utility; by contrast, men of the eighteenth century were led by the spectacle the old royalty offered them to admit that individual reason must give way before such decisions, provided that they were founded on science.

If it is easy to understand how the most scandalous sophisms of the calculation of probabilities arose, it is harder to understand how they were able to hold sway so long. First we must consider the ideas our predecessors formed about the duties of the scientist towards science. Often science made its appearance by reasonings of a doubtful or even completely false value, but people were not discouraged; they sought to reduce the very obvious faults one way or another; more than once an important domain was definitively mastered by dint of perseverence. Experience thus seemed to favor the bold; any retreat would have been a betrayal.

One can also say that any retreat would have been contrary to the interests of the scientists, because it would have seriously compromised their prestige in the eyes of society people; until the middle of the nineteenth century, the latter remained the audience whose praises the scientists avidly sought. Arago was one of the last great scientists who sought an important worldly position from his scientific fame; thus, one should not be surprised that he was also one of the last defenders of the theories Condorcet had transmitted to nineteenth-century geometricians.[56] This situation becomes clearer when we recall this story of the famous hypothesis of the nebula: when Laplace believed that he could present a theory of the formation of the world, astronomers found it very difficult to reject it completely because men of letters believed that this doctrine occupied an important position in science.[57]

---

[56] Perhaps one could also point out several weaknesses in Berthelot's writings that are due to his slightly outmoded way of thinking.

[57] Laplace wished to show that the intervention of a creative intelligence could

As long as the encyclopedic ideas of the eighteenth century endured, it was believed that there must be some science contained in them which would be capable of quelling the anxieties of the statesmen who wondered what their plans would produce. As we have seen, Madame de Staël had a confidence in the calculation of probabilities which greatly resembles that of certain of our contemporaries in sociology: in the two cases it is a matter of predicting by means of reasonings capable of giving at least the illusion of being scientific instead of relying on the instincts of experienced men. There is one great difference between our period and Condorcet's: that sociology is not cultivated by true scholars. The latter study the history of institutions. But once, true scholars believed that they should work in the direction indicated to them by society people. We should state that sociologists succeed in impressing only those people whose manner of living makes them resemble men of the eighteenth century.

As mathematicians have become liberated from the shackles the former society oligarchy had imposed on them, they have been able to discuss the questions of the application of science in a more serious way and to reject all that did not have a true scientific value. This emancipation of science is one of the most important—perhaps even the most extraordinary—aspects of the whole ideological history of the nineteenth century; it took place when large industry made extraordinary advances. Simultaneously, science and production rose above the caprices of the aristocracies, which, for a long time, had seen in science a means of satisfying their curiosity above all and had seen in production a means of satisfying their extravagance.

Among all of the indictments that can be leveled against the eighteenth century, the "scandal" furnished by the calculation of probabilities is not one of the least.

---

be dispensed with in explaining why the orbits of *all* the bodies of our solar system are near the ecliptic and why *all* of the movements are in the same direction. Today, we know that there are exceptions to these two empirical laws. The hypothesis of the nebula is found in a final footnote of the *Exposition du système du monde* ("Exposition of the World System"), that is, in a literary work; it is of no use to celestial mechanics.

CHAPTER IV

The Boldness of the Third Estate

I. *Rousseau's prudence in the face of practical questions. Turgot's increasing boldness. Confidence given to the ideologues by the American Revolution.*

II. *The return to nature. The importance of enlightenment. The transforming influence of education.*

III. *Literature on the savages. Father Charlevoix's descriptions. Indifference toward the existing order.*

IV. *Economic progress. New administrative preoccupations. Increase of revolutionary momentum with material progress.*

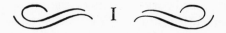

Modern historians are extremely astonished to discover with what daring lightheartedness our fathers approached the most radical problems of social reform. Formerly, the transformations that overthrow a complete social order were not clearly differentiated from those that operate slowly and allow for easy corrections in proportion as experience shows the advantages or the disadvantages of each action. In the following chapter, we shall see from whence comes the currently accepted opinion regarding what is called evolution.

Tocqueville said that in summing up all the demands included in the *Cahiers* of 1789, he saw "with a kind of horror that what was demanded was the simultaneous and systematic abolition of all of the existing laws and customs in France." And these demands gave the impression of being entirely natural; nobody foresaw the dangers of a revolution. "Those who would be tomorrow's victims had no inkling of their fate; they believed that a sudden and complete transformation of a very complex and ancient society could occur without disruption, by dint of reason and by its efficacy alone. The poor dupes!"[1]

This foolhardiness appears all the more extraordinary when we note that the man who passes for having been the great dealer in political absolutes, Rousseau, was always very cautious whenever he spoke of reforms. Lichtenberger says,[2] "If we examine briefly the advice that Rousseau gave to the legislators and the opinions that he expressed of the various constitutions of his time, we notice his extraordinary moderation in actual practice, his care to accommodate his precepts to the necessities of reality, and, all told, the slight use that he makes of his early radical theories." Lichtenberger thinks that if Jean-Jacques had been concerned with France, he would have spoken primarily of moral reforms.[3]

The plans Rousseau had formulated for Corsica were very well suited to a region that had remained unusually primitive economically and that would remain outside of the great European movement as long as it was not annexed to France. Rousseau was acquainted far better than his contemporaries, with the long-standing customs of mountain folk, for he had observed them in Switzerland. He saw nothing strange in his desire to export those customs into regions with backward economies. He would have liked to guarantee sufficient property to all Corsican families, give prestige to agricultural work, and render a money economy all but useless.[4] In the end, however, he wondered if he had perhaps created a utopia.[5]

In his plans for Poland, Rousseau shows even more restraint, if that is possible, and Lichtenberger thinks that here we have proof of the enormous difference between pure speculation and actual practice in the minds of the men of that time.[6] Here again we are

---

[1] Alexis de Tocqueville, *L'Ancien Régime*, p. 144.
[2] André Lichtenberger, *Le Socialisme au XVIIIᵉ siècle* ("Socialism in the 18th Century"), p. 166.
[3] Lichtenberger, *XVIIIᵉ siècle*, p. 173.
[4] Rousseau wanted the state to be rich and the individuals poor. This is a very old idea, which Machiavelli regarded as axiomatic (*Discourses on Titus Livy*, Bk. I, 37). If the state is rich, there is no need of taxation.
[5] Lichtenberger, *op. cit.*, pp. 168–170.
[6] Lichtenberger, *op. cit.*, p. 170.

stuck by Rousseau's reliance on his recollections of Switzerland. Chapter VI of this work contains some surprises, for here he points out the enormous dangers that Poland would risk in immediately freeing the serfs. In Chapter XIII he presents a plan for "opening a door to the serfs to obtain liberty[7] and to the bourgeoisie to obtain nobility." We are indeed far removed from the deed soon to be accomplished by his alleged disciples in abruptly abolishing slavery in the colonies!

During the half century before the Revolution, there was a very rapid movement toward recklessness. Turgot's works show this clearly. When Turgot left the Sorbonne at an age when the usual tendency is to believe that anything is possible, he showed discouragement at the difficulties of legislation in a civilized society. He wrote that, like Lycurgus, the "very mediocre" Jesuits of Paraguay "and William Penn, whose principal power was his virtue, experienced almost no difficulty." But Solon, "with much more intelligence, was less successful than Lycurgus, "and his achievements were less durable because his nation was more advanced and had more pretensions. . . . In Europe's present condition, the tasks of the legislator and the degree of skill required of him are so great as to intimidate a man capable of discerning them and make a good man tremble. These duties demand the greatest efforts, the most diffused and at the same time sustained attention, and the most constant diligence on the part of the courageous man whose penchants lead him to public duty and whose experience there makes him devoted to it." Turgot hoped, however, that the study of economic principles would lead to simplifying the science of government and to putting it within the reach of ordinary men.[8]

When Turgot had acquired experience in worldly affairs and had become a minister, he considered it an easy matter to make a radical change in the French mind by means of civic education— and in a mere several years. "Instead of the corruption, cowardice,

---

[7] This would be carried out by committees, called *censoriaux* by Rousseau, which would be given the responsibility of choosing "the peasants who distinguish themselves by good conduct, good farming, good morals, good care of their families, and by satisfactorily fulfilling all of the duties of their position." The landlords would not only be indemnified, but "it would be absolutely necessary to proceed so that instead of being burdensome for the master, the emancipation of the serfs could become praiseworthy and to his advantage."

[8] Turgot, II, 674–675.

intrigue, and greed which [the king] has found everywhere, [he] would find virtue, disinterestedness, honor, and zeal. To be an upright man would be the usual thing."[9]

This movement toward unwarranted boldness cannot be differentiated from the movement toward dominance by the bourgeois oligarchy, which sensed that the hour of its dictatorship was near. Daily experience shows us how swiftly politicians change from the moment they are near the seats of power. Starting modestly enough in the Parlements, they no longer doubt their universal capacities as soon as they are named by the newspapers as possible choices for cabinet ministers. In acquiring the honors of the aristocracy, the third estate also acquired the frivolity and complacency of the titled class.

In his statement to the king on municipalities, Turgot tells us that it was indeed a dictatorship of which the bourgeois oligarchy dreamed. "As long as your majesty does not stray from the path of justice [that is, stray from the advice that Turgot is going to give him], he may consider himself an absolute legislator, and he may count on his good nation for the execution of his orders."[10] The dictatorship would be provisionally exercised in the name of the king.

The unpublished correspondence between Condorcet and Turgot, brought out in 1883 by Ch. Henry, shows us curious examples of the philosophical world's self-conceit: during his friend's ministry, Condorcet made himself the chief director of public works and called the illustrious Perronet ignorant, useless, and I believe also a rogue.[11] He was indignant about the opposition to his projects arising from the esprit de corps of the engineers. He had only contempt for Borda, who was concerned with *physicaille* and who wrote treatises that will never be discussed.[12] He was violently opposed to Lavoisier, who did not approve of his system of measuring the capacity of barrels.[13] It must not have been easy to live under the thumb of this philosopher. Sometimes the question has arisen whether, by doing away with such a great number of men who

---

9 Turgot, II, 549. Cf. Taine, *Ancien Régime*, pp. 309–310.

10 Turgot, II, 503.

11 Perronet was the creator of the Neuilly Bridge, long regarded as the masterpiece of civil engineering.

12 Nevertheless, they are discussed a bit more than Condorcet's.

13 *Correspondance inédite de Condorcet et de Turgot*, pp. 253, 263, 215, 273.

were learned and obsessed with ideology, the Terror did not perhaps render a service to France. Perhaps Napoleon might have found the task of restoring the administration more difficult without the great purge that preceded his regime.

We have seen what the encyclopedic science of the eighteenth century was: a body of knowledge derived mainly from books of popularization and intended to enlighten the masters who put the specialists to work. In every sense of the word, this is truly what can be called a bourgeois science. Several facts seemed to uphold the position of the proponents of this system and to show that things could advance smoothly with such a hierarchy: at the top, men of society who knew how to speak in an engaging manner on any subject whatever; at the bottom, men who had been trained in detail and who were supposed to carry out the lofty conceptions of their masters.

To approach the questions from above, through principles, was the masters' goal: the principles were vague utterances that could serve as the themes for any number of dissertations by lettered men used to developing a subject. The further the questions were removed from daily experience, the greater became the attractiveness of the principles. Thus, in the theories on public law, the tendency was to totally disregard the facts. Taine said, "Destitut de Tracy, in commenting on Montesquieu, discovered that the great historian remained too slavishly grounded in history, and he went about remaking Montesquieu's work by constructing the society that ought to be rather than observing the society that is."[14]

Historical studies were thus completely neglected. Already at the end of the seventeenth century, Huet was complaining that there were no longer any scholars.[15] The situation grew worse. Renan is mistaken in blaming Voltaire for this decline: "Voltaire did more harm to historical studies than an entire invasion of barbarians. With his witty frivolity and his deceiving facility, he discouraged the Benedictines from writing history, and if for fifty years the dom Bouquet collection was sold in grocers' shops for its weight in paper,

---

[14] Taine, *Ancien Régime*, p. 264. It is all the more comical that de Tracy's commentary was written after the experience of the Revolution. Laboulaye says it was the work of a disciple of Condillac and Condorcet, who believes only in logic and holds history in contempt. "If de Tracy had wanted to prove he did not understand a word of what Montesquieu intended to say and do, would he have written any differently? (Laboulaye in his edition of Montesquieu, III, lxii–lxiii).

[15] Taine, *Ancien Régime*, p. 243.

if *l'Histoire littéraire de la France* ceased to publish for want of readers, it was indeed his fault."[16] But no! It was the fault of the entire French bourgeoisie, which could work up no interest in anything that was neither amusing nor an occasion for being officious. Hearing about primary principles is what interested this class, because it believed them necessary to overthrow the then existing body of law.

At the end of the ancien régime, a great historical event seemed to justify the position of the ideologues: "The Americans seemed merely to be putting into practice what our writers had conceived; They gave the substance of reality to what we were only dreaming about."[17]

This is how Condorcet spoke of American independence: "For the first time we see a great people, free from all bonds, peacefully adopting the constitution and the laws that it thought best suitable for creating its happiness." The thirteen state constitutions had "as their foundation a solemn recognition of the natural rights of man and as their principal goal the preservation of these rights." Thus, at last, there existed a positive system of law clearly founded on the primary principles. But all was not yet perfect in the work of the Americans, because their legislators were not sufficiently steeped in the lofty philosophy of the French salons. Condorcet adds: "We will show what [these constitutions] owe to the progress of political science and also what remains in them of the old errors, due to the prejudices of education. We will show why, for example, the system of the balance of powers damages the simplicity of these constitutions[18] and why their guiding principle was unity of interests rather than equality of rights. . . . We will insist on this purpose because this [last] error is the only remaining dangerous one, for it is the only one that still deceives truly enlightened men."[19]

For the Americans had preserved the property qualification for voting, founded on the assumption that there is such a close solidarity between men that the interests of the upper classes can be assumed to be identical to the nation's. According to Condorcet, "the

---

[16] Renan, *Nouvelles études d'histoire religieuse* ("New Studies in Religious History"), p. 462.

[17] Alexis de Tocqueville, *L'Ancien Régime*, p. 146.

[18] This is a good example of an ideologue's argument, which nowadays would seem to constitute the height of absurdity.

[19] Condorcet, *Tableau historique*, 9th epoch.

British Constitution is made for the rich, the American Constitution for the well-to-do, while France's must be made for all men."[20]

France appeared to be much better prepared than any other country for a faultless application of political theory, for it had the most truly enlightened philosophers. And besides, the existing legislation was "sufficiently beneath the level of the public mind so that no national pride or predisposition would bind [the country] to its ancient institutions." The supposed true enlightenment was possessed by the men of letters who held forth in salons and were lionized by the ladies for their original or startling ideas. . . ."[21] To gain this reputation, there is no need of legal, historical, or social knowledge. Siéyès, a man of extremely limited intellect, achieved an extraordinary reputation due to his art of manufacturing unrealizable constitutions, founded on the most abstract principles.

Condorcet himself tried his hand at this art, and consequently we owe to him a draft constitution, which he presented to the Convention on the fifteenth and sixteenth of April, 1793. According to Taine,[22] it was "the last word and the masterpiece of theory . . . a more ingenious and intricate mechanism would be impossible to design on paper." Several months later, hunted down by the Jacobin dictatorship, Condorcet still was impelled to celebrate the glories of constitutional drivel: "We will show why the principles on which the Constitution and the laws of France have been devised are purer, more precise, and more profound than those by which the Americans were guided . . . how the limitation of powers has been substituted for that ineffectual balance of powers so long admired; how . . . we have been the first to dare to preserve the right of popular sovereignty—that of obeying only those laws whose means of formation, if entrusted to representatives, are legitimized by the people's immediate consent. The people, furthermore, can always obtain reform by a regular action of its sovereign will if the laws harm its rights or interests."[23]

---

20 Taine, *La Conquête jacobine* ("The Jacobin Victory"), p. 383.

21 Geoffroy published some curious extracts from the correspondence of Gustave III with the Countess d'Egmont (the daughter of Marshall de Richelieu), the Countess de La Marck, and the Countess de Boufflers (*Gustave III et la cour de France*, Chap. IV). All of these women displayed an extraordinary knowledge of the principles of statecraft. Madame de Boufflers sent the king a dissertation with the title: "The Effects of Despotism if It is Established in Sweden."

22 Taine, *Ancien Régime*, p. 387.

23 Condorcet, *Tableau historique*, 9th epoch.

And yet, after reading this magnificent accumulation of nonsense,[24] we are still amazed that all our revolutions have ended in dictatorship! Our theoreticians had not the slightest idea of the necessary conditions for assuring liberty and law. They could only have had an idea if they had been willing to admit that the truth is not endowed with the beautiful simplicity attributed to it by the world of philosophy. The manufacture of such constitutions was an easy thing, and our fathers fancied that, since social reform consisted in an easy application of extremely simple and certain principles, it would be wrong to fear the great innovations.

We will now examine several compelling factors that led the men of the eighteenth century to believe that a radical alteration of institutions could easily be put into practice. First of all, we must speak briefly of their remarkable ideas on the nature of man—ideas whose origins were principally religious.

"The rights of men are founded not on their history but on their nature. . . . The greatest force of all is a pure and enlightened conscience in those to whom Providence has invested authority." These are Turgot's words to the king—words apparently inspired by Rousseau which, in the mouth of a minister, astonish us today.[25]

a. Some of Rousseau's ideas on nature are essentially biblical and Calvinist. This fact explains why his contemporaries sometimes found them very difficult to understand. To comprehend thoroughly his somewhat paradoxical discourse on the arts and sciences, it is best to refer to what Renan wrote on the *Jehovist* accounts of the book of Genesis: "The Jehovist has what amounts to hatred for civilization, which is considered a *decay of the patriarchal state.*

---

[24] In his *Histoire socialiste, La Convention,* p. 1792, Jaurès finds this admirable. His admiration for Condorcet's verbiage is natural enough. The words "pure," "precise," and "profound," which he uses indiscriminately enough himself, have clearly seduced him.

[25] Turgot, II, 503. Ch. Henry points out this opinion as being particularly curious (*Correspondance inédite de Condorcet et de Turgot,* p. xvii). Turgot wrote to Condorcet in 1773: "I'm grateful to Rousseau for almost all of his works" (*ibid.,* p. 146).

Each step forward in the path of what we would call progress is to him a crime inevitably followed by immediate punishment. The punishment for civilization is toil and strife. Babel's attempt at a worldly, secular, monumental, and artistic culture is the height of crime. Nimrod is a rebel. Whoever is great in whatever endeavor before Jehovah is his rival."[26] "The Jehovist is a somber thinker, at the same time religious and pessimistic, like certain philosophers of the new German school, such as Hartmann. . . . This conception of a primitive, dogmatic man, who knows neither death, toil, nor suffering, astonishes us by its boldness."[27]

Perhaps less with the intention of making his sophisms more palatable than of creating high-sounding oratorical phrases, Rousseau worked hard at establishing confusion among his various ideas on nature. At times he thought of travelers' tales of the savage life, at times he was under the influence of the accounts of classical heroes, and at times he was thinking of the so-called preternatural state that Adam enjoyed in the terrestrial paradise.[28] Civilization made man fall into nature as we know it now. In response to his detractors, Rousseau seems to be thinking of the fall of man. At the end of his letter to the King of Poland, he expresses himself thus: "To no avail would you try to destroy the sources of evil; to no avail would you remove the inducements of vanity, idleness, and luxury. Even to no avail would you bring men back to that primal equality which preserves innocence and is the source of all virtue; *their hearts, once spoiled, will always remain so*. There is no longer any remedy, short of some great revolution (to be feared almost as much as the evil it would cure), a revolution reprehensible to desire and impossible to foresee."

In all of this pessimistic literature, Rousseau clearly shows a great deal of guile. It is very possible that he adopted the course of denouncing the arts and sciences because this course allowed him to include the personification of Fabricus, composed by him in the Bois de Vincennes. The Calvinist idea of sin was not at all in keeping with Rousseau's profound thinking. We learn from Rousseau himself that Father Hemet, Rousseau's and Madame de Warens' Jesuit confessor, had calmed down the terrors that the reading of

---

26 Renan, *Histoire du peuple d'Israël*, II, 341.
27 *Ibid.*, II, 357.
28 Cf. Didiot, *Morale surnaturelle fondamentale* ("Fundamental Supernatural Morality"), p. 7.

Jansenist works had given him. Madame de Warens, who likewise did not believe in original sin, also reassured him.[29] It was thus completely natural that Rousseau should eventually abandon his pessimistic literature.

Many eighteenth-century men of letters had been brought up by the Jesuits and knew only by name the Jansenist (or Calvinist) doctrine of sin. Society people rarely understood it well. Wishing to influence his contemporaries in order to make them accept what he regarded as worthwhile in Christianity, Rousseau was led to adopt a less despondent attitude than is found in his first discourse. He believed that world redemption was possible by the action of mankind alone. *Emile* became the gospel of the state of nature regained.[30]

The idea of returning to the state of nature was not a novelty for Rousseau's contemporaries. In 1744 Father Charlevoix observed that it was very difficult to make the converted Indians understand that they must not give in to their inclinations freely, that the state of nature was corrupted and no longer allowed such liberty, and that "the law which restrains us brings us nearer to our original liberty while appearing to rob us of it."[31] In 1751 Turgot wrote to Madame de Graffigny: "In every way we have stifled instinct, while the savage follows it without recognizing it; he lacks sufficient intelligence to free himself from it. Nevertheless, it is necessary that the savages be educated, and this fact is realized before the art of educating the Indians is mastered, because the rules are based on false assumptions. It is only after a long time that, by consulting nature, we are able to help the savages, while being spared the drawback of going against nature."[32]

In our fathers' opinion, the history of modern art was founded on

[29] Rousseau, *Confessions*, Bk. VI. In his time, furthermore, Calvinism was in a state of decline, and the ministers of Geneva no longer believed in much of anything (*Deuxième lettre écrite de la Montagne* ["Second Letter from the Mountain"]). Rousseau presented almost all of the tenets of current liberal Protestantism in an excellent form. He clearly derived them from the body of Protestant thought, to which no one had yet been able to give coherent expression.

[30] According to Catholic theologians, a preternatural state today can be found exceptionally in saints. Protestants believed that the state of grace of the mystical monks could be extended to all Christians (*Réflexions sur la violence*, 4th ed., p. 399 [*Reflections on Violence*, Collier Book ed., New York, 1961, p. 254. Page numbers of this work refer to the American edition.—Trans.]). Rousseau played down the idea of salvation, diluted it somewhat in order to universalize it.

[31] Charlevoix, *Histoire et description générale de la Nouvelle France* ("History and General Description of New France"), V, 402.

[32] Turgot, II, 788.

a recent return to nature. Such a return was Boileau's great thesis.[33] Turgot strongly defends this theory in his discourse of 1750: the caprices of Gothic architecture were not the works of true primitives.[34] At the beginning, "the acquisition of knowledge and the formation of taste walked hand in hand, so to speak. Guided by instinct and imagination . . ." men had grasped "these relationships between man and the objects of nature, which alone are the foundations of beauty." Later, during the Middle Ages, great progress had been made in everyday skills, but "nature and feeling had been lost sight of. It was necessary to return by way of perfection to the point where the first men had been led by blind instinct; and who is there that does not know that herein lies the supreme effort of reason?"[35]

b. The church blamed the mistakes and the troubles of nations on their religious infidelity. When heresy gained ground, moral, intellectual, and political decadence was certain. When the kings relied on their confessors to bring their people back to the virtuous path, prosperity returned as if by magic. This extraordinary philosophy of history has not gone out of fashion; we can still read many dissertations on the subject in religious periodicals. The philosophers had only to change a few words of this doctrine in order to blame the errors and troubles of the world on the obstacles posed to the spread of enlightenment by the crafty politics of princes and priests.

When he left the Sorbonne, Turgot explained these mistakes in terms of psychological causes: "indolence, obstinacy, and the spirit of routine, all that is conducive to inaction."[36] But he did not look for the origin of these character defects. The philosophers believed they were going to the very heart of things when they denounced the church as being the source of all evil. Taine was justified in saying that eighteenth-century philosophy could be summed up in the slogan, *"Ecrasons l'infâme."*[37] In 1774 Condorcet wrote to Turgot, "The colossus is half destroyed, but we must liquidate it. . . . It is still doing great harm. Most of those ills that afflict us are the work

---

[33] Brunetière, *Evolution des genres,* pp. 96–102, 108–109.
[34] Gothic architecture seemed to Turgot to exemplify how progress can be independent of taste. He recognized the technical worth of medieval construction, but he did not like it (Turgot, II, 666).
[35] Turgot, II, 610.
[36] Turgot, II, 672.
[37] Taine, *Ancien Régime,* p. 302.

of the monster and can only be abolished when it is abolished."[38] When the writers of that time spoke of the struggle of the mind against authority, they almost always had in mind the struggle against the church.

The sometimes extraordinary admiration the eighteenth century revealed for Descartes had no other origin. At that time their conception of Descartes was rather inaccurate; he was pictured as exuding encyclopedic passions. At the end of his eighth epoch Condorcet celebrated the glory of three great men who liberated the human spirit: Bacon, Galileo, and Descartes.[39] In speaking of Descartes, he said, "He excited minds which the wisdom of his rivals had been unable to arouse. He told men to loosen the yoke of authority and to recognize henceforth only what might be acknowledged by reason. He was heeded because people were captivated by his boldness and swept away by his enthusiasm." This description is a little too fanciful; one would think that the author was speaking of Diderot and not of Descartes!

In Condorcet's view, even the fine arts suffered from tyranny; he was convinced they would make great progress under the influence of philosophy and science if "the prejudices that have restricted their scope and that still hold them under the yoke of authority, already broken by philosophy and science," could be destroyed.[40]

In his tenth epoch, in the midst of prophesying, Condorcet exclaimed: "When *maxims* that encourage action and energy have succeeded those that tend to restrain the dynamism of the human faculties, we doubtless will need no longer fear that there remain places on the earth inaccessible to enlightenment or that arrogant despotism can still raise its long insurmountable barriers to the truth. The moment will then arrive when the sun will shine only on free

---

[38] *Correspondance inédite de Condorcet et de Turgot*, pp. 205–206.
[39] Condorcet said that Descartes had given mankind "the method of finding and recognizing the truth." Too bad the formula has been lost. As for Bacon, he admitted that his principles "did not at all alter the course of science" (*Tableau historique*, 8th epoch). Galileo is the true father of modern science.
[40] Condorcet, *Tableau historique*, 10th epoch. What does the author mean to say? Condorcet is unintelligible here, as in many other instances. One rather wonders if the influence of the friends of the Enlightenment was not fatal to art during the end of the 18th century. This influence helped to ruin professional traditions and to set art on an artificial path with a view to expressing philosophical fantasies.

men who recognize no other master than their reason. The tyrants and the slaves, the priests and their dull-witted or hypocritical lackeys, will exist only in history books and on the stage."

Now we understand why our predecessors believed institutions to be responsible for all evil and why they assumed that it was so easy to transform these institutions. The reason is that, since they saw the whole world of the past as dependent on the church and since the church had lost nearly all of its vigor, it could be hoped that with a little good will and energy a radical change could be wrought in a short time. Now that we no longer attribute to the church such importance and have seen it rise up from ruins, we find it difficult to understand the extreme optimism of the eighteenth century.

c. It was from the church that the philosophers borrowed their ideas on the power of education to change society. More than once, missionaries had told of extraordinary results obtained very quickly in working with the savages. In their view, several of their settlements resembled the communities of apostolic times. A Jesuit compared the large villages of Paraguay to monasteries, in which people led a completely innocent life and practiced weekly communion.[41] Condorcet believed that the nations remaining outside the European movement would enter into it rapidly: the great Oriental religions were in a state of decline and "no longer threaten to entrap human reason in a bondage without hope and in an eternal childhood." Progress would be extremely rapid because the Europeans would bring these peoples the fruits of long and painstaking investigations.[42]

After becoming minister, Turgot proposed to the king a master plan for public education, which was an exact imitation of the clerical proposals. Until that time, man was concerned with "molding scholars and men of intellect and taste," but one must now concern oneself with the others: "to form in all social classes virtuous and useful men, just souls, pure hearts, and zealous citizens." For the

---

[41] André Lichtenberger, *Le Socialisme au XVIIIe siècle*, pp. 58–62.

[42] Condorcet, *Tableau historique*, 10th epoch. The author does not consider what would happen if Oriental peoples adopted only the material civilization of Europe. His illusions are great. He says elsewhere, "In connection with the invention of explosives, civilized people no longer must fear the blind courage of barbarians. The great conquests and the revolutions that followed them have become almost impossible" (7th epoch).

primary national bond is constituted by morality, and it depends on the education given to the young "on all of the duties of man in society." It is therefore necessary to give children "moral and social education."[43] "The civic education that the board of education would give . . . the enlightened books it would write and require all teachers to use, would contribute still more to the formation of an educated and virtuous people. These books would plant in the hearts of children the principles of humanity, justice, charity, and love for the state, which qualities, finding their application as the children matured, would continually grow. They would bring patriotism to that high degree of enthusiasm of which only the ancient nations have given several examples, and this enthusiasm would be more prudent and more solidly based because it would rest on a greater degree of genuine happiness."[44]

This lay and civic catechism would rapidly show results. Turgot said to the king, "I dare to answer him that in ten years time, his nation would be unrecognizable, and that with enlightenment, high moral standards, and enlightened zeal to serve king and country, his nation would be infinitely superior to all others. Children who are now ten years old would be men who are prepared for the state, loving their country, obedient to authority, not from fear but from reason,[45] charitable toward their fellow citizens,[46] accustomed to recognizing and respecting justice, which is the primary foundation of societies."[47]

Contemporary democracy has kept all of these beliefs of the third-estate oligarchy. It also has conceived of primary instruction as a means of teaching a lay, patriotic, and bourgeois catechism. It believed that it could thereby render the masses more receptive to all

---

[43] Turgot, II, pp. 506–508. "There are methods and institutions for training geometricians, physicists, and painters; there are none for training citizens" (*ibid.*, p. 506).

[44] *Ibid.*, II, 549.

[45] Taine, who quoted this passage from Turgot's report (*Ancien Régime*, pp. 309–310), should have been warned by this sentence that the author was clearly speaking of a catechism to produce automatic obedience. Turgot understood education in a Napoleonic way. He told the king it was necessary to develop "a spirit of order and union to make all of the strengths and resources of your country unite for the common good, to consolidate them in your hands, and to make them easier to control" (Turgot, II, 506).

[46] We know how much pauperism then preoccupied all the economists and the men of state.

[47] Turgot, II, 508.

the nonsense uttered by politicians. It has already very conveniently succeeded in developing credulous and servile puerility. Our fathers, who lacked our experience, were unable to distinguish between the things that the lay catechism could and could not teach. They did not know that this catechism is only really effective in facilitating the domination of charlatans.

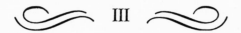

The literature on the savages had a great influence on the men of the eighteenth century. It can be said that America was discovered twice: the first time by the *conquistadores*, who were eager for pillage, and later by missionaries, who revealed the existence of a new type of humanity that seemed to them to have a great future before it. The Franciscan Bernardino de Sahagun, who wrote a book of great interest on Mexican antiquities, hoped (in 1569) that the Indians would compensate the church for the losses heresy made it undergo in Europe.[48] I think a similar opinion could be found at the basis of the thinking of the majority of missionaries; seeing the savage peoples more obedient to the orders of the clergy than the Europeans, they were disposed to attribute to them greater virtue.

The missionaries generally were committed to defending the oppressed Indians; they were led to maintain that the advantages brought to the conquered peoples by civilization could not compensate for the evils which they thereby suffered.[49] Bernardino de Sahagun's translator observed that he voluntarily limited himself to giving the information on the conquest of Mexico, which he had learned firsthand among the natives, "without even omitting what was critical of his fellow countrymen."[50]

In all of this literature on savages, I believe I should choose Father Charlevoix's book on New France because it was widely read in the

---

[48] Bernardino de Sahagun, *Histoire générale des choses de la Nouvelle Espagne* ("General History of New Spain"), p. 10. He went to America eight years after the conquest of Mexico.

[49] Bernardino de Sahagun said that the Mexicans were injured as the Jews had once been and that they had lost every semblance of what they had previously been (*ibid.*, p. 7).

[50] Bernardino de Sahagun, *Histoire générale*, p. xviii.

eighteenth century and because, since it appeared in 1744, its influence on Rousseau and Turgot was probably especially great. It seems to me even more useful to call attention to this work because Lichtenberger did not use it in his *Socialisme au XVIIIe siècle*.

Speaking of the Indian chiefs' councils, he said, "We must admit that in these assemblies they proceed with a wisdom, a maturity, a skillfulness, and I would even say an integrity, generally speaking, that would have done honor to the Council of Athens or the Roman Senate in the finest days of these republics. There no conclusions are arrived at in haste. . . . The principal moving forces of all their endeavors are usually the glory of the nation and considerations of honor."[51] With respect to diplomacy, "Everything is conducted with a dignity, an attention, I would even venture to say a capability, worthy of the most important matters."[52]

Here we very clearly see one of the great reasons that distorted the judgment of the Jesuits in their evaluation of savage life. Used to attaching tremendous importance to good manners in their schools, they believed the development of ceremony to be proof of the greatest wisdom. Only in our time has it been acknowledged that ancient ceremony is the product of magical superstitions, so that ceremony very often played an important part in the life of peoples with the lowest forms of culture.

This passage also draws our attention to the tone of the work, which was a defense of the savage life whose qualities were contrasted to the vices of the refined life. These portrayals led to the belief that the poor classes, having a less complicated life than the rich classes, are more capable of virtue. This idea completely dominated the end of the eighteenth century.

I will now cite several traits of the savage life, given by Father Charlevoix. "We note in them a society spared from nearly all of the faults that so often mar the tranquility of our own. . . . They give the appearance of leading the most miserable life in the world, and they were perhaps the only happy people in the world before knowledge of the things that stimulate and seduce us awakened a greed in them that had been held in check by ignorance.[53] Born free

---

[51] Charlevoix, *Histoire de la Nouvelle France*, V, 397–398.
[52] *Ibid.*, V, 399.
[53] Charlevoix recognized elsewhere that the taste for spirits has brought on many disorders. "Drunkenness has made them self-seeking and has disturbed the tranquility they had enjoyed in their home life and in everyday affairs" (*ibid.*, VI, 31).

and independent, they have a horror of even a hint of despotic power, but they rarely deviate from certain principles or customs based on common sense, which take the place of laws and which in a sense replace institutionalized authority. They rebel against all restraint. But reason alone keeps them in a sort of subordination that attains the goal they set for themselves and is nonetheless effective for being voluntary."[54] Thus, conscience is a sufficient guide for the savages. Why not try to apply to civilized societies these principles which succeed so well when applied to savages?

"As they are not slaves to ambition and self-interest (these passions have done more than anything else to weaken the sentiment of kindness, which had been graven in our hearts by the author of nature), inequality of conditions is not necessary to uphold their society. . . .[55] In this country, all men are considered as equals, and what is esteemed most in a man is his humanity—no distinction of birth, no privileges based on rank, which discriminate against individual rights, absolutely no preeminence attached to merit, which only inspires pride and makes others feel inferior. They have, perhaps, less delicacy in the sentiments than we do, but more uprightness and less affected niceties and what makes them ambiguous, less indulgence in self-examination."[56]

One experience had made a strong impression on Father Charlevoix: Some young Indians, who had been raised in the European way, fled to the woods. In addition, an Iroquois who had become a lieutenant in the French forces ended up by returning to his tribe. Frenchmen who lived with the savages "never could prevail on these runaway Indians to go back to the French colony, although they could have lived very comfortably there."[57] Here, then, we have actual proof that the poverty of Indians could be preferred to civilized comfort. "The liberty they enjoy is for them a great compensation for the material commodities of which they are deprived. We see every day in professional beggars and in some rural people

---

54 *Ibid.*, VI, 59–60.

55 In his letter of 1751 to Madame de Graffigny, Turgot maintained that inequality is necessary to assure the division of labor (Turgot, II, 786). Father Charlevoix praised the savages for not knowing the difference between mine and thine; "these cold phrases, as St. John Chrysostom called them, extinguish the flame of charity in our hearts and kindle that of greed" (*Histoire de la Nouvelle France*, VI, 11).

56 Charlevoix, *Histoire de la Nouvelle France*, VI, 61–62.

57 *Ibid.*, VI, 32–33.

a clear proof that it is possible to be happy in the midst of poverty. Now the savages are even more truly happy, primarily because they believe themselves to be happy; secondly, because they are in the peaceful possession of the most precious of all of nature's gifts; lastly, because they are completely unacquainted with and do not even seek the knowledge of those fraudulent blessings that we revere so much, that we buy at the price of the real blessings, and that we enjoy so little in reality."[58]

It is not difficult to see that Father Charlevoix found material for preaching in this subject and that his penchant for preaching prevailed by much over his gift for observation (which was meager enough, anyway). The eighteenth century enthusiastically accepted this doctrine of compensation. Lichtenberger notes an almost paradoxical example in Bougainville. The latter, in describing the miserable natives of the Tierra del Fuego, said that one cannot "pity the fate of a free man who is his own master, without duties or concerns, and content with what he has, because he knows no better."[59] The seafarer echoed the sentiment of the missionary: It would be impossible to count the times the observers of that period repeated the same lessons.

I do not think that the significance of this literature is generally clearly understood. The greatest impression has always been made by the principles which it provided to authors who advocated moral reforms. Rousseau no doubt adopted his ideas on maternal suckling and on the gentleness which should be employed in education from this literature. Moreover, it is probable that the missioneries' favorable judgments on the morals of the savages led to the belief that sexual restraints could be modified advantageously: in Europe, the reign of greater freedom in natural relations would probably produce the same cold temperament which had often struck the missionaries in the Indians.[60]

---

[58] *Ibid.*, VI, 31–32.
[59] André Lichtenberger, *Le Socialisme au XVIIIe siècle*, p. 360.
[60] Charlevoix, *Histoire*, VI, 37–38. Lafitau, *Moeurs des sauvages américains* ("Customs of American Indians"), I, 582–583, 593–603. Elsewhere, however, Father Charlevoix speaks of the lasciviousness of the women. This corruption supposedly extended from Louisiana as far as the Iroquois territory. He also reports the homosexuality of the Indians, which somewhat embarrassed the admirers of nature. Diderot wrote superficial explanations on this subject, which would be fit for a university extension lecture (Diderot, VI, 452–453).

Above all, this literature must be considered as having induced an attitude of indifference for the civilization achieved. The savage life inspired many fanciful novels. Undoubtedly, these stories were often less projects of reform than diatribes against society. We know this was true in the case of the Platonic utopias. In such compositions, we do not usually look for indications of what reforms should be accomplished until the works fall into the hands of a class or a generation other than that which the author intended to inform. The eighteenth-century writers more than once plunged headlong with a genuine furor into dreams for a new society, and their arguments are not easily understood by our contemporary historians. Lichtenberger regards the *Supplément au voyage de Bougainville* as a "fancy-whim with which Diderot was carried away on a reckless philosophical binge."[61] This evaluation diminishes considerably the importance of such a work.

Fourier wanted to resume the arguments against civilization after the Revolution. He hoped his contemporaries would tire of the new regime just as the preceding generation had wearied of the ancien régime. Completely lacking in taste and having slight success, he found scarcely anyone to applaud him except mediocre minds, eccentrics, or deranged women. He could never understand why people did not take him seriously though they had taken the Encyclopedists seriously. This difference depended not only on the difference in talent but on the fact that France had changed completely in the course of the Revolution: the wars of liberty had brought so much glory to the new regime that it could not be seriously menaced by any sort of literature. This was not the first time our ancestors showed indifference to the past. During the first centuries of our era, a great number of men ceased to attach even the slightest importance to political or family affairs. They abandoned their public responsibilities and advocated celibacy. Renan said that "it was they who abolished the Roman Empire. They sapped its vitality and took away the elite personnel from its offices, particularly the army. It is not enough to say that someone is a good citizen because he pays his taxes, is charitable and steady, when he is really a citizen of heaven and considers the earthly city only a prison where he is chained side by side with wretches."[62]

---

[61] André Lichtenberger, *Le Socialisme au XVIIIe siècle*, p. 257.
[62] Renan, *Marc-Aurèle* ("Marcus Aurelius"), p. 428.

The admiration of the men of the Renaissance for classical civilization now seems very naive. But in order to understand it, we must note that this enthusiasm for the ancients was a way of expressing their disgust for the Middle Ages. We might compare the admiration of the sixteenth century for the Greeks with the love of the savages in the eighteenth century. In both cases, the immediately preceding civilization was being condemned and found almost no defenders.[63]

IV

We will now deal with a third class of reasons that were as decisive as the previous ones in producing the extreme temerity of the third estate at the time of the Revolution. This third class of reasons is economic.

The beginning of the eighteenth century had been a very unhappy time. But from the middle of the century on, there was a general revival in agriculture. In 1772 Turgot wrote to Condorcet that the decree of 1764, by permitting the grain trade, was very beneficial, and that the tenant farmers had been able to recover. Progress was due, not solely to this factor, but even more to the technical changes then undertaken. Turgot himself refers to the development of clover fields.[64] D'Avenel tells us that in 1768 it was declared in the Orne that clover had been grown for twenty-six years, and in 1760 on the English Channel violet clover had been part of the crops for several years.[65] The tax farmers raised the amount they collected at each improvement. Necker said in the census of 1781 that ". . . we can estimate that the revenue from all taxes on commodities increases about 2 million a year." Arthur Young declared that in 1788 Bordeaux was a larger commercial

---

[63] In 1772, Turgot wrote to Condorcet that he was shocked with Raynal's "incoherent arguments," which were a conglomeration of the most bizarre things he found in the books he consulted. Condorcet answered that Turgot was too severe (*Correspondance inédite de Condorcet et de Turgot*, pp. 93, 95). Raynal's tenets did not shock the Paris *literati*, but Turgot lived in the provinces.

[64] *Correspondance inédite*, p. 81.

[65] D'Avenel, *Histoire économique de la propriété, des salaires, des denrées, et de tous les prix depuis l'an 1200 jusqu'a l'an 1800*, I, 296.

center than Liverpool, and he added that in recent years maritime commerce had made more rapid advances in France than even in England and that French trade had doubled in ten years.[66]

Not all of the classes in society profited equally from these advances. Pauperism does not seem to have been abolished. It is, however, sufficient for our purposes to examine the phenomena that had a direct and decisive influence on the thinking of the third estate. From this point of view, we may study the value of arable lands in order to shed light on the economic movement of the eighteenth century, especially as land value underwent an extraordinary increase at that time. In spite of the criticisms made of d'Avenel's statistics, we may make excellent use of them for our purposes because we are examining a very rapid economic advance.

The price of land increased in the first seventy-five years of the seventeenth century.[67] Then began a rapid collapse of the market. D'Avenel notes that, about 1725, the price of land was at the lowest point since the reign of Henry II. Starting from 1750, "the increase accelerated and expanded with an intensity that far surpassed what has happened in our time . . . with the result that, all things considered, it was perhaps in the second half of the eighteenth century that we had the most rapid increase ever recorded." It was rare that the price of land merely doubled between 1700 and 1790; rather, it tripled on the average. The author even cites a case in which the price increased four and a half times. Revenues did not increase as fast, and the interest rate fell from five percent to 3.5 percent.[68]

The consequences of this state of affairs were considerable. "In 1780 it could not longer be maintained that France was in a state of decline. On the contrary, it was said that there were no limits to her progress. It was then that the doctrine of the continuous and unlimited perfectibility of man was born. Twenty years earlier, there had been no faith in the future; in 1780 there was no fear of it. Leaping ahead of this imminent and unheard-of good fortune,

---

66 Tocqueville, *L'Ancien Régime*, pp. 173–174.

67 From 1625 to 1650, there was an interruption in this prosperity. In 1641, the ambassador from Venice believed that France was unable to meet her obligations (D'Avenel, *Histoire économique*, I, 379–380).

68 D'Avenel, *Histoire économique*, I, 374, 384, 387–389, 394–396. D. Zella gives several tables on the land revenues in his *Etudes d'économie rurale* ("Studies in rural economics"), pp. 415–417.

people were indifferent to the benefits of the present and instead precipitated toward new things."[69]

As always happens, there were ideologues who continued thinking in line with past conditions. Indeed, experience shows that philosophers, far from being in advance of the common herd and showing them the path, are almost always behind the public. According to a famous saying, philosophy is like the bird of Minerva—it bestirs at night.

Helvetius was one of these late thinkers. He wrote in his book, *l'Homme*: "My country has finally acquired the yoke of despotism, which stifles thought in the mind and virtue in the soul. . . . This degraded nation is today the scorn of Europe. No salutary crisis will give her liberty. It is by consumption that she will perish. Conquest is the sole remedy for her trouble." In 1773, these somber predictions greatly disturbed Parisian society.[70] In a letter to Condorcet, Turgot, who saw things from the vantage point of his province, protested against the statements of Helvetius, whom he called a "speechifier." He contended that France had not "reached the last stage of oppression and degradation" and said that he found only "vanity, partisanship, and hotheadedness" in Helvetius' book. Regretfully he saw that such a work was extolled out of a spirit of partisanship. In it he saw "neither love of humanity nor philosophy."[71]

Compelled by public opinion, the administration modified its procedures. Formerly, intendants were concerned solely with maintaining order, raising militia, and assuring the collection of taxes. "The intendant of 1780 . . . had other cares: his head was filled with a thousand projects for increasing the public wealth. Roads, canals, manufacturing, and commerce were his principal preoccupations.

Agriculture, especially, drew his attention. Sully became popular among the administrators. "Certain memoranda from this comptroller general read more like treatises on the art of agriculture than government business letters."[72]

According to the experts of social reform, such a regime ought to have been excellent for consolidating the government. The third

---

[69] Tocqueville, *L'Ancien Régime*, p. 177.
[70] Rocquain, *L'Esprit révolutionnaire*, p. 310.
[71] *Correspondance inédite*.
[72] Tocqueville, *L'Ancien Régime*, p. 172.

estate prospered and the administration devoted itself to helping it prosper. And yet, "as France's prosperity increased, the general mood seemed more and more to be one of discontent and unrest; public dissatisfaction became more embittered; hatred grew against every old institution. The nation was obviously heading for a revolution."[73] "[Forty years before the Revolution] a sort of interior disturbance, hitherto unnoticed, could be discerned in all parts of society. . . . Everyone was in a ferment, restless with his lot, and trying to change it; a search for the better life was universal, but it was a search fraught with impatience and vexation. People cursed the past while imagining an utterly different world from that of the present."[74]

This astonished Tocqueville, who seems not to have ever reflected much on the influence of economic conditions on thought: "The most dangerous time for a bad government is the time when it begins to make reforms." People supported an evil without complaint if it appeared to be necessary. "Every abuse that is remedied draws attention to the ones that remain, and they are now more galling. The evil is mitigated, but awareness of it is greater."[75]

The essential reason for this fact is the total abandonment of the notion of necessity. With regard to the future, "nothing is feared. Imagination makes people indifferent to the benefits of the present and precipitates them toward new things."[76] To use more technical language, I will say: When economic necessity has disappeared and it is thought that the time has come to make bold experiments in social affairs as well as in technology, reformers and inventors bring forth their projects, and the politicians and industrialists let themselves be easily persuaded because they think that the huge profits to be accrued in the immediate future will be such that mistakes will not matter.

In a general way, we can say that the revolutionary spirit gains ground whenever the belief in economic necessity is weakened. Hence these obvious paradoxes: that social legislation, introduced with the purpose of calming socialist ardour, often results in promoting socialism; that the concessions made by employers following

---

[73] *Ibid.*, p. 175.
[74] *Ibid.*, p. 171.
[75] *Ibid.*, p. 177.
[76] *Ibid.*, p. 177.

a strike generally constitute one of the factors in the progress of revolutionary syndicalism; in a word, that social peace almost always feeds the class struggle.

Observation of contemporary society shows that economic necessity is very difficult for intellectuals to understand. This is why university teaching was so often denounced in the past as bound to lead the bourgeois classes to utopia. At present we see a very curious spectacle: many university men are undertaking to replace socialism with social science. But they claim to be creating this science with a view to abrogating the effects of economic necessity; as a result, they are thinking of a truly antiscientific science, which would exist without rigid connecting links between things.[77] This is one of the most obvious proofs of the intellectuals' difficulty in understanding economics.

It is often asked why rich Jews are so sympathetic to utopian ideas and sometimes even give themselves socialistic airs. I naturally disregard those who see in socialism a new means of exploitation, for there are some who are sincere. This phenomenon cannot be explained by ethnic reasons.[78] These men live on the margins of production—literature, music, and financial speculation are their interests. They are not aware of the forces of necessity in the world, and their outspoken boldness has the same origin as that of so many eighteenth-century gentlemen.

Furthermore, great landowners have been known to compose social utopias. We know that the possessors of vast agricultural

---

[77] Lassalle understood the true character of science when he spoke of the "iron laws" governing the social world. He did not wonder if there really is a science that permits one to proceed to sure deductions in all the branches of social knowledge. The existence of such a science appeared obvious to him. On the contrary, it seems very unlikely at present. Nevertheless, the more we search for the economic basis of the world, the more we find necessity.

[78] Guglielmo Ferrero has written several interesting pages on this subject in a book published in 1897. He was struck with encountering so many wealthy Jews in socialist circles in Germany. These people did not have personal complaints of injustices. They were similar to other members of the bourgeoisie in their cupidity. And yet, contrary to the expectations of their manner of life, they rediscovered the traditional path of their race, determined in its protests against the faults of humanity. Marxist tenets seemed to them to be an echo of the ancient prophetic scriptures and to be new revelations (*Europa giovane*, pp. 361–362). Cf. the pages concerned with Jewish pessimism, with the pride, the overstatement, and the idea of mission in the Jewish people, and finally, with their need of proselytism (pp. 363–371). It seems to me that almost all of this can be explained without bringing in atavism.

domains have often been more interested in literature than the science of agriculture. Hence, they so often fail in the cultivation of their lands and neglect obvious improvements for fanciful projects. It is not in the least rare to encounter among them men who have had their heads turned by economic novels; these men fancy that prices are regulated by the will of a few men, and they dream of enormous cooperative trusts. Like the men of the eighteenth century, they think with their imagination. Consequently they, too, are foolishly attached to the idea of the enlightened will.

Our fathers of the eighteenth century were all the more aware of the slackening of economic necessity as they saw no great value in historical necessity. It is only during the nineteenth century that the role of tradition began to be understood, and that only happened following the great upheavals that marked the end of the Napoleonic Wars. In the eighteenth century, the breakneck speed with which progress accelerated indeed served to promote the belief that everything was possible in the future as long as the instincts of human nature were followed.

CHAPTER V

Theories of Progress

I. *Turgot's discourse. Differences with Bossuet; bourgeois preoccupations. Development of progress in the midst of life's unforeseen
circumstances. Material progress in the Middle Ages.*

II. *Madame de Staël's defense of the new order. The new principles
of literary criticism. The fusion of different civilizations. Christianity. Violence.*

III. *The birth of the idea of evolution at the end of the wars of national independence. The historical formation of law and juridical
conscience. Evolution is the opposite of progress.*

IV. *Tocqueville and the necessary march toward equality. Proudhon's and Marx's objections. Proudhon's abandonment of the idea of
necessity; moral progress.*

V. *The idea of progress in democratic literature. P. Lacombe's theory: its naive illusions; what it reveals about democracy.*

VI. *Natural progress or technical progress in production. A glance
at the progress of machines. Contemporary ideology.*

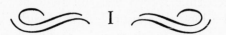 I

In the middle of the eighteenth century, it was easy to believe that
there was going to be a radical transformation of the French state.
As early as 1753, d'Argenson considered a revolution inevitable.[1]
In 1774, after having left the ministry, he wondered if circumstances

---

[1] Rocquain, *L'Esprit révolutionnaire avant la Révolution*, p. 114.

were leading toward the establishment of a republic. The festivities at the time of the peace of Aix-la-Chapelle (1748) showed how great the discontent was. The people did not shout: "Long live the king."[2] Incessant conflicts brought the government and the Parlements to grips with each other on taxes that the ministry required to be maintained although the war expenses no longer existed. In 1751 d'Argenson believed that revolution would come about by acclamation.[3] In 1753, the Parlement reminded Louis XV that "kings owe obedience to the laws, and it is the alteration of the laws that [causes] revolutions in states." At that time began to be put forth the symbolic images of justice, truth, and law which would be so successful at the end of the century.[4] The chief justice seemed to take the attitude of a leader of a senate that derives its power from the nation and not from the king.[5] Exiled Parlementarians fervently studied public law; they conferred about it amongst themselves as they might have done in the academies, and some men said that if ever the French nation found a day to give them its confidence, they were a ready-made national senate.[6]

Rocquain thinks it was perhaps just as well that nothing happened in 1754: "The Parlement without a doubt would have taken the leadership of the movement. From a political point of view, it should not be thought, as d'Argenson did, that the trend would have been towards a regulated democratic government. In all probability it would have been restricted to limiting the authority of the sovereign."[7]

It was during this troubled period that Turgot wrote his essays on progress. The first is a speech given at the Sorbonne on December 11, 1750. Turgot was then twenty-three years old. It does not seem probable that he thought that he was introducing great novelties, for this academic speech was not published by Dupont de Nemours until a long time after Turgot's death. The young student had always given much thought to economic questions. At the time that he was taking courses in theology, he also was prepar-

---

[2] *Ibid.*, pp. 123–128.
[3] *Ibid.*, p. 146.
[4] *Ibid.*, pp. 171–172.
[5] *Ibid.*, p. 165.
[6] *Ibid.*, p. 177.
[7] *Ibid.*, p. 180.

ing to enter the magistrature.[8] His education was broad, and every-thing leads us to believe he sought to give a successful formulation to concepts dominating bourgeois thought. Consequently, his speech should be considered as having a much greater historical significance than if the author had felt he was expressing a personal doctrine.

This speech must not be separated from the three fragments written a little later and meant to prepare for a more important work. Dupont de Nemours has left us some valuable information about the intention of his friend: "Turgot gave to Bossuet the homage that the loftiness of his thoughts and the boldness of his expression deserved. He admired the noble and brisk manner, the wealth of expression, the grandeur and harmonious dignity of his style. But after paying this tribute to the excellent writer, he regretted that the *Discourse on Universal History* was not richer in perspective, reason, and true knowledge. . . . He [intended] to rewrite the book to give it the desired breadth and to put into it the principles the illustrious Bishop of Meaux had silently passed over, perhaps had not thought of, and perhaps would not have adopted."[9]

The first of the fragments refers to the formation of governments and to the relations of nations, the second to the progress of the human mind (as in the speech of 1750), and the third to the periods of progress and decline in the arts and sciences. This last fragment (which stops at the time of Charlemagne) was written at a time when Turgot saw he could not carry out his original plans.

Clearly Turgot intended to remake Bossuet's work by replacing theocratic dogma with a theory of progress in harmony with the aspirations of the enlightened bourgeoisie of his time.

For Bossuet, the Dauphin's teacher, the main purpose was to teach his pupil "the continuing course of religion," to reveal to him that the titles of legitimacy of Catholicism trace back to the origins of the world, and to make him understand the duties of a king. The sovereign must defend tradition and use the power of the state against the unfaithful: "Let your august dynasty, the most digni-

---

[8] In 1749, he wrote a dissertation on paper money. He left the Sorbonne at the beginning of 1751. He was named assistant to the attorney general on January 5, 1752, counselor on December 30, and master of requests on March 28, 1753. He allied himself with Quesnay and Cournay in 1755 and wrote articles for the Encyclopedists in 1756.

[9] Turgot, II, 625–627.

fied in the whole world, be the first to defend the rights of God
and to extend throughout the universe the reign of Jesus Christ, who
permits you to rule with so much glory."[10]

Later, on the other hand, the bourgeois oligarchy for which
Turgot wrote concentrated all its attention on the progress of the
arts and sciences; it is not without reason that Turgot ended up by
limiting his work to this study alone.

Bossuet had conceived of history as a teaching. At the beginning
of his book he said: "When history is useless to other men, princes
should still read it. There is no better way to show them the effects
of passions and self-interest, historical circumstances and contin-
gencies, and good and bad advice. Histories are written only by
the acts that take place in them, and everything in them seems to
be done for their use."

It seems to me that Turgot also had teaching very much in mind,
because he called all the attention of his contemporaries to the reasons that bring on the ruin of great civilizations. He obviously was
thinking of the errors that could compromise his civilization when
he explained Roman decadence by the tyranny that debases the
spirit, the blind extravagance that transforms works of art into
signs of opulence, the desire for fancy goods which distracts men
who do not have enough genius to be creative, the imitation of
the faults of the ancient authors, the multiplication of writers in the
provinces, the deterioration of the language, and the mixing of the
traditional philosophy with empty allegories and magic.[11] He judges
the Middle Ages from the perspective of a future royal magistrate:
then kings were without authority, there were no restraints on the
nobles, the people were slaves, the countryside was frequently rav-
aged, there was no commerce, the artisans were uncompetitive, the
aristocracy was lazy, and general ignorance prevailed. The author
notes that progress began in the cities, which are "in all lawful countries the center of commerce and of the main forces of society."[12]
It is the bourgeoisie that carries the future of the world.

At the end of the *Discourse on Universal History*, Bossuet presents his idea thus: this long series of particular causes that make and

---

[10] Bossuet, *Discours sur l'histoire universelle* ("Discourse on Universal History"),
2d part *ad finem*.
[11] Turgot, II, 606.
[12] Turgot, II, 607–608.

unmake empires depends on the secret orders of divine providence. From high in the heavens, God holds the reins of all realms; he has all hearts in his hands; at times he holds passions in check, at times he unleashes them, and consequently he stirs the whole human race. . . . It is he who determines the effects in the most distant causes and who strikes those great blows whose echoes are heard everywhere." Thus only the acts of kings and their ministers should be considered; but Bossuet also knows that it is necessary to explain these actions by other than individual motives alone. Thus he makes a kind of supernatural psychology intervene; there is a divine will operating outside of all human expectations. "All those who govern feel that they are themselves subject to a major force. They do more or less than they think, and their decisions have never failed to have unforeseen effects. Neither are they the masters of those factors past centuries have put into the state of affairs, nor can they force the course which the future will take, so far are they from controlling it. God alone holds everything in his hands, who knows the name of what is and what is to be, who presides over all epochs and anticipates all decisions." Finally, history is an impenetrable mystery for man.

With Turgot, we move to an entirely different ground. This is how he represents the task to be accomplished: "To reveal the influence of particular, general, and necessary causes and the free actions of great men; to show the relationship of all this to the very constitution of man; to show the scope and the mechanics of moral causes by their effects—all this comprises the role of history in the eyes of the philosopher."[13] We no longer find divine intervention necessary to fulfill the princely will. The problem is posed in an inverse form from Bossuet's. Writing for a prince acting under divine right, Bossuet sees only the decisions of the king and the resolutions of God as having any real importance in the world. Writing for a class that furnished many assistants to the government but never governed, Turgot regards as accident everything that happened outside of the third estate and everything it accepted passively; true history is that whose active principle is found in his social class. "Empires rise and fall; laws and forms of government come and go; the arts and sciences develop and are perfected. Al-

---

[13] Turgot, II, 628.

ternately retarded and accelerated in their progress, they pass from region to region. Self-interest, ambition, and vainglory perpetually change the face of the world and inundate the earth with blood; in the midst of their ravages, customs become refined, the human mind becomes enlightened, and isolated nations draw near to one another. Commerce and politics finally unite all parts of the globe, and the total mass of the human race, by cycles of calm and unrest, good and evil, slowly but surely marches to a greater perfection."[14]

Thus the great events Bossuet wanted to discuss with the dauphin became accidents in the midst of which the third estate pursued its impersonal work. It is this work alone that merits the attention of philosophers. We pass from political history to the history of civilizations. But by what mechanism is this movement generated? Here again we will find Turgot adopting a viewpoint completely opposed to that of Bossuet.

In the providential system there is no room for chance. "Let's speak no more of chance or fortune," says Bossuet, "or let us speak of them only as words with which we conceal our ignorance. That which we call chance with respect to our uncertain plans is a concrete design in a higher plan—that is, in the eternal plan, which includes all causes and all effects in a single design. In this way, everything works to the same end. Because we fail to understand the whole, we find chance and irregularity in particular circumstances."

On the contrary, when one no longer intends to reason on the "eternal plan," which is not accessible to historians, chance is found to be the great law of history, the very condition of the regularity that permits the philosophical study of history. There is a canceling out among the forces created by the acts of rulers. But in the third estate, forces act in a constant sense and produce a definitive work by successive approximations. "In the midst of this varied combination of events—at times favorable and at times perverse— whose opposing actions must eventually destroy one another, nature has bestowed genius on a few men interspersed almost evenly among the whole human race. This genius acts unceasingly, and by degrees its effects become apparent. . . . Always uneasy, incapable of finding peace except in the truth, always excited by the image of this truth, which it thinks it has grasped and which flees before it, men's

---

[14] Turgot, II, 598.

curiosity multiplies the questions and the disputes and obliges them to analyze ideas and facts in an ever more exact and thorough way. ... Thus, by groping, by multiplying the systems, by working out the errors, so to speak, knowledge of a greater number of truths is finally arrived at."[15] Contemporary philosophy would change almost nothing of this statement of the origin of knowledge.

Turgot's essays seem much superior to the *Tableau historique*, in which Condorcet undertakes to treat the same question as his friend. It is even very fortunate for Condorcet that he was obliged by circumstances to limit himself to tracing a simple outline of the progress of the human mind, for he announced so many things that it would have been impossible to keep most of his promises. His book, written when the Revolution had triumphed, is above all a hymn to the new regime and an indictment against superstition.[16]

Turgot shows himself to be much more modern than his successor, not only because he judges the past with more seriousness, but also because he has a more exact feeling for the importance of economic phenomena. This is so odd that it would be useful to dwell an instant on it. According to Turgot, the invasion of the barbarians did not make the arts and crafts antiquity had practiced completely disappear, because the demand for their products never ceased. During the Middle Ages, there was much perfection of the mechanical arts, commerce, and the customs of civil life. "Accomplishments were amassed in the shadow of the Dark Ages, and the sciences, whose progress, though hidden, was nonetheless real, would reappear one day enhanced by these new riches."[17] After the Renaissance, the mind, thus well-prepared and having become more alert, profited from the slightest chance to make discoveries.[18]

Condorcet also mentions, in the seventh epoch of *Tableau historique*, the changes the Middle Ages produced. He does not, however, seem to give them their true place; between Scholasticism and

---

[15] Turgot, II, 600–601.

[16] Thus the rapid decline of the Arabs "warned our contemporaries to neglect nothing so as to preserve and augment enlightenment if they wish to become and remain free and to maintain their liberty if they do not want to lose the advantages enlightenment has procured for them" (*Tableau historique*, 6th epoch). History should serve "to maintain us in an active vigilance in order to be able to recognize and suppress under the weight of reason, the first germs of superstition and tyranny, if they ever dared to appear again" (10th epoch).

[17] Turgot, II, 608; cf. p. 666.

[18] Turgot, II, 610.

Italian poetry he speaks of silk, paper, the magnet, and cannon powder.[19] Farther on, at the end of the ninth epoch, he seems even to want to reverse the natural order of things and base the recent progress of arts and crafts on the very old attainments of pure science. Here we find the oft-quoted sentence: "The sailor whose exact observation of longitude saves the ship from shipwreck owes his life to a theory which, by a chain of truths, goes back to discoveries made in the school of Plato and were buried for twenty centuries in complete uselessness." One might think that he wanted to take the opposite stand from Turgot.

Here is a thought of the latter to which I call the reader's closest attention: "Skills are only the putting to use of nature, and the practice of skills is a succession of physical experiments that reveal nature more and more."[20] I believe the influence of crafts on science has rarely been expressed so strongly.[21]

Finally, I call attention to an observation by Turgot relating to printing, which was introduced in the discourse of 1750 and which is more developed in one of the unpublished essays. He says in this piece that technical books were printed at first for the instruction of artisans, but men of letters read them. They "became acquainted with a thousand ingenious techniques of which they had been unaware, and they pictured themselves being led to an infinite number of ideas, full of benefits for physics. It was a new world in which everything stimulated their curiosity. From this grew the taste for experimental physics, in which great progress would never have been made without the help of the inventions and procedures of mechanics."[22] In writing that, Turgot probably wanted to bring back to their rightful significance the pretensions of the entrepreneurs of the Encyclopedia, the prospectus of which appeared in

---

19 Condorcet even seems to be trying to diminish the importance of this progress by insinuating that they were all due to imports: "The mechanical arts began to approach the perfection that they had preserved in Asia." As great as the contributions of these imports were, they cannot explain all the technical progress of the Middle Ages: metallurgy seems to have been transformed in Germany, Gothic art was born in France, etc.

20 Turgot, II, 608.

21 Turgot's concept is not entirely precise because it assumes that science arrives at a perfect knowledge of nature. But it is not long ago that we began to understand the difference between "artificial nature," created under the influence of the crafts, and "natural nature," which envelops it. I have developed this idea at length in my book on the use of pragmatism.

22 Turgot, II, 667; cf. p. 610.

1750. He knew that the results that could be expected from a description of the crafts were already attained. Moreover, it does not seem that the *Encyclopedia* brought about any new advancement in any art or science.

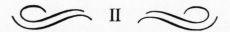

Now we find ourselves at the beginning of the nineteenth century with Madame de Staël's famous book, *Literature Considered in its Relation to Social Institutions.* Here the doctrine of progress is going to be affirmed with much more vividness than in Condorcet's effort. At the time she was writing, the ideas of the *philosophes* were under strong attack in France. The Revolution had hardly fulfilled its promises: the humanitarian ideal, which had enchanted its promoters, gave way to bloody fights among factions. While it had been hoped that all men would be brothers in a superior civilization, there was actually a great intellectual decline. After so much was spoken about the reign of virtue, the country was reduced to the disgraces of the Directory. Thus we understand how many people were inclined to maintain that "enlightenment and all that is derived from it—eloquence, political liberty, and the independence of religious opinions—troubles the peace and the happiness of mankind."[23]

It was difficult, however, to believe that France had acquired in the wars of liberty so much glory to no purpose. It was probable that force had settled the question in the direction of the modern regime and that all the regrets of the old royalists were henceforth superfluous, but France no longer had its old supremacy in elegance and gaiety: "No one contests," said Madame de Staël, "that literature has not lost much since the time that the Terror cut off lives, spirit, feelings, and ideas."[24] One could hardly be expected to see the old literature arise again, for it had depended too much on the definitely extinct aristocratic way of life to be able to adopt radically different

---

[23] Madame de Staël, *Oeuvres complètes* (1820 ed.), IV, 586.
[24] *Ibid.*, IV, 408.

customs. How does one reconcile progress with such an admission of facts?

Madame de Staël was in a situation similar to Perrault's. She had to prove the superiority of her time through considerations of a literary nature. For men of the seventeenth and eighteenth centuries had believed that the greatness and decline of peoples was measured by the taste with which the major works were composed. The Middle Ages horrified them because, according to them, the period totally lacked taste. Chateaubriand tried to lead his contemporaries back to Catholicism by making parallels between pagan authors and Christian authors, showing the superiority of the latter.

The new regime could not yet oppose to the authors of monarchical times its own great men; Mme de Staël, therefore, would not proceed by way of parallels like Perrault and Chateaubriand. She sought to show that literature could find causes of rebirth in the new conditions and that the theatre, philosophy, and eloquence would reach unforeseen brilliance.[25]

"The new literary and philosophical progress I propose to outline will continue the development of the system of perfectibility I have traced from the time of the Greeks."[26] If she succeeded in convincing her contemporaries, she justified the Revolution. The Revolution was not condemned to join the school of the seventeenth century and to be judged in comparison with the time of Louis XIV; it could have opened a new era producing great works that would be appreciated in themselves or, better yet, in relation to new historical conditions.

In order to make her defense easier, Mme de Staël fought the prejudices governing all previous criticism. Condorcet had declared that "the rules of taste have the same generality and the same constancy but are susceptible to the same kind of modifications as the

---

[25] The estimates and advice of Mme de Staël are not always rewarding. She writes that the satire against abuse is going to lose its importance, "if the Constitution of France is free and its institutions are philosophical"; humor, then, will be useless and uninteresting (de Staël, IV, 480 ff.). "*Candide* and writings of that type are harmful in a republic," because, "the most noble interests in life are ridiculed. Henceforth, comedy should attack the "vices of the soul which harm the general good" and especially "those which destroy good qualities," because "the republican spirit requires positive virtues" (p. 487). Seduction would be ridiculed on the stage, etc. (p. 489). We must remark once again how little history follows the dictates of ideologues.

[26] De Staël, IV, 410.

other laws of the universe, moral or physical, when it is necessary to apply them to the immediate practice of a craft."[27] Brunetière observes very justly that, for our author, "the part of the absolute decreases, that of the relative increases,"[28] and thus one is led "to doubt the rules of the old criticism, founded as they were on a literary experience whose inadequacy seemed startling to its readers";[29] but he does not see that this new conception of criticism is motivated by Mme de Staël's plan of defense.

If she put the English characters of Shakespeare and the German characters of Goethe so well in relief, it is not because she used the comparative method but because she had to prove the possibility of a great literature free from the rules of classicism. In her work, the method is governed by the expediencies of her argument. By establishing that there exist great works specifically English and others specifically German, Mme de Staël hopes to lead her readers to admit that it would be entirely reasonable to expect some specifically republican masterpieces from the new France. In the presence of such an exquisite argument, every true rationalist would be as convinced of the existence of these marvelous products of the republican mind as if they had already been on the library shelf for a long time. Thus the new regime would be fully justified.

The society produced by the Revolution lived in a way that was inimical to all the ideas of the eighteenth century; the traditional reputation of French manners was strongly attacked. Mme de Staël says: "During the course of these ten years we have often seen enlightened men governed by ignorant ones: the arrogance of their tone and the vulgarity of their style were even more revolting than the limitations of their minds."[30] "Since the Revolution, a revolting vulgarity in manners is often found united with the exercise of any authority."[31] "In the long run, this revolution can enlighten a great number of men; but for several years the vulgarity of language, manners, and opinions must cause taste and reason to retrogress in many respects."[32]

Quite a considerable part of the book could be called an exhorta-

---

[27] Condorcet, *Tableau historique*, 9th epoch.
[28] Brunetière, *Evolution des genres*, p. 179.
[29] *Ibid.*, p. 177.
[30] De Staël, IV, 437.
[31] De Staël, IV, 420.
[32] De Staël, IV, 408.

tion to civility, and we must compare the ideas expressed by Mme de Staël on this subject with the efforts the emperor would make to force the new society to conform to rituals that imitated the old court. She says, "How much bad taste pushed to the point of grossness opposes literary glory, morals, liberty, and everything good and exalted in human relationships! ... People boldly joke about their own vulgarity and vices, admit them shamelessly, and ridicule those timid souls who still shrink at this debasing gaiety."[33] "Urbanity of manners is an effective way to succeed" in bringing people together.[34]

Commentators were naturally led to compare the Revolution with the fall of ancient civilizations: the nobility, having become as weak as the Romans, were ousted by a vulgar horde "whose education is several centuries behind that of the men they conquered."[35] The barbarian invasions constituted a very great difficulty for theorists of progress. Turgot pointed out that actually in "this apparent destruction, the seeds of the supposedly lost fields of knowledge were spread to a greater number of nations."[36] Mme de Staël goes much further, for, distinguishing this perfecting of all mankind from the progress of the mind, she claims to show that the Middle Ages fostered the latter.[37]

It was the mixing of races and Christianity that produced this fortunate result. Mme de Staël seemed to be entirely free from the passions of the *philosophes* on the subject of religion. This was not due solely to the influence of Rousseau,[38] but also to the obligations imposed on her by her defense of her own times. She hoped that the mixing of the classes would produce an effect similar to the mixing of the races, and she did not despair at seeing some new doctrine play a role like that of Christianity. She says: "How wonderful if we would find, as at the time of the invasion of the peoples from the north, a philosophical system, a virtuous enthusiasm, a strong and

---

[33] De Staël, IV, 420–421.

[34] De Staël, IV, 441.

[35] De Staël, IV, 199.

[36] Turgot, II, 672.

[37] Brunetière seemed to believe that Mme de Staël only considered the perfecting of mankind by means of the dispersion of knowledge (*Evolution des genres*, p. 176).

[38] This influence was grand enough for her to dare to write that "in the countries in which the Reformation took hold, the good influence of Christianity on morality is still noticeable today" (de Staël, IV, 206). We know that, for Diderot, morality is corrupt everywhere a god is recognized (cf. Reinach, *Diderot*, p. 170).

just system of laws which would be, as the Christian religion was, the belief in which victors and vanquished could unite!"[39] Napoleon thought that it was quite useless to seek afar for such a philosophical system; he could be satisfied with Catholicism by imposing a spirit of tolerance on it.[40] Condorcet would have been very surprised if he had been told that it could be written, so soon after him that "the religious meditations of Christianity, to whatever object they have been applied, have developed the faculties of the mind for the sciences, metaphysics, and ethics."[41] Mme de Staël thought that the mind would not have concentrated on abstract studies if it had not at first been led by religious fervor to occupy itself with theological subtleties.[42] The Renaissance showed the immense progress that had taken place: "Bacon, Machiavelli, Montaigne, Galileo, all four almost contemporaries in different countries, suddenly emerged from these obscure times and nevertheless showed themselves to be several centuries in advance of the last writers of ancient literature and especially of the last philosophers of antiquity."[43]

The exigencies of her argument led Mme de Staël to present a defense of violence. She did not dare to touch frankly on the very subject of the Revolution, but she took the accusations hurled by the *philosophes* against religious fanaticism[44] as a pretext to show the considerable role passion can play in history. I think it useful to present here an important extract from her defense (even though the doctrine is extremely lacking), because it is interesting to see, once again, how historical conditions control the thought of ideologues:

"Although strong passions lead to crimes indifference would never have caused, there are circumstances in history in which these passions are necessary to revive the mainsprings of society. Reason, with the help of the centuries, takes hold of some of the effects of these great movements. But there are certain ideas that are revealed by passions and that would be unknown without them. Violent

---

[39] De Staël, IV, 200–201.
[40] That is Condorcet's principal aim: the emperor, by his choices of bishops, imposed on the church the obligation of forgetting the curses hurled against the constitutional priests.
[41] De Staël, IV, 190.
[42] De Staël, IV, 209.
[43] De Staël, IV, 211.
[44] She said that the *philosophes* praised paganism because of their aversion for intolerance (de Staël, IV, 206).

jolts are necessary to expose the human mind to entirely new objects: these are the earthquakes and subterranean fires that show men the riches time alone could not have revealed."[45]

It is indeed remarkable that Mme de Staël abandons the ground of rationalism here. Her contemporaries easily admitted that philosophy can be obliged to use coercion (even rather brutal at times) in order to make triumph the truth it has recognized. But our author proclaims a *mission of creation native to violence*. Undoubtedly, she does not yet detach herself from the idea of natural law; in her eyes, violence is a way of finding this law hidden from the efforts of reason. But her thesis is nonetheless noteworthy because of this.

It is very probable that, in writing these lines, Mme de Staël had especially in mind the struggles of the Reformation. Before her time, and often since, Protestant writers have pleaded extenuating circumstances in support of the leaders of the Reformation and have sought to play down the violence of the sixteenth century. Mme de Staël, led by the exigencies of her polemic, is shown to be much more perspicacious than the historians of her religion generally are; the present gives her a clear understanding of the past.[46]

All of the new tenets of this book are found to have been thus dominated by historical conditions, a very interesting fact from the Marxist point of view.

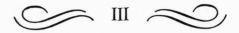

III

We must now interrupt the course of this history of the idea of progress to speak of a doctrine which, while contradicting that of progress, has nevertheless had a very great influence on it. I am speaking of the doctrine of evolution, which is connected with the wars of independence.

These wars have too often been compared to those fought by our revolutionary armies. In truth, they correspond to an opposing ideological movement. Wherever the French armies penetrated,

---

45 De Staël, IV, 206.
46 We have seen previously that the same fact holds true for Augustine Thierry.

people were eager to imitate France in suppressing old institutions and creating others according to principles regarded as conforming to natural law. There came a day, however, when the peoples revolted against this system of improvement and refused, with arms in hand, the happiness we had brought to them. "The idea of nationalities," says Renan, "of which the eighteenth century offers no trace, solely occupied as it was with its general philosophy, and of which the conquests of the beginning of this century were the negation,[47] dates from the revolt the unifying tendencies of the Revolution and the empire produced in the peoples who were brought to consciousness of themselves by the yoke of the foreigner."[48]

Henceforth, evolution would be opposed to progress, tradition to creation, and historical necessity to universal reason. This does not mean, as admirers of the eighteenth century have upheld at times, that the defenders of the new ideas wanted to immobilize the world. But they did want to show that there is a *local historical law* of change, and they thought it very essential that the governments respect it. The first great manifestation of the new concept was that of Savigny, and it concerned law.

For a long time, statesmen intended to regulate the activity of the courts by writing important ordinances; Napoleon believed that his civil code would assure him more glory than his great battles; it seemed natural that Germany, given back her freedom, would assert the consciousness she had acquired of her strength and her unity by setting up a system of law. Savigny disputed this opinion in 1814, thus founding the historical school.

The mission of this school was to refute those who, never doubting the infinite wisdom of modern legislators, thought that law would henceforth be the expression of will enlightened by philosophy. Savigny and his students opposed to this doctrine of the rationalistic creation of law a doctrine of spontaneous creation: the juridical conscience of the people replaced universal reason. Here it would be useful to refer to a well known passage of the *Profession de foi du vicaire savoyard*: "The conscience never deceives us; it is

---

[47] Note the change of the meaning of the word "patriot": during the wars of liberation, a patriot is the one who aids the French against their sovereign; later, it is one who fights to restore the power of the prince.

[48] Renan, *Essais de morale et de critique* ("Moral and Critical Essays"), p. 117.

the true guide of man; it is to the soul what instinct is to the body";
and Rousseau adds as a note: "Modern philosophy, which admits
only what it explains, is far from admitting this obscure faculty
called *instinct*, which seems to guide animals towards some end
without any acquired knowledge. Instinct, according to one of our
wisest philosophers, is only a habit devoid of reflection, but is acquired by reflection." This theory seems absurd to Rousseau. The
juridical conscience of the people is also a sure instinct; it is "by
itself the law."[49]

Savigny's students imagined that, at the beginning, law was
formed by itself out of custom. Later, legislation appeared which
was able to have a beneficial effect by assuring to law transformations that had become necessary more rapidly and more surely than
could "the invisible forces that had created primitive law." Finally
the work of the legal experts intervened.[50]

Thus we have a regular movement of instinct towards more and
more intellectualized forms of human activity. It is still the spirit
of the people being manifested, but in a less and less direct way; in
proportion as we rise on this ladder, we have more to fear that arbitrary solutions, due to metaphysical speculations or the importing
of foreign ideologies, might disturb the truly national product.
Common law would present then a certain superiority, as the expression of juridical instinct. As a result of these opinions, Savigny
and Puchta have been reproached for professing "a veritable idolatry
for this method of forming law"; they regarded as a very serious
outrage against the law every measure of legislation that "arbitrarily
limits the necessary effects of custom"; customs should always be
able to modify or repeal the law by disuse.[51]

Many serious objections have been made to this doctrine, about
which we must say a few words.

Many people think law could have originated according to the
ideas of Savigny and Puchta only during primitive times, when the
distinction between the rules of law and religious and moral rules
did not exist.[52] On the contrary, Ihering wondered if primitive law

---

[49] Tanon, *L'Evolution du droit et la conscience social* ("The Development of
Law and Social Consciousness"), p. 18.

[50] *Ibid.*, pp. 13, 15–16.

[51] *Ibid.*, pp. 17–18. Here the similarity to Rousseau's ideas is striking: conscience
is above the law.

[52] *Ibid.*, p. 32.

was truly formed out of custom.[53] It seems to me that the spontaneous formation of law is shown above all in the commercial domain; we observe it there even today. This body of law depends much more on usages resulting from agreements that have been tried between particular individuals than on rules and theories. If we admit this role of commerce, we must admit that common law was superimposed, during a period of reflection, on something older; for it is easy to regard everything that concerns commerce as not belonging to the reflective period of human activity.

When the whole sweep of a long period of time is considered, it seems plausible that each people produces the law it needs. "Seen from above and from afar the acts of the legislator seem no more than an accident in time, and the law seems to grow by its own force and by the power of the idea of which the legislator is only the instrument and the carrier. . . . It is different when viewed more closely at hand. When we consider positive law at a given moment in its history we see immediately, in many things, rules that do not agree at all with the spirit of the nation."[54]

But it is especially when we study present-day changes and when we try to surmise about the near future that the historical doctrine becomes unsatisfying. Every attempted effort to adapt it to these problems is in vain.[55] "The founders of the school have left the future law outside of their speculations." I do not believe that this attitude can be explained by saying, with Tanon, that "their very conservative personal inclinations led them to consider by preference one of the aspects of this evolution: that which ties the law of the present to that of the past."[56] Rather we must say that all research on the future is impossible for anyone who accepts the historical doctrine without falling into the absurdity of trying to calculate the future by means of the alleged tendencies of the past.

Newman, in his researches on the development of Christian dogma, took the same viewpoint as Savigny's school: he was concerned only with what existed. He wanted to answer the objections

---

[53] Ihering, *Histoire du développement du droit romain* ("History of the Development of Roman Law"), p. 12.

[54] Tanon, *L'Evolution du droit*, pp. 31–32.

[55] It is absurd to try, as several authors have done, to establish as identical, juridical conscience and the will of the people as revealed in the vote.

[56] Tanon, *L'Evolution du droit*, p. 40.

of Anglican controversialists, who accused the Catholic Church of
not having faithfully preserved the repository of the faith during
the Middle Ages. The Anglicans admitted that during the early centuries the councils had defined the dogmas correctly. Newman
found in the history of the early church the types of development
(or flowering) to which he compared the subsequent work of
Roman theology in order to prove that this work had been irreproachable. He never thought of drawing from these studies a
theory that would permit him to make theology progress. Thus a
greater error could not be committed than to confuse him with
those who call themselves his disciples and who are concerned with
the history of dogmas only in the hope of showing that there are
similarities between modernist tendencies and the positions taken
by certain fathers of the church. They write about the past, but
they are dominated by dreams of the future.

It is necessary to apply here a distinction I have made elsewhere
between two ways of conceiving history:[57] One may look toward
the future and note all the seeds of development which are supposed
to give a complete explanation of events; this approach is concerned
then with creations. On the other hand, one may look toward the
past to find how adaptations have arisen; this is the doctrine of
evolution. Savigny changed the spirit of history by introducing this
new method. Inextricable difficulties occur when progress and
evolution are mixed.

It has been observed several times that there is a great similarity
between the points of view proposed by Savigny and Darwinism.[58]
Many contemporary naturalists reproach Darwin for not having
studied what Alfred Giard calls the primary factors of evolution,
that is to say, the forces that create the new species. Darwin studied
an already finished natural history, and he wanted to show us how
the elimination of certain forms can be connected with the conditions under which the search for food and mating (the struggle for
life and sexual selection) take place. In pure Darwinism the variations in the species are undetermined. The pretensions of Alfred
Giard, who wishes to reconcile Darwinism and Lamarckism by
combining the secondary factors of the first with the primary factors

---

[57] Cf. Georges Sorel, *Système historique de Renan* (Paris: Marcel Rivière, 1906),
pp. 5–23.
[58] Tanon, *L'Evolution du droit*, p. 22.

of the second, is the artless notion of the naturalist who is little accustomed to philosophizing.[59] It is necessary to choose between two systems; the two cannot be mixed under the pretext of making a higher science.

Law is no less amenable to change than are living species. There is not one big incident which does not give evidence of the existence of forces calculated to modify the law: lawyers, judges and professors, in their defenses, their decisions and their commentaries, always touch on the existing system to a slight extent, due to their personal views. Very often, also, the public at large intervenes in order to exercise pressure on the professionals. In the midst of all these causes, which it would be absurd to try to analyze, there arises a movement: this movement is the fundamental idea of history, and it is this which informs us of the juridical conscience of the people.

In the history of law, then, it is not necessary to demand that the juridical conscience be defined as if it were a force whose effects could be foreseen according to law. The juridical conscience is an image destined to embrace all of the conditions under which is made the acceptance (or the refusal) of a new system of relations. For a long time, the peasants of the south of France have given earnest resistance to the laws of inheritance of the civil code. Here we have a striking example of a struggle between tradition and new solutions. All of the elements of this struggle can be observed easily enough. Thus, it is not exact to say that the juridical conscience "is not at all able to be determined";[60] it is determined to the extent that the role of traditions in negative adaptation can be known.

In this connection, it is suitable to observe that naturalists do not all interpret adaptation in the same way. Bergson says that "for some, external conditions are capable of directly causing variations in organisms in a definite way, by physiochemical modifications which they determine in the living substance: this is the hypothesis of Eimer, for instance. For others, more faithful to the spirit of

---

[59] One should repeatedly inform the people of the sociological thoughts which inspired Giard to form the theory (such an unlikely one) of *telegony,* according to which the offsprings of a female retain something of the traits of the first male mate. He thought the inferior classes of Europe had been happily transformed by the practice of *Jus primae noctis* accorded to the nobility. This idle talk did not prevent Alfred Giard from being a naturalist of the first rank; but learned men are not always skillful in the art of drawing general conclusions from their experiences.

[60] Tanon, *L'Evolution du droit,* p. 28.

Darwinism, the influence of conditions is exercised only in an indirect way, by favoring, in the life struggle, those representatives of a species whom the chance of birth has better adapted to the environment. In other words, the former attribute a positive influence to exterior conditions and the latter a negative influence: in the first hypothesis, this cause would give rise to variations; in the second, it would only eliminate them."[61] Once again, Darwinism is related to the historical method.

Bergson says that "the Darwinian idea of an adaptation coming about by the automatic elimination of the unadaptable is a simple and clear idea." I think that, in the same way, the theory of the juridical conscience can be applied in a way which makes the history of law simple and clear. But we must not ask of it what it cannot give, namely, the explanation of the progressive development of an institution following a given line. Darwinism demonstrates the same powerlessness in biology, as Bergson says.[62]

The theorists of historical law have not always presented their doctrines in a satisfying way. A great deal of practice in the most severe disciplines of science is necessary in order to arrive at the understanding that the mind can content itself to reason about negative adaptations. In Savigny's time, all change was conceived under forms similar to those provided by biology: it is thus entirely natural that the juridical conscience of the people was so often regarded as being a sort of vital force. Thus, the philosophy of law merits the bitter criticism which Ihering made of it:

"The origin of law is an impenetrable mystery; so what good is any further search? This doctrine has the merit of cutting short any question about the reason of things. Its answer is always the same: popular soul, national juridical feeling. . . . It is fatality presiding over the elaboration of the law. . . . The theory of emanation is the soft pillow on which science has only to fall asleep. Let us take it away so that it wakes up—so that it finally opens its eyes and sees things as they are in reality."[63]

If the principle of evolution has been understood in so many dif-

---

61 Henri Bergson, *Evolution créatrice*, pp. 59–60 [Creative Evolution (New York, Modern Library ed.), pp. 62–63. All page references to Bergson will be to the American edition.—*Trans.*].

62 *Ibid.*, p. 63.

63 Ihering, *Histoire*, p. 12.

ferent and arbitrary ways, it is because a majority of its advocates
had been led to admit it, not for intellectual reasons, but for political
ones. People were tired of all the struggles that had put Europe in
turmoil. They were disposed to accept as superior all the processes
of ideological formation which did not entail struggle.[64] They were
thus very happy to hear common law praised and to liken it to the
development of language. Later, Ihering would point out very rightly that this likening of law to language is contrary to history, considering that philology does not show conflicts similar to those which
appear every time a new rule hurts someone's interests.[65] But this
false analogy was, on the contrary, of such a nature as to charm
Savigny's contemporaries.

The historical school threw light on a close interdependence of
the diverse manifestations of the national spirit.[66] Thus it compared
a nation to a living organism, in which all parts are solidly tied to
each other and are harmonized. The popular conscience seemed to
have a reality. Thus, it is not astonishing that the likening of history
to a living being had so much influence on the thought of political
writers during a great part of the nineteenth century. I believe this
was the most popular heritage of historicism.

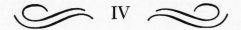

For about forty years after the Restoration, the liberal world was
very much occupied with scientific studies of the past. The frivolity
of the century of Enlightenment was contrasted with the seriousness
of the historical schools. The doctrine of progress could only have
survived by absorbing many ideas from the concept of evolution.
We note that the comparison of history to an organism engendered
a great number of important theses.

---

64 We know what importance the distinction between *critical* and *organic* periods
has taken in France; the Saint-Simonians proposed to make the French come out of
the purgatory of criticism and to lead them to organization. This idea surely harkens
back to Napoleon, who announced that he had closed the era of the Revolution
and introduced into our language the term organic law with the meaning of fundamental law of an administration. [See n. 30, chap. 2.—*Trans.*]

65 Ihering, *La Lutte pour le droit* ("The Struggle for Law"), pp. 6–11.

66 Tanon, *L'Evolution du droit*, p. 13.

First, primary importance was attached henceforth to the slowness and regularity of the movement of history. Occasionally, people went so far as to look with pity upon the revolutionaries, who did not understand that such a progression is alone compatible with science! They went so far as to pay a superstitious respect to this pace, whereas formerly the slowness of progress was solely looked upon as a measure dictated by prudence.

Second, the idea of necessity was strongly reenforced. Madame de Staël called attention to the great evils that would result from a policy having for its goal the arrest of the progress of enlightenment, and she looked upon such an attempt as necessarily fruitless.[67] But this was only a judgment based on the evaluation of political sagacity, whereas today we regard the continuity of historical movement as being as necessary as that of a living evolution.

Third, the progress of the mind or the growth of the intelligence was no longer speculated on. Institutions were viewed as being the organs of a living being. By Cuvier's method, dominating characteristics were chosen, and history was studied by following their variations.[68]

We find a very remarkable application of these new points of view in Tocqueville's *Democracy in America*, the first edition of which was published in 1835 and which exerted such a great influence on the thought of the nineteenth century. We learn from the first few pages of Tocqueville's book that equality of conditions appeared to him to be the dominating characteristic of American institutions. It was "the generating factor from which each particular fact seemed to evolve" and the "central point to which all observations should lead." He teaches us also that he had been led to recognize that the movement toward equality is definitely not peculiar to the United States and that it was happening everywhere, generated by unconscious causes. "Everywhere we have seen the diverse occurrences of the life of nations turning toward the advantage of democracy; everyone has aided it in their efforts: those who have consciously gone along with its successes and those who would not dream of helping it; those who have fought for it and even those who have declared themselves to be its enemies. All have

---

[67] De Staël, IV, 586.
[68] Cf. Pierre Marcel, *Essai politique sur Alexis de Tocqueville* ("Political Essay on Alexis de Tocqueville"), p. 107.

been pushed pell-mell in the same direction. All have worked in common for it, some in spite of their best efforts, and others, even though they do not know it, have become blind instruments in the hand of God."

Tocqueville expressed the idea he had acquired of this necessity in a language which he tried to make shocking: "This whole book that you will read has been written under the influence of a kind of religious awe produced in this writer's soul by the sight of that irresistible revolution that has advanced for so many centuries despite all obstacles and that is still advancing in the midst of the ruination which it has caused. . . . If from long observations and sincere meditations, the men of our day could be brought to recognize that the gradual and progressive development of equality is both the past and future of their history, then this discovery alone would give to this development the sacred character of the divine will. To attempt to struggle against democracy, then, would seem to resist the will of God; and the nations would then be constrained to accommodate themselves to the social lot awarded to them by Providence."

The movement is looked upon as being like an organic movement. The conclusion is drawn that democracy is necessary in the future: the wise man should seek in the experience of the nations who are most advanced on the new road for those experiences which are capable of guiding the legislator who is trying to facilitate the passage from the past to the future.

Tocqueville succeeded in imparting his convictions to his contemporaries. Le Play deplored this; he regarded *Democracy in America* as a "dangerous book" having "done much evil."[69] "Honest men who attached themselves to the past or who remained indecisively between good and evil gradually took confidence in his prediction. Since then they believe in the inevitable triumph of the American regime noted as the prototype of equality and democracy."[70] Le Play did not want to admit the necessity of a

---

[69] Le Play, *La Reforme sociale en France* ("Social Reform in France"), III, 327.
[70] Le Play, *Organisation du travail* ("Organization of Labor"), 3d ed., p. 367. According to Le Play, Tocqueville thought the decline of the European peoples was inevitable; "he believed, moreover, that this decline could scarcely be accelerated by importing the American regime" (p. 377). We learn that Le Play only came into contact with Tocqueville during the Second Empire. Like nearly all the old liberals, Tocqueville regarded the imperial regime as being the result of a decline.

development which appeared obvious to Tocqueville. Le Play persuaded himself that the world could be changed by the example of several old families who would preserve patriarchal ideas. The notion of historical necessity was absolutely foreign to Le Play. He still thought in the style of the men of the eighteenth century, which can be attributed to the fact that for the most part he remained ignorant of the works of nineteenth-century legal and enonomic history.[71]

I think *Democracy in America* had a considerable and perhaps decisive influence on Proudhon's earlier works. The pamphlet, *La Célébration du dimanche*, which appeared at the end of 1839, contains aggressively equalitarian statements, but these did not stem from the traditions of our eighteenth-century writers. The author took care to warn that he did not want to "warm over the theories of the celebrated discourse on *Inequality of Conditions* [and] shore up the ill-conceived thesis of the Genevan philosopher."[72] Neither can we say that Proudhon is influenced by the French communists. He is referring to them when he says: "The question of equality of conditions and fortunes has already been raised, but only as a theory without principles: we must raise it again and probe it in all its truth. . . . [73] But a problem is presented immediately: to find a state of social equality which is neither communism, nor despotism, nor expropriation, nor anarchy, but liberty with order and independence in unity. And with this first point resolved, there remains a second: finding the best means of transition."[74]

The following year Proudhon resumed his equalitarian ideas in his first essay on property. He was certain of the final condition of humanity because Tocqueville had affirmed the march to equality. He had only to present a formal proof. When we read his essay with this in mind, Proudhon appears much more interesting than our contemporaries think; they find him too little concerned with the facts.

Proudhon's contemporaries were widely exposed to the ideas put abroad by Tocqueville and were extremely impressed by the essay of 1840. On this point, we have the testimony of Marx and Engels

---

[71] Le Play seemed never to have perused the historical works, except to take a few notes from them. Perhaps even the notes were supplied to him by friends.
[72] Proudhon, *Oeuvres complètes*, II, 144.
[73] Proudhon affirmed that "equality of conditions conforms to reason and is incontrovertible in law" (*ibid.*, II, 49).
[74] Proudhon, II, 151.

in *The Holy Family* and especially that of F. Vidal. The latter devoted a special chapter to Proudhon and to Constantin Pecqueur[75] in his book on the redistribution of wealth, published in 1846. He refers to them as equalitarians and distinguishes them from the other socialists (Saint-Simonians, Fourierists, and communists).

The *Economic Contradictions* were written in order to develop this same equalitarian theme by showing that equality arises out of economic development like a hidden law. It seems to me that if Proudhon so often used a providential language in this work, it was because he had been struck by the great effect produced by Tocqueville's concepts. Marx was taken in by appearances, and in *The Poverty of Philosophy* he regarded Proudhon as a latter-day disciple of Bossuet instead of seeking the very nearby source from which this manner of exposition originated. Marx said: "In the first place, the end goal of the guiding social spirit that speaks through the words of M. Proudhon is to eliminate the evils in each economic category in order to have only the good remain. For Proudhon, the good—the supreme blessing—the true, practical aim is equality. . . . Every new category is a hypothesis of the social spirit, in order to eliminate the inequality produced by the preceding hypothesis. In short, equality is the primal intention, the mystical tendency, the providential end that the social spirit constantly has before its eyes in spinning around in the circle of economic contradictions. Therefore, providence is the locomotive that pulls M. Proudhon's whole economic baggage better than his pure and featherbrained reason. He has devoted an entire chapter to providence which follows the one on taxes."[76]

It is obvious that Marx must have read this chapter very superficially (if at all), for Proudhon rejected as clearly as possible "the providential government whose nonexistence is sufficiently established by the metaphysical and economic hallucinations of humanity, in a word, by the martyrdom of our species."[77]

---

[75] Pecqueur published his *Théorie nouvelle d'économie politique et sociale* ("New Theory of Political and Social Economy") in 1842.
[76] Marx, *Misère de la philosophie*, pp. 164–165 [*The Poverty of Philosophy* (Moscow: Foreign Languages Publishing House), p. 133. All page references will be to this English-language edition.—*Trans.*]. A little later on he refers Proudhon to Villeneuve-Bargemont's *Histoire de l'économie politique* ("History of Political Economy"), which transforms history into a Catholic apology (p. 135).
[77] Proudhon, *Contradictions économiques* ("Economic Contradictions"), I, 360–361.

Marx was right for not wishing to admit that one could make a synthesis of human history in subordinating it to the development of a particular characteristic. His criticism is very accurate and destroys the systems of progression used so widely by the Saint-Simonians. "A tendency toward equality belongs to our century. To say now that all previous centuries with entirely different needs, means of production, etc., worked providentially for the realization of equality, is first to substitute the means and men of our century for the men and means of previous centuries and to belittle the historical movement for which successive generations transform the results acquired from preceding generations."[78] History cannot be molded into an illusory ideological unity. In order to follow an evolution scientifically, it is necessary to take in only a period whose economic conditions present enough constancy so that we may find a genuine unity.

But Proudhon did not intend to demonstrate the existence of a historical movement toward equality of conditions. He received this fact from Tocqueville and he wanted to find a metaphysics in it by establishing a philosophical order in economics. He took the world as a whole and tried to extricate from it an order that could take account of the law proclaimed by Tocqueville. His very complicated idea is rather strange to our present habits of thinking,[79] but it would have appeared completely natural to a man who had been slightly acquainted with the vast Hegelian syntheses. Proudhon said, in his chapter on machines: "We do not make history according to the order of the times, but according to the succession of ideas. The phases or economic categories are in their manifestations sometimes contemporary and sometimes reversed. From that comes the extreme difficulty economists have always felt in trying to systematize their ideas. From this comes the chaos of their works. . . . But the economists' theories haven't lessened their logical succession and their range of understanding: it is this order that we presume to

---

[78] Marx, *The Poverty of Philosophy*, p. 134.
[79] It is even more difficult to accept Proudhon's views when we see that the contemporary facts are in full contradiction to Tocqueville's historical law. No visitor to the United States today admires the equality of conditions which the French writer of 1832 observed. The United States was then an agricultural country. Now it has become an industrial nation, and speculation has produced the most incredible inequalities there.

disclose and that will make of this work a philosophy and a history at the same time."[80]

Proudhon believed that he proved to be much more scientific than the Hegelians with whom he had associated in Paris. The Hegelians wished that humanity had made millenial efforts to give evidence in favor of the chosen metaphysics. Thus they denatured reality. But Proudhon, strengthened by the authority of Tocqueville, could not imagine that people accused him of neglecting reality.

We are not straying from our subject when we call attention, at this point, to several very curious theses he soon presented which greatly clarify the doctrine of contradictions. These theories did not impress Proudhon's contemporaries very much, because the latter thought of philosophy in a completely different way. In examining them, we understand why Proudhon's language is so often obscure in his works of this period: an author, as great as he may be, cannot succeed in giving a clear exposition of his intuitions if he does not have the collaboration of his public.

The ancient Greek metaphysics had as its aim the contemplation of the absolute, which was constructed by sculptors and architects who were used to carving in marble, works their contemporaries regarded as being destined for immortality. Proudhon maintained that it was necessary to take the opposite view from the ancients. "The true, in all things—the real, the positive, the practicable—is what changes or at least what is capable of progression, conciliation, and transformation; whereas the false, the fictitious, the impossible, and the abstract is all that is presented as fixed, whole, complete, inalterable, without defect and not capable of modification, conversion, augmentation, or diminution and consequently refractory to any higher combination or any synthesis."[81]

Economic contradictions result from the illusion of our abstract understanding, which wishes to follow logically all the consequences of judgments that have only a relative value. Proudhon says: "I have proved that most of our notions on which at this time industrial

---

[80] Proudhon, *Contradictions économiques*, I, 148.

[81] Proudhon, *Philosophie du progrès* ("Philosophy of Progress"), p. 21. Here are several theses that are worth noting because of their similarities to contemporary theories. "Movement is a primary fact" (p. 27). When we speak of a point of departure or principle and a point of arrival or an end, we formulate an illusion. A second illusion makes us regard the principle as being the cause or generator of the end. "Movement is: that is all" (pp. 29–30).

practice rests (and accordingly the whole economy of modern society) are . . . analytical concepts, parts, mutually deduced from one another by way of opposition, of the corporate group, its ideas, and its law and each developed separately, without restraint or limit. The result is that society, instead of resting on harmony, is seated on a throne of contradictions. Instead of progressing with certainty in wealth and virtue, it presents a parallel and systematic development in misery and crime."[82]

It does not seem that Proudhon ever made a very serious effort to give to these beautiful philosophical laws a somewhat systematic organization. The conclusions he drew from his thoughts on movement are very far from being in line with the promises he made to us.

The coup d'état of 1851 caused Proudhon to understand better his vocation as a moralist. In the presence of a society which, intoxicated by good fortune, no longer wanted to discuss anything but success, progress, or pleasures, he made known the magnificent protest of *La Justice dans la Révolution et dans l'Eglise*. He didn't want to admit that a law exists making civilizations succeed one another as do human beings. He had been duped "formerly by this physiologico-political toy." He thought that dissertations on such a movement served no purpose. "As for me," he said, "I say that if progress does not provide us with anything more than that, it is not worth the trouble of becoming so agitated and upset. The best thing would be to go along living as it pleases God and to follow the advice of the monk: "Mind your own business; do not malign the government. Let the world go as it will."[83] Indeed, the doctrines of progress were flourishing at the time, because the French bourgeoisie felt the desire to "go along living as it pleases God," in benefiting from the good times.

As had already happened at the end of the seventeenth century, a society content with its lot held up the idea of progress to the moralists; the latter remained alien to the new way of living, reproached the society for its frivolity, and wished to remind it of the principles of the great philosophers.

The question, for Proudhon, was entirely a moral one. There is progress when "the redemption or the perfecting of humanity by itself" is produced. Then humanity believes in liberty and justice in

---

[82] Proudhon, *Philosophie du progrès*, p. 49.
[83] Proudhon, *La Justice dans la Révolution et dans l'Eglise* ("Justice in the Revolution and in The Church"), III, 255–256.

developing its faculties, resources, and power. It "rises above what is inevitable in it." Decline consists in "the corruption or dissolution of humanity by itself as manifested in the successive loss of traditional morality, liberty, and creating spirit, by the diminution of courage and faith and the weakening of races, etc."[84] It is hardly necessary to call attention to what such a picture contains of allusions to the condition in which France found herself during the first years of the second empire.

According to Proudhon, history ought to bring forth a double testimony; it ought to show us that progress is the "natural condition of mankind" and that accordingly "justice is by itself stronger than all the forces that battle against it."[85] It ought to explain decline by psychological illusions: man, recognizing that the system of justice is imperfect in practice, loses his faith in justice, follows an ideal that appears to be able to procure his happiness, and makes the ideal serve his concupiscence."[86] For Proudhon, what appeared most difficult was the eclipse of the moral sense, which was then noticed in France and which came after a time when so many hopes of renewal had been conceived. Proudhon didn't want to believe that this regime could last for a long time. "Work and law are the two great principles on which all creations of the ideal should depend henceforth. The idols have been overturned: contemporary debauchery has dealt them a final blow. The hour will soon come of perpetual courts and incorruptible judgment."[87]

As long as the defeated parties of 1851 remained apprehensive about the future, they greatly admired justice and maintained their hopes of the common people by assuring them that justice always triumphs in the long run. Such language appears very old-fashioned today. The victorious democrats have relegated to the pawnshop all the old liberal literature that could inconvenience them in their work in the government.

---

[84] *Ibid.*, III, 271.

[85] *Ibid.*, III, 277.

[86] *Ibid.*, III, 297–299. According to a theory he probably derived from the Hegelians, Proudhon thinks that "Christianity only propounded a myth from which philosophy was later to extract the truth and explain it" (p. 281). Man is moved to follow justice because he is upheld by the ideal he has constructed. It is this that the theologians have expressed in their theory of grace (p. 280). Sin consists in man's more or less accidental separation from what is highest in himself, the just and the ideal (p. 296).

[87] *Ibid.*, III, 299.

Since democracy believes itself assured of a long future, and the conservative parties are discouraged, democracy no longer feels the same need as before of justifying its right to power by using the philosophy of history. Thus, the notion of progress has lost much of its importance in the eyes of the men who hold a great place in the bourgeois science: thus two excellent *blocards*, Professors Langlois and Seignobos, devote only fifteen lines (and these are disdainful at that) to the question of progress in their *Introduction aux études historiques*. It is easy to see, however, that progress is still not expunged from the democratic dictionary.

Democracy is based on the existence of a strong hierarchy. The oligarchy of gross success seekers must have an eager troop of underlings who never cease to work in the interest of their leaders and who derive little material profit from their activity. It is necessary to keep this type of petty nobility in a state of excitement by lavishing them with tokens of friendship and by arousing them with feelings of honor while speaking to them in idealistic phrases. National glory, the domination of natural forces by science, the march of humanity toward enlightenment—this is the nonsense which is heard constantly in the speeches of democratic orators.

In a speech given before the League of Education at its Angers Congress in August 1906, the Minister of Education said: "The exercise of power in my opinion is only interesting insofar as it allows a man, not to enjoy the honors which go with position, but to obtain for himself that deep and intimate satisfaction one experiences when he can realize his own thinking." This stoical language was used by the austere Aristide Briand! A few moments before, he had said: "It is we who love this country. If it is to live, to develop, to grow, to flower, it will be because of us—because we are republicans. It would be useless to say this to the conservatives; they do not understand you."[88]

Thus, the good apostle speaks as if he were the principle author of everything great in this country, and he finds listeners who accept

---

[88] Cited from the *Débats*, August 7, 1906.

his charlatanism! He deplores the fact that the conservatives are not impressed with this. Nowadays the politicians no longer address the educated public, for whom the fathers of democracy wrote. They speak to types of people who have undergone a special training and who have been molded for the purpose of admiring the oracles that come out of the mouths of the politicians.

Every effort of the republican administration for the last thirty years has gone into enlisting teachers into this petty nobility, which makes the fortunes of the heroes of our contemporary democracy. Efforts have been made to inculcate in them a superstitious respect for grandiose words, which are almost devoid of meaning and which serve as the bourgeois philosophy. Hence results what Léon Daudet calls the "primary-school philosophy." This term is inaccurate because the jumble of words is not a spontaneous creation of men who have received only primary education, but an intentionally sophistic creation of their masters, calculated to dupe them, to exploit them, and to make an income on the public treasury, which their devotion opens for the politicians.[89]

Somewhere in this world, there are always a few polite souls who refuse to see things in their true light, which they find rather repellent. Consequently, they exercise their wits to fabricate theories that can give a little respectability to democracy. Thus, we should not be astonished at again coming upon theories of progress, very artificial theories in which the author tries to delude himself. In ending this study, I think it would be useful to present the reader with the doctrine which P. Lacombe outlined a dozen years ago. This will be all the more instructive as Lacombe is a conscientious scholar[90] as well as a longstanding republican. We will find in his writing an extraordinary naiveté that corresponds well to this double condition. The author believes that the world lives from the passions that dominate the collector of learned *ibids.*, and he wants to encounter in the world only what suits his republican conscience.

P. Lacombe observes that one can formulate two very different

---

[89] It is easy to see that the teachers are making laudable efforts today to emancipate themselves. The democrats redouble their audacity in order to maintain their prestige. But by dint of abusing the heavy-handed means they have at their disposal, they might well become the laughingstock of those whom they fooled for so long a time.

[90] Langlois and Seignobos invited those of their readers who wished to probe the notion of progress to consult the work of P. Lacombe (*Introduction aux études historiques* ["Introduction to the Study of History"], p. 249).

ideas on progress, depending on whether one considers it "under the simple form of an accumulation of riches and knowledge" or rather as having for its end "a more perfect equilibrium, a more successful conciliation" among the diverse emotions.[91] "What matters in reality is the attitude which one has with regard to one's destiny."[92]

Le Play often insisted on this distinction. It can sometimes happen that the second type of progress is in doubt at the same time that the first exists incontestably. Thus, speaking of the imprecations which Arthur Young had hurled against the great French lords who left their lands in their old condition, he said, "To justify this criticism completely, the author should have proved that the peoples who lived on these fallow lands were not any happier than those on the nonfallow lands of his county of Suffolk."[93] Le Play believed he saw in the course of his travels that perfect equilibrium, which for Lacombe equals true progress, has been achieved in the peoples of the great steppes of Asia. "The inhabitants of the steppes, when they have not been corrupted by contact with 'civilized people,' have inspired affection and respect in the traveler to a greater degree than any other people in the human race. All westerners who have sojourned to the lands of the steppes have experienced the same impression. They all have acknowledged to me that in returning to sedentary people, they experienced regret and disillusion."[94]

The ideas P. Lacombe formed on the subject of happiness are based, not on the observation of actual historical groups, but uniquely on the type of life best suited to a man who, like him, has been used to shuffling old books in libraries all his life. He said that "the intellectual feelings generally are less intense than the sentimental or sensual emotions, but . . . duration and repetition do not weaken them. The mild and tranquil happiness that comes from intellectual feelings can be constant and can fill almost any moment. . . . The most sure rule of the art of living or art of happiness consists in following, to a large degree, the intellectual sense."[95]

[91] P. Lacombe, *De l'histoire considérée comme science* ("On History as a Science"), p. 276.
[92] P. Lacombe, *ibid.*, p. 280.
[93] Le Play, *La Réforme sociale en France* ("Social Reform in France"), I, 278.
[94] *Ibid.*, II, 513.
[95] P. Lacombe, *De l'histoire*, pp. 281–282. The author, believing he had seen that intelligence is always being expanded, judges that "the course of things, if it does not confirm our wishes, does not contradict them any more positively" and that "our lot is not deplorable if we recognize and accept it" (p. 282).

The author passes from this pleasant scholar's philosophy to a completely different consideration. He imagines that the historian is called to give prizes for wisdom to nations that have permitted themselves to be governed by men who have best practiced the fine art of happiness.[96] "The historian who wishes to measure the relative distance between societies on the path of progress has no more accurate yardstick to employ than the part played in each of the societies by the intellect itself, art, and science."[97] A new difficulty presents itself at this point, for there are two intellectual yardsticks, one scientific and the other artistic. But a former inspector of libraries could never have too much doubt in his mind; the first is the good one. He concludes: "I ask that civilizations be compared first of all by the criterion of the science each one has developed, while we may also take account, on a secondary level, of the artistic, literary, or moral superiority one of them may have over the others."[98] Thus here we are reduced to an academic contest!

We must not believe this conception was absolutely unattached to democratic tendencies. It is easy to see that P. Lacombe has revealed to us several secrets of the contemporary world.

First of all, we should note the difficulty in which the author finds himself on the subject of material progress, for P. Lacombe speaks often of technology in terms a disciple of Marx would not repudiate. Thus, we might expect that he would arrange civilizations according to the level of their production methods. But while considering the priority of economic development as empirically valid, P. Lacombe did not use economics in order to judge the "relative merit of civilizations."[99] This attitude corresponds perfectly to the situation of the contemporary democracies. They exist in countries that are becoming more and more wealthy as a consequence of causes foreign to the concerns of the democratic leaders and very often even in spite of the activity of these leaders. Thus, it is natural to view the progress of production as being the fundamental condition of all modern civilization, but also to place the essential of this civilization other than in economics.

---

[96] For P. Lacombe admitted that he intended to be concerned only with the conditions of life of the highest social strata (*ibid.*, p. 283).

[97] *Ibid.*, p. 283.

[98] *Ibid.*, p. 288.

[99] *Ibid.*, p. 283.

We note further that P. Lacombe gave only a small place to moral concerns. To him the progress of morality led only to inspire neutral feelings.[100] The success of democracy requires emotions of a more positive type. We know by the slightest observation of contemporary phenomena that democracy has the most profound scorn for everything that recalls the constraints morality tries to impose on men.

We have seen that P. Lacombe is concerned with only the ruling group in society. Everything is subordinated to the well-being of this elite. Here again we find a valuable admission: nothing is more aristocratic than the aspirations of democracy. The latter tries to continue the exploitation of the producing masses by an oligarchy of intellectual and political professionals.

There is such a great contradiction between the conditions of the joyous life sought everywhere by democracy in imitation of the old society and the conditions of the well-ordered life that P. Lacombe describes that we at first find it hard to understand how he was able to view scholarly moderation as adaptable to historical evolution. In order to understand this very strange paradox, we must remember that democracy likes to receive the compliments it merits least. I will give some examples taken from a recent work by one of the most illustrious flatterers of contemporary society.[101] Alfred Fouillée asserts that along with democratic progress there is "a progressive consciousness of human dignity, liberty, and independence," and he concludes that "in spite of too many frequent deviations, democracy is by itself edifying."[102] It would be hard to compound such huge lies with greater audacity: it is sufficient to look around us in order to recognize that democracy is a school of servility, venal denunciation, and demoralization. Fouillée does not do a bad job of insulting the intelligence of his readers when he claims that goodness is an efficacious moral force capable of leading our contemporaries.[103] One would hardly suspect goodness to be

---

100 *Ibid.*, p. 281.
101 This evaluation does not appear at all severe to persons who know the strange corrections made in the latest editions of the *Tour de France* in order to please the anticlericals. Notre Dame de Paris had ceased to be the masterpiece of French art. Saint Bernard and Bossuet have been struck from the pages of history (cf. *Chambre des Députés* ["Chamber of Deputies"], Jan. 17, 1910, morning session).
102 Alfred Fouillée, *Morale des idées-forces*, p. 375.
103 *Ibid.*, p. 360.

a widely spread virtue in the world. It even seems that it is not a democratic virtue at all,[104] but democracy wants people to extoll the excellence of its heart. This type of flattery is inherited from the ancien régime.

In giving intellectual things such an important place, P. Lacombe could have been believing that he expressed the deepest wish of democracy. The latter never ceases to vaunt its supposed passion for truth. In his speech in Angers, Aristide Briand asked teachers to mold "the real man, the citizen of the true democracy, whose brain is not jammed by preoccupations with mystery and dogma; a man who looks clearly before him, a man who sees life as it is, beautiful and worth living, and who lives it." And indulging himself in all the exaggerations of democratic eloquence, the minister emitted this astonishing sentence: "The divine is embodied in such a man! And if this god has been, until now, so often powerless, wavering and stooped under the burdens of life, it is because lies and ignorance have chained his efforts for too long a time. It is up to us to liberate him."

It is my opinion that it is difficult to push any further the audacity of the politician, happy to have reached finally an unhoped-for situation and taking unfair advantage of the naïveté of his audience, trained to admire the hollow metaphysics of successful parvenus.[105]

At the beginning of our investigation, we found a petty philosophy of men of the world who meant to enjoy their wealth with relish and who no longer wanted to hear of the prudence long imposed on their fathers. Louis XIV's contemporaries boasted of the wonders of their century and were enthusiastic at the thought of the beautiful things being created spontaneously in order to assure an ever-increasing happiness to mankind. Later, a philosophy of

---

[104] *Le Cri de Paris* of August 4, 1907, points out an entirely democratic method of practicing goodness: many philanthropic works are electoral works: "Politicians tap the great stores, banks, and famous millionaires who are all obliged nowadays to have a special budget for this type of operation. This does not prevent the politicians during electoral periods from energetically condemning the commercial monopolies, the great banks, and the plutocracy." It is this fraud which Alfred Fouillée probably mistakes for goodness.

[105] A biography of Aristide Briand would be very informative for knowledge of the democracy and socialism of politicians, a variety of which has generally not much to recommend it. The old "knight of labor" who was happy to find at Pontoise an unorthodox bar association to enable him to take the title of lawyer is today the Minister of Justice. We may hope, for the beauty of the ending, that he will become chief justice of the Supreme Court of Appeal.

history appeared which took its definitive form at the time of the liberal bourgeoisie and which had for its object to show that the changes undertaken by the champions of the modern state possess a character of necessity. Now we have descended to the arena of electioneering tommyrot that permits demagogues to have all-powerful direction over their supporters and assure themselves a successful life. Sometimes, polite republicans try to conceal the horror of this political system under philosophical appearances, but the veil is always easy to tear aside.

All ideas related to progress combine together in an extraordinary and sometimes ridiculous way, because democracy has very few ideas it can properly call its own and because it lives almost entirely on the heritage of the ancien régime. One of the tasks of contemporary socialism is to demolish this superstructure of conventional lies and to destroy the prestige still accorded to the "metaphysics" of the men who vulgarize the vulgarization of the eighteenth century. This is what I try to do whenever possible in this work.

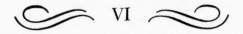

We cannot leave these questions without noting a very remarkable characteristic apparent in modern society which seems to many people to be in contradiction with the principles of the class struggle.

In the capitalist world, there is a material progress that allows the rulers to enjoy themselves but that, at the same time, is the necessary condition of the socialist revolution. This material progress, which bears on the techniques of production, is applauded equally by the bourgeoisie, who welcome a bigger and better life, and the socialists, who regard it as a guarantee of a revolution capable of suppressing the masters. Thus Marxists have always denounced as dangerous reactionaries those philanthropists who, to spare the people the suffering caused by any great economic transformation, would like to restrain this material progress by regulation.

Intellectuals find it very difficult to understand how the owners and the revolutionaries can agree to this extent on the value of material progress. It seems to them that what is advantageous to the first ought to be odious to the second for they believe all historical conflicts are like party struggles over the fruits of power: what one gains another loses. Many believe that the admiration our contemporaries show for material progress could well be a sign of a harmony of interests. All social philosophy would be concerned with knowing whether each group benefits according to its merit. The true question for the revolutionaries is to judge the facts of the present in relation to the future for which they are preparing; it is this way of thinking which our professional idealists can scarcely understand.

I do not believe anyone has yet probed in a satisfactory way the conditions of the progress of production to the extent that it is possible to formulate general laws about them. I will confine myself to indicating the points of view which, it seems to me, should be taken into consideration.

We should first concern ourselves with types of machines in order to determine what the new properties are which the engineers demand of them. This will certainly be the easiest part of our task. Here are several general observations whose importance can be verified by anyone with mechanical inclinations. Engineers are using more and more geometric formulas.[106] They are trying to obtain very rapid rotations, which are very close to uniform movement. They are reducing by many methods the role of passive resistance, not only to economize on power, but also to diminish sporadic movement.[107] Everywhere, they try to automatically regulate input, either of the means of production or of the consumer goods, so as to achieve a very regular pace. When accidental exterior forces disturb movement, one attempts to obtain oscillations at long intervals on which short perturbations have only a slight influence.[108]

We can compare machines with living beings, as Bergson does. According to him, life manufactures explosives that are expended by the sensory motor system. "What do these explosives represent if

[106] The law that Reuleaux gives (in *Cinématique*, p. 243) is more precise. But his statement can be understood completely only by readers familiar with the ideas of this great engineer.

[107] The reduction of passive forces is mentioned in the analysis below. When one reduces friction, one also reduces its variations.

[108] Modern locomotive boilers are placed very high, which gives them the same advantages as large steamships. The oscillations are longer and the machines are also more stable, contrary to what has long been believed. Scientists seem to have had great difficulty in understanding this and have hindered progress in France.

not a storehouse of solar energy, energy whose reduction is temporarily suspended in several of the points where it is expended. Of course, the usable energy the explosive contains expends at the moment of explosion, but it would have been expended sooner if an organism had not been there to arrest its dissipation in order to retain it and store it up."[109] Hydraulic motors are propelled by water that would have wasted its energy along the banks of rivers; economies of friction are gained on the fall of the water. Likewise in steam engines, the boiler receives part of the heat produced by the combustion of pit coal, heat that would have been lost by radiation or by the mixing of the warm gases with the atmosphere. Engines are thus devices placed on the natural or artificial paths of the dissipation of energy,[110] designed to retain something of it and capable of dispensing what they have retained for the benefit of man.

Modern engineers are very attentive to the dissipation of energy. That is why they make such great efforts to obtain very powerful motors with very high speeds, in which the cooling losses are substantially reduced. Furthermore, in a general way we can say that in all the industries that use heat it is good to have mechanisms of large dimensions and very rapid output.

Related to the same order of ideas is the capture of gases that metallurgical furnaces formerly lost, and their utilization for the heating of boilers.

The questions relative to the dissipation of energy offer an interest of the first order for the economist, for immense present-day installations have, from this point of view, an enormous superiority over former systems. The advantage of the powerful steam engine was impressive from the very beginning of large industry, and all the progress accomplished in the chemical arts has better shown this value of size. Authors (and especially socialist authors) have often forgotten the technical origin of this value of size. Thus they have attributed to any extended enterprise a superiority they would have much difficulty justifying scientifically. It is most extraordinary that so many so-called Marxists have reasoned about the statistics establishing industrial concentration without going back to the technical bases of this concentration.

---

109 Bergson, *Creative Evolution* (Modern Library ed.), pp. 268–269.
110 The firebox of a steam engine is an artificial channel of energy dissipation.

Lastly, we must examine what relation exists between the machine and the worker. This part of industrial science has always been treated in the most superficial manner. It has always been surprising to see how the expenditure of muscular force diminishes in proportion as the mechanism is perfected: some applaud the disappearance of a work force too well-qualified and consequently too expensive. Others celebrate the triumph of intelligence over matter and dream of workshops in which work will resemble a game of skill. These are bourgeois thoughts and consequently without interest for us. I believe that we must rather focus our investigation on the following points:

First of all, we should point out the feelings of attachment inspired in every truly qualified worker by the productive forces entrusted to him. These feelings have been observed particularly in rural life. The peasant's love of his field, his vineyard, his barn, his cattle, and his bees has been celebrated. Generally this attitude has been connected with property, but it is not difficult to recognize that there is something more fundamental here. All the virtues attributed to property would be meaningless without the virtues engendered by a certain way of working.

In general, facts of rural life have been very badly understood because philosophers are almost always city dwellers who do not realize the place of agriculture on the hierarchy of work. There is a rough form of agriculture in which one would look in vain for the virtues attributed to property. But there is another type which, for many centuries, has been very superior to the majority of urban occupations as qualified work. It is the latter which poets have celebrated, because they perceived its esthetic character. Property seems to have as its principal advantage the fact that it puts the peasant in the position to become an artist. The importance of this consideration is very great for socialism.

The modern workshop is an experimental field which continually incites the worker to scientific research. The same goal can be attained by different methods, and these are always regarded as provisional. Thus it is always necessary to have one's eyes open to the difficulties the current method of production presents. Here again we must appeal to observations made long ago about agriculture. It has often been pointed out how much the winegrower is an observer, a reasoner, and is curious about new phenomena; he resembles much more the worker of progressive workshops than the laborer. It would be impossible for him to be content with routine, for each year brings a burden of new difficulties. In the great wine-producing regions, the winegrower follows with minute attention all the life stages of each plant.

Modern technical education should have as its goal to give the industrial worker something of this spirit. It is a matter much less of teaching him the services rendered by machines than of preparing him to recognize their imperfections. This point of view is entirely opposed to that which we see in men of letters who laud the realized marvels of progress without understanding the conditions under which this progress was produced. The perspective of men of letters has had, very naturally, a great influence on the people who are responsible for directing education, and it seems that the technical schools are much more occupied in teaching routine than in awakening a true scientific spirit.

We are thus led to invention, which is the great activity of every modern industry. I have pointed out at the end of *Reflections on Violence* that it seems to me that art should be regarded as being an anticipation of the highest form of production as it tends to be manifested more and more in our society. I believe there are many significant conclusions to be drawn from this thesis, which concentrates probably almost all that can be said which is truly interesting on the spirit of invention.[111]

Science has almost completely emancipated itself from the direction men of letters tried to impose on it. The latter still suppose they serve the cause of science because they indulge in noisy parades in honor of modern discoveries. But their prattle has practically no listeners among the men who are informed about scientific works. Every day it becomes clearer that science has as its object to superimpose on nature an ideal workshop formed of mechanisms functioning with a mathematical rigor, aiming to imitate with a close approximation the changes taking place in natural bodies. Just as experimental physics progresses only because of the competition of the builders of machines, mathematical physics seems called to ask, more and more, for formulas for its needed hypothesis from kine-

---

111 The art of which I am speaking is the one based on the practice of artisans and not the art taught in our schools in order to satisfy the modern bourgeoisie.

matics. Science and crafts are thus much closer than the great geometricians of past centuries suspected.

I said that not much attention has been paid to the relations between the worker and the machine, but a great deal has been written
on the relations of the bourgeoisie with their businesses, their pleasures, and the social organs that protect their interests. Books on
collective psychology, which abound today, speak of nothing else.
This literature is greatly appreciated by our contemporaries because
they regard it as an excellent preparation for the elaboration of
an official morality, which would be taught in the schools in order
to assure the government of the people by intellectuals of every
category.

One cannot help but be struck by seeing what a small place contemporary philosophy accords to questions that seemed the most
serious to our fathers: religion is treated in the most superficial
manner, and morality is reduced to a training in docility intended
to assure order.

The more I reflect on these questions, the more I am persuaded
that work can serve as a basis for a culture that would give no cause
to regret the passing of bourgeois civilization. We know the war
that the proletariat should conduct against its masters is suited to
developing in it noble sentiments that are today completely lacking
in the bourgeoisie. The latter has borrowed much from one of the
most corrupt aristocracies that has ever existed; the guides of its
conscience are no less cynical than the men of letters which formed
what Rousseau called the Holbachian circle. All our efforts should
tend to prevent the bourgeois ideas from coming to poison the rising
class; that is why we cannot do enough to break any connection
between the people and the literature of the eighteenth century.[112]

---

[112] I cannot recommend enough reading the excellent observations that my
book has suggested to Jean Bourdeau (*Entre deux servitudes* ["Between Two Servitudes"], pp. 95–104); they very well complete the preceding conclusions. They
bring to light the value that I (like Proudhon) attach to the purity of customs and
classic culture.

CHAPTER VI

Greatness and Decline[*]

I. *Cyclical development in Greek philosophy. The law of apparent regression. Significance of primitive communism and of socialist programs.*

II. *Degeneration of the law; penal system; divorce; influence of commercial practices and of liquid capital.*

III. *Unique occurrences in history. Reasons for Roman law. The Renaissance and the French Revolution. General views on revolutions.*

IV. *Genius and mediocrity. Arts and entertainment. Corruption of the educational and political arts. Religions: the modern role of mediocrity. Philosophies.*

V. *Conclusions on democracy.*

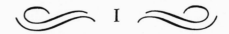

The subtle Greek mind, equally at home in poetry and in mathematics, was fascinated by the marvels observation of the heavens revealed. The ancients could not tackle the great problems of terrestrial physics (which comprises the pride of science today) for lack of an instrument of precise measurement, but their astronomical tools were perfected enough to enable them to reason about the movements of heavenly bodies. They liked to suppose that human things ought to imitate the movements of divine things. Conse-

---

[*] *Translators' note*: This chapter was originally added as an appendix to the 1910 edition.

quently, if institutions were abandoned to their own forces, according to them, they would be seen to obey laws similar to those ascertained in astronomy. Thus provided that catastrophies brought about by exterior causes do not upset the historical order, changes would take place in a closed cycle; after long adventures, societies would return to a regime requiring for its harmony the same principles of public law as the regime at the point of departure.

In his *Discourse on the Origin of Inequality Among Men*, Rousseau adopted the point of view of Greek philosophy. He used all the resources of his eloquence to describe the divisions that have never failed to aggravate the ills of humanity since it ceased to respect the laws of nature. Despotism finally ends this era of calamities (without the reasons for its necessity having been realized), and the author concludes with the statement: "This is the last stage of inequality, and the extreme point that closes the circle and touches on the point from which we have departed." Rousseau did not at all claim that despotism leads people whose lives have become very refined to the customs of the nomad savages in the American forests. The similarity he intends to bring to light between the beginning and the end of the movement is of an entirely ethical order: "The notions of good," he said, "and the principles of justice die away once again."

In our day many sociologists, posing as having advanced ideas, have tried to combine the old notion of astrological cycles with the modern one of progress. In their reveries, humanity would not be condemned to retrace its steps; it would rise continually towards more noble regions. True, such considerable similarities existed between two civilizations that are separated by a very long space of time that they could be defined by the same generic name. Social conditions might be greatly improved, however. Thus the movement could no longer be schematically represented by a circumference; it must be represented by a spiral.

This idea greatly pleased socialist writers who wanted to show proof of lofty knowledge. Often defenders of capitalism reproached them for pursuing a stupid utopia in aspiring to lead the world to communism. For, they said, communism has been the system of the most savage hordes. The socialists accepted this comparison, but they added that the new communism would occupy a much more elevated place in universal history than the present-day capi-

talist order. The aim sought by the socialists would thus conform
to the so-called law of apparent regression, which governs all evolution, and the defenders of the bourgeois economy would be defeated
by ignorance.[1]

This law of apparent regression is very suited to muddle the
questions to which it is applied. In order to understand fully the
meaning of the realities concealed by this law, it is necessary first
of all to determine what the word "communism" signifies.

The juridical labels that should be applied to the life of savages
have been heatedly discussed. It is not very reasonable to apply to
beings who are entirely foreign to our ways of thinking notions
borrowed from the most intellectualized regions of the civilized
mind. Now, unquestionably, law belongs to this very exceptional
region. If it were wished to establish at any price a vague similarity
between the life of the hordes of hunters and modern law, it would
be fitting to compare, as did professor J. Flach, the lands on which
these hordes pursue their game to the area occupied by a nation,
rather than to the lands on which different families exercise the
rights of use regulated by custom.

I do not yet see any rudimentary private law in the life of the
nomads, who mark with magic signs the trees whose fruits they
want to reserve for the day when they take up the old camping
grounds again. The savages, whose wives cultivate roots in a crudely
reclaimed soil that they abandon at the first opportunity, do not yet
possess the spirit of the proprietor. Thus we would not expect to find
juridical thought in them. Private law can appear, for the first time,
in an incontestable way only in the countries where the heads of
family, having received from their ancestors regions that were improved by addition of numerous productive forces, work to leave
new improvements to their successors. Moreover, this economic
condition is not sufficient for the law to take on a perfectly determined body.

The evolutionists were unable to accept this historical manner of
understanding the origins of law. They need to establish that there

---

[1] Enrico Ferri believes that he deserved the credit for giving a definitive form
to this law in 1892, which was only under conjecture or outlined before him
(*Socialisme et Science positive*, p. 94). Tchernichewsky, however, made a very
paradoxical and even unusual use of this so-called law in his *Critique des préjugés
philosophiques contre la possession communale du sol* ("Critique of the Philosophical Prejudices Against Communal Land Ownership") in 1858.

exists a close connection between modern law and the life of the most savage peoples. Thus they must attribute a fictitious juridical system to the latter; for want of anything better, they attribute communism to them, finding no other term that can be taken in such a vague way. This "primitive communism" has thus been invented for sophistic reasons; we are going to see that the future communism of the socialists also corresponds to sophistic maneuvering.

We know with what vigor Proudhon battled against the utopias that were so successful in his time. The violence with which he so often conducted his polemics can be attributed to the horror he felt for social reformers who worked to remove any preoccupation with law from the popular consciousness. His criticism has forced contemporary socialists to present their ideas in a more covert form than those of the old utopians. Formerly the dreams that had been formed for reorganizing the world were naively described; now, socialists are limited to saying that the Party aspires to the realization of a communist society, and they avoid giving explanations of this obscure statement.

If we are not definite about the direction of the ideal program, we can, at least, reason about the immediate reforms that the socialist parties demand and that, according to socialist theoreticians, must prepare the coming to power of the communist society. In France, for a long time, numerous sects quarreled intensely about these reforms. But today they seem to agree since many socialist deputies have entered parliament. Some writers, apparently inspired by Belgian ideas in particular, asked that the state gradually take the responsibility of all large businesses whose modern forms were created by capitalism.

The workers of the most advanced enterprises would thus become government functionaries. In 1883, the *Guesdistes* opposed this "gradual absorption of private industries by the state," which they called "the socialist baggage of shoddy pseudo-communists." They limited themselves to demanding the cancellation of contracts with the Bank of France and the railroad companies, as well as the suppression of mine concessions. The exploitation of these sources of public wealth should be entrusted, according to their program, to the workers occupied with them.[2] It does not seem that the social-

---

[2] Guesde and Lafargue, *Le Programme du parti ouvrier* ("The Program of the Workers' Party"), commentary on Article 11 of the economic section.

ist deputies of today have the confidence in the economic capacities of the workers themselves which Guesde and Lafargue had in 1883. Parliamentary socialism demands the indefinite extension of the economic powers of the state.[3]

We must ask ourselves what juridical future the execution of such a program can provide the world. Twelve years ago, Saverio Merlino reproached the socialists for not having reflected enough on the guarantees that should be applied to the management of large enterprises entrusted to the state. He said there must "be assured this justice in the administration, of which we have at present a vague idea," and to him the problem seemed to be bristling with difficulties.[4]

Experience teaches us that administrative law can only have a certain effectiveness in societies that possess judicial organizations capable of ruling on private rights in an especially satisfactory way. It is the moral authority acquired by judicial bodies which makes administrative bodies fearful of committing arbitrary acts. According to the ideas of contemporary theoreticians of parliamentary socialism, private rights are destined gradually to lose their authority: these theoreticians say that the state will leave the management of lesser enterprises to private individuals for a long time to come; the small rural property, the small workshop, the small business are destined to disappear because of the slow ruin that strikes down out-of-date economic forms. The prestige of private law would obviously follow the same descending path as the prestige of private production. If administrative bodies were no longer being restrained by the desire to follow the examples of very respected judicial bodies, what would become of this "justice in the administration" which Saverio Merlino had recognized as so necessary? In proportion as the state would absorb new productive forms, the need for this justice would become greater and the means of realizing it weaker.

The Belgian deputies Destrée and Vandervelde seem to me to have perceived the immense difficulties that result from an indefinite

---

[3] In an interview published by *Matin*, June 1, 1910, Jules Guesde said that he would be resigned to state monopolies if these monopolies were necessary in order to find the needed funds for social expenses.

[4] Saverio Merlino, *Formes et essence du socialisme* ("The Forms and Essential Nature of Socialism"), p. 198.

extension of public administration. It is undoubtedly because of the lack of confidence they felt in thinking of the consequences of their program, that they have written the following sentences: "This is certainly not our ideal. We ardently aspire to the moral transformations that will make possible the cooperation of all workers, and perhaps also . . . create the anarchist community, overflowing with fraternity and wealth, in which everyone doing what he wants, as in the Abbey of Thélème, would give according to his abilities and would take according to his needs."[5] In this way they invite the socialists to console themselves through dreaming: undoubtedly, "justice in administration" would be lacking, but one would ardently hope for an ideal regime in which law would become unnecessary.

Thus we finally succeed in discovering the secret thinking of the sociologists who speak of apparent regression: they want judicial concerns to become as foreign to the civilized world as they have been to the primitive. They do not dare to admit frankly that law seems to them a burden created during the Dark Ages. In order to express the aversion they feel for judicial ideas, they use a form that enables their friends to understand their thoughts without exposing them too easily to criticisms of philosophers. When we look for the reasons parliamentary socialism is so successful in society today, we see that it is because it expresses better than any other democratic doctrine the aversion present-day society feels for the law. Indeed there no doubt exists at the present time a general degeneration of the law which corresponds to the new directions of customs.

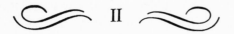 II

We cannot speak about this phenomenon in a clear way by using abstract terms. In order to obtain satisfactory results, it is well to

---

[5] Destrée and Vandervelde, *Le Socialisme en Belgique* ("Socialism in Belgium"), 1st ed., p. 283. In 1883, Guesde and Lafargue maintained that it is absurd to compare future society to the Abbey of Thélème, that in the future the abundance of products will undoubtedly permit free consumption, but that production will never be able to be free (*Programme du parti ouvrier*, p. 35). These observations are not to be found in the present edition of this pamphlet.

proceed to descriptions, by taking examples from various types of law.

a. When Rousseau traced the picture of a society that, after having been long torn by factions, finds peace in submitting to despots who abolish every principle of justice, he was obviously thinking of the tragic destinies of Rome, which fell under the yoke of grotesque and ferocious tyrants. Two facts seem to me to dominate the history of the Roman decline: (1) the privileges wealth procured had become enormous; (2) the descendants of the conquerors were treated like the descendants of the conquered.

On the first point, here are some observations of Renan: "The Roman Empire, in humbling the nobility and reducing the privilege of birth to almost nothing, increased on the other hand the advantages of fortune. Far from establishing the effective equality of its citizens, the Roman Empire, opening wide the gates of the city, created a great division between the *honestiores*, the notables (the wealthy), and the *humiliores* or *tenuiores* (the poor). By the proclamation of the political equality of all, the inequality of the law was introduced, especially in penal law."[6]

This change is especially illuminating when it is likened to the transformations produced by modern capitalism. Experience seems to show that the abuses of power committed for the profit of an hereditary aristocracy, in general, endanger the respect for the law of a people less than the abuses provoked by a plutocratic regime. It is unquestionably true that nothing is as liable to ruin respect for the law as the spectacle of misdeeds committed with the complicity of the courts by adventurers who have become rich enough to be able to buy statesmen. The boldness of the American financiers constitutes an ideal for all our stock market speculators. The present orientation of the rich classes is a subject of fear for the people who believe in the importance of respect for the law.

The degeneration of the law, which was the consequence of the assimilation of the Romans with their former adversaries who had undergone conquest, filled Ihering with indignation: "The provinces," he said, "were the experimental laboratory of the empire. It was the provinces that hastened the transformation of criminal procedure. . . . The provinces were at first the scorned victims of

<hr />

6 Renan, *Marc-Aurèle*, pp. 598–599.

these experiments; in their turn, subsequent Roman generations payed an enormous price for the crime of their ancestors. Under the Republic the provinces had suffered from the arbitrariness and inhumanity of Rome. From the provinces the empire brought home to Rome the era of cruelties."[7] The causes and the effects are to be distinguished in this history of imperial law; no doubt the same results will not be found again in just the same way, but the basic cause of this degeneration can recur in any period. This cause is the equalization of the classes on the level of the lowest class.

Very often, we hear denounced as reactionary judges who seek to quell criminal affairs, which they think would dishonor families that had always been respected. In order to satisfy the intransigent admirers of the rights of man, every delinquent should be treated as if he belonged to the dangerous classes. Equality would then be realized on the level of the lowest classes. The lawyers reason otherwise, because they always strive to have a criminal arrest contribute to the enhancement of respect for the law in the people. They think that this attitude is attained when the moral failings that take place in houses where one meets the social authorities can be displayed to all. Indeed, experience seems to bear out the opinion of the lawyers. But the newspapers feel that they are deprived of their rights when they are prevented from exploiting such scandals, so useful in selling their papers. Thus they cry out violently in the name of equality;[8] their interests generally win over the interests of law.

b. The origins of monogamous marriage are very obscure. Engels was mistaken to think that this institution is characteristic of civilization.[9] The idea of monogamy remained foreign to peoples who have had an important place in history. Such was the case for the Semites. "It is only under the influence of the modern codes derived from Roman law," writes Renan, "that polygamy disappeared in the

---

[7] Ihering, *Histoire du développement du droit romain*, p. 37.

[8] I find in the *Guerre Sociale* ("Social War") of July 12, 1910, an article that deserves to be noted here because similar ones are hardly ever found in the advanced press. The author condemned magistrates who, on an anonymous denunciation, prosecuted an aristocratic girl for infanticide, and the jury that condemned her. The previous day, a peasant woman accused of the same crime had been acquitted by the same court. The social resentment that inspired justice in this affair is regarded as an execrable thing by the author who is undoubtedly an anarchist.

[9] Frederich Engels, *The Origin of the Family, Private Property, and the State*, pp. 72, 95.

Jewish people."[10] Up until the time when the Jews in Algeria were assimilated with the French, they were not bound to practice monogamy.[11] Ihering thought that Roman marriage was at first not only monogamous, but even indissoluble.[12] Not finding any reason in the theories that usually serve to explain matrimonial customs which could justify customs so similar to those of the Christians, he created the famous hypotheses of the *Indo-européens avant l'histoire*. Earliest Roman marriage was related to the conditions under which the migration of the armed Aryans was made.

The best present-day socialist writers are rather at a loss when they are led to speak of the future of the sexual union. In this matter, they dare not apply the law of apparent regression, whose application to economic development seems certain to them. Engels does not think of announcing to us the reappearance of any of the old forms that he encountered in the books of Lewis Henry Morgan. His forecasts seem to me to have been carefully presented with a mind toward satisfying the tender sentiments of German women readers: "Monogamy, instead of being in jeopardy, will become a reality, even for men." Domination by the man and the indissolubility of marriage will disappear: "People will be spared the futile wading in the mud of a divorce trial" when love will have ceased to unite them.[13] Thus socialism would end up by establishing a matrimonial system very analogous to that which existed in the Rome of the decadent period.

The rule of the indissolubility of marriage is certainly destined to disappear from the laws of every country. But it is possible for divorce to exist in two very different ways: either the court pronounces it because of criminal or almost criminal acts that destroy the dignity of the partners and render the maintenance of the family impossible, or the divorce expresses only the will to break a union that has become tiresome. It is toward this second form that divorce is heading in the most civilized countries, as a consequence of the ever-increasing ease given by the courts to those married persons who wish to separate. It can be expected that in a very few years

---

10 Renan, *Marc-Aurèle*, p. 548.
11 *Eben Haezer*, I, 42–47.
12 Ihering, *Histoire*, p. 68.
13 Engels, *Origin of the Family*, pp. 97, 109–110.

ideas about marriage will be based on the hypothesis that this type of divorce will be the rule. Henceforth every union will be considered as normally being dissolved the day erotic desires are extinguished. Lasting unions will be suspected as being maintained only for financial reasons and in spite of secret discord. People will no longer be persuaded that the destiny of man is to ennoble the sexual union by the sacrifice of the instincts to a duty. It is impossible for respect for law not to undergo a prodigious diminution when the Roman hypothesis of the dignity of the family has disappeared,[14] but there is no forewarning capable of stopping the current drift.

c. Proudhon pointed out several times that commercial practice exercises an ever-increasing influence on civil jurisprudence. This observation is even truer today than in his time. I find in this fact one of the principal causes that have weakened respect for law in our contemporaries.

It is very easy to suspect that there is a tremendous difference of spirit between civil and commercial law. One has only to consider how greatly their jurisdictions differ: the merchants are very fond of their consulary courts, which are composed much less of real judges than of arbitrators who determine to what degree each litigant has been a loyal merchant.[15] But the difference seems truly basic when we go back to the economic sources.

Civil law historically belongs to the rural domain; it supposes the existence of a head of family who farms without supervision, much less in view of the pleasures that he can derive from it than for the financial benefit of his distant heirs. If this master contracts obligations, in the mortgage he gives to each of his creditors an isolated right by virtue of which each one can, in case of a sale, come according to his terms of contract to claim the sum of what is owed him on the value of the property. The case is entirely different for the businessman. His suppliers and lenders are not separated into neat pigeonholes but implicitly united in a hidden association. In the case of a failure, this association makes itself explicitly known, since the

---

[14] We know that Proudhon was strongly opposed to divorce.

[15] Today there exists a strong current of opinion that it be a condition of contracts that difficulties will be settled by means of arbitration. According to the interpretation given today by the courts to Article 1006 of the Code of Civil Procedure, it cannot be agreed to regulate by arbitration a dispute that does not yet exist.

Code de commerce states that creditors are incontestably in a state of union. Two economic-judicial systems could not be more opposite than those which I have just described.

The conditions concerning this hidden association take into account the rules on bankruptcy. The bankrupt merchant can be condemned to forced labor if he does not produce accounts kept in a manner completely above board, "without there being any fraud." This is the same punishment given to public civil servants who destroy records with which they are entrusted (*Code de commerce*, 586, # 6; *Code pénal*, 402 and 173). The law severely punishes the delinquent member of the secret association who would put the latter in a position of not being able to establish its account.[16] This likening of the bankrupt and the government official who destroys records is very legitimate because, in both cases, the criminal could not be watched by the people whose interests he has gravely injured. More unusual, perhaps, are the following offenses constituting simple bankruptcy and leading simply to prison: having made exaggerated personal expenditures, having lost large sums in gambling or in devious operations on the stock market, having entered into financially ruinous contracts in order to obtain funds with the aim of postponing catastrophe, and having favored one creditor to the detriment of the others after the cessation of the payments (*Code de commerce*, 585; *Code pénal*, 402); thus the merchant betrays the common interests of the secret association that has been established around his business.

When social reformers state that there exists a natural association between work and capital, advocate profit sharing, or ramble on about interdependence, they apply to the workshop ideas that commercial practice has vulgarized. If Léon Bourgeois were to the slightest extent a legal authority, he would see that his so badly established doctrine of the quasi contract is capable of taking on a special meaning when it is applied to commercial law. Before 1856, Article 51 of the *Code de commerce* imposed on the members of a commercial association the obligation of having recourse to arbitration to settle their disputes. In this, the code did nothing but bring

---

16 It should be pointed out here that Article 439 of the Penal Code likens to the destruction of public records the destruction of "negotiable instruments containing or bringing about obligation, disposition or rebate"; the punishment is solitary confinement with hard labor. It decreases to imprisonment for two to five years if the destroyed notes are not of this exceptional nature.

into use an old rule, and one can say that even today there exists a prejudice in favor of this way of judging such matters. Thus, we should not be surprised to hear frequent advocacy of compulsory arbitration to regulate differences that arise between employers and workers. This arbitration is derived from the idea that social reformers have about the occult association that exists between work and capital.

It is clear that all these associationist doctrines, which are derived from commercial practice, destroy the historic principle of civil law that supposes economic isolation.

Each day, for still other reasons, the rich bourgeoisie is losing more and more respect for the principles of civil law. It admires the great deeds done in the course of the nineteenth century by powerful corporations much more than the modest works of rural families who have preserved the traditional economy, which corresponds essentially to civil law. In the new economy that the rich bourgeoisie considers the noblest, direction by the head of family has completely disappeared. Having become a stockholder, he is content to hold a certificate giving him the right to a variable revenue.

People who do not possess a considerable number of liquid assets are regarded today as being bad managers of their wealth. The principal preoccupation of the rich bourgeois is to put into his wallet the stocks that are regularly expected to increase in value. Thus the farsighted head of a family counts on bettering the situation of his heirs no longer by the improvement he brings on his rural property, but by the normal play of the stock market.

In the formation of the large fortunes of today, speculations on the stock market have played a far more considerable role than have the beneficient innovations introduced into production by able heads of industry. Thus wealth increasingly tends to appear detached from the economy of progressive production, and it then loses all contact with the principles of civil law.

The transformation of judicial ideas which results from the changes that have developed in the composition of bourgeois fortunes is expressed in a particularly clear way in the system of inheritance taxes. Formerly, in the rural domain that served as the economic model to the theoreticians of civil law, everything was organized with a mind toward heirs in such a way that it could be said of the latter that they were the hidden lords of the land, the proprietor of the time being only their proxy. Today everyone thinks the contrary, that the stockholder has no moral connection that makes him depend on heirs; consequently, he can spend everything as he likes. Those who will receive his estate will be expected to consider themselves lucky, like people who have won a lottery. Inheritance is thus a sort of windfall, on which the state makes no scruples about imposing taxes so heavy that they have been compared sometimes to a partial confiscation. Opinion accepts these fiscal measures without protest, which proves to what an extent all ideas of civil law have been forgotten.

One could cite many more examples, and it would be discovered that, in each category, there is a deterioration similar to those that have just been described.

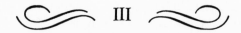

III

When we realize that, in our time, there are numerous disparate and strong causes that connive to bring about the degeneration of law, we then wonder if Proudhon was not victim of a strange illusion when he assumed that our nature leads us toward justice. On the contrary, it would seem that law was imposed on man by historical accidents and that peoples make all kinds of attempts to shake off a yoke that artificially has come to multiply the difficulties of life. We are used to viewing the greatness of law as being the best sign of historical greatness. Thus, historical greatness is a condition against which humanity struggles.

Modern scholarly studies that have shown the importance of magic in ancient institutions tend to show, also, that law was very exceptional in the ancient world. Magic consists of a group of tricks that enable a man who is rich enough to pay the possessor of mysterious formulas to acquire the help of exceptional forces and thus triumph over any adversary. On the other hand, law assumes that the individual engaged in struggle upholds his claims fortified only by his own resources.

I do not think that the Greeks were great masters of the law.[17]

---

[17] Renan, in enumerating everything we owe to the Greeks, speaks of "international and maritime law" but not of civil law (*Histoire du peuple d'Israël*, I, ii).

Professor Glotz has affirmed that our 'basically secular and democratic society" would find "great profit in occasionally abandoning
Roman law, which is rigid, formal, imprisoned in forms and rules of
religious and aristocratic origin, in order to reinvigorate itself in a
living, free, fluid, and sympathetic law in which justice is capable
of being roused and takes the name of humanity."[18] This folderol
can only make very suspect a law that is, moreover, little known
according to its apologist.[19] A law that is sympathetic and fluid does
not sound like such a great thing. In order not to run the risk of
getting lost in the midst of futile dissertations, we must return to
the opinion of past jurists who saw in Rome the homeland of law.

The idea that this could be a unique creation in history shocks
many contemporary evolutionary assumptions. But Judaism is most
certainly a unique creation in spite of the efforts of the Orientalists
to fit it into the mainstream of Semitic religions. Renan believed
that the existence of Judaism was not as extraordinary as was the
"simultaneous appearance made in the Hellenic race by everything
that comprises the honor and adornment of the human spirit." According to him, the Roman conquest would be placed on the same
footing as the Jewish religion and Greek civilization.[20]

If anything unique has been produced in history, it is because
chance plays an enormous part in the life of peoples. It sometimes
happens that the union of powerful causes produces results that are
of an entirely new type.[21] The historian must seek to determine
those new types to which the most important causes are related.
But he would be on the road to the absurd if he purported to teach
us why, in a given place and at a given date, this unique conjunction
of causes came about.

We can suppose, for example, that the conquering destiny of
Rome was due to the fact that an aristocracy, remarkably gifted in
commanding, inherited from Greece military institutions, a fiscal
system, and a policy of judicious exploitation of the conquered.
Force organized according to a plan, which could have been given

---

[18] Glotz, *Etudes sociales et juridiques sur l'antiquité grecque* ("Social and Juridical Studies on Greek Antiquity"), p. 299.
[19] He thinks that scholarly research ought to concern itself presently with re-
constituting Greek law (*ibid.*, p. 279).
[20] Renan, *Israël*, I, iv–vi.
[21] With regard to the origins of capitalism, Marx wrote: "This confirms the law
stated by Hegel in his *Logic*. According to this law, simple changes in quantity
having reached a certain degree induce differences in quality" (*Capital*, I, 133).

by a Greek tyrant,[22] would in the long run extinguish the anarchy of the Italian villages, which no doubt greatly resembled Berber villages. But how the Roman patricians were able to receive, accept, and preserve a regime so foreign to Italian customs is a question the genuine historian never poses, and never posing it, has no reason to be astonished at the exceptional character of the Roman conquest.

It is possible to recognize what preponderant causes must have acted together to form Roman law. But it would be ridiculous to try to explain why these causes were found only in Rome.

All those who study this history are struck by the great intelligence in agricultural matters possessed by the old patricians. It is extremely probable that the usage of their domestic records went back to a very early period.[23] Everyone knows that agricultural cultivations, of which the masters keep exact day-to-day records, have an economic value much superior to others less carefully recorded.[24] Ihering greatly admired the primitive Romans for having admitted no other disruptions of property than those needed for good cultivation. The future of the domain was thus protected against errors and caprices.[25] The distinctions established between the *res mancipi* (productive forces) and the other forms of wealth[26] proves that the Romans formed sophisticated economic ideas at a very early time. This incessant preoccupation with the proper forms of production had, among other results, that of suppressing magic, which is as much the enemy of true civil law as of science.

The organization of the Roman family was another very efficacious cause of the organization of Roman law. Ihering stresses the ideas of liberty and power, which, in his eyes, dominated the whole Roman juridical system, and he shows at the same time that the will of the citizens was strongly controlled by customs that could not be violated without danger.[27] The *pater familias* was thus very

---

[22] The legend of Servius Tullius has preserved a trace of this importation.

[23] Ihering, *Esprit du droit romain*, II, 14–15.

[24] Thorold Rogers said that, in the 18th century, English agriculture often experienced miscalculations because bookkeeping was often neglected, and he insists, with Young, on the importance of good bookkeeping (*Histoire du travail et des salaires en Angleterre* ["History of English Labor and Wages"], p. 415.

[25] Ihering, *Esprit du droit romain*, II, 226–227, and IV, 330.

[26] *Ibid.*, II, 160, and *Histoire*, pp. 77–82.

[27] Ihering often returns to this central question (*Esprit*, II, 136–139, and *Histoire*, pp. 85–86. *Du role de la volonté dans la possession* ["The Role of Free Will in Ownership"], pp. 104–105).

similar to a king who should serve as an example of obedience to the laws. On the contrary, the tyrant governs according to his whim. Thus, the whole life of the Roman family was accompanied by judicial majesty one would probably look for in vain in other ancient land.

But above all, it is necessary for us to examine the subject of war in order to understand the reasons for the exceptional juridical genius of Rome. Rome never retreated before her enemies. She did not buy peace by cowardly compromises. She was always certain of triumphing in the long run.[28] The patrician entered into the struggle for law with a feeling of inflexibility which he took from the policy of the Senate. Everyone thought that war would perpetually increase Roman power. And likewise the heritage protected by Roman law would continually become enriched. The foundations of Rome, protected by legions reputed to be invincible, seemed built for eternity. Thus, law took on the character of an eternal thing, and this character conferred on it a dignity similar to that of science in Hellenic thought.

The men of the Renaissance were amazed at reading the great works of Roman law. The works of the medieval jurists seemed miserable compared to the great words of the *Digeste*. Rabelais' Pantagruel says: "There are not in the world any other books as beautiful or as elegant as the texts of the *Pandectes*. But in their margins, that is to say, in the glosses of Accursius, one finds so much dirt, so much squalor and so many bedbugs that it is only filth and villainy."[29] The works of the canonists could not greatly please jurists who had such literary passions, and Rabelais in the fourth book of *Pantagruel* ridicules the "decree-givers" at length. Besides, we cannot regret that the magistrates of the time worked to make solutions inspired by Roman law triumph. For the canonists, wanting above all else to defend the ecclesiastical interests, had not thought of the management of production. Thus their actions often

---

[28] "No one could have predicted the existence of a force like that which Rome now showed to the astonished world. Military deployment was not considerable. What was terrible was the resolution, obstinacy, and energy that one felt behind these legions and their ambassadors—representatives of an irresistible force" (Renan, *Israël*, IV, 267).

[29] Rabelais, *Pantagruel*, II, 5.

resulted in doctrinaire pettiness, which permitted many arbitrary measures[30] and sometimes absolutely absurd solutions.[31]

The triumph of Roman law cannot be explained solely by the merits of its solutions, there are more tangible reasons. The Roman theory of property gave the lords the means of liquidating to their best advantage the confused customs that existed on the uncultivated lands of the country. The princes' counselors found in the imperial tradition magnificent precepts that helped them justify the great strengthening of power which took place at this time and which all the politicians of the time regarded as an absolute necessity. The troops began to maneuver skillfully, and the authority of the general became the prototype of authority, as was true in Rome. This renaissance of the military idea reinforced the regard then held for a law created by the conquerors of the ancient world.

The seventeenth century inherited the Renaissance notions of law. The men of this time have often been reproached for lacking sensitivity, but law is hardly a school of sensitivity. Bossuet's theology is conducted rather generally like a legal theory. I am persuaded that the majesty with which our great classics are expressed is very largely due to the majesty of the *Digeste.*

The French Revolution revived a hegemony of juridical ideas, which had lost much of their authority during the sentimental years of the eighteenth century. Nonnoble lands were freed from feudal services that could not be justified by civil law, and thus the Roman independence of the principal cultivator reappeared. A great number of citizens were brought to ownership and became energetic defenders of the law. The new social order was defined, proclaimed, and imposed by the most fabulous general the world had known since Alexander.[32] In theory, France was completely Roman: each head of family was supposedly a master of a rural domain, a citizen participating in the sovereignty, and a good soldier.[33] It is easy to

---

[30] We find a rather large amount of the nonsense on the canon law in the study made by Professor Esmein on the promissory oath.

[31] For example, in the name of morality, the canonists demanded for prescription that the possessor had always possessed in good faith.

[32] Historians should render to the civil code the name of *Code Napoléon* ("Napoleonic Code"), which offers the immense advantage of recalling one of the essential reasons for the establishment of modern law.

[33] Georges Sorel, *Insegnamenti sociali della economia contemporanea* ("Social Teachings of Contemporary Economics"), p. 109.

recognize that respect for the law has greatly weakened in us since warlike ideas, originating from the Napoleonic tradition, are less popular.

Several years ago, I proposed to determine the general character of these two great transformations by means of a precept that could be applied equally to the hypotheses I have made on syndicalism. I said that, in these three cases, we pass from a *system of duties* to a *system of rights*.

At the dawn of modern times, anyone who held any authority whatever aspired to liberate himself from the responsibilities that archaic conventions, customs, and Christian morality had, until then, imposed on the masters for the benefit of the weak. Since the new jurists affirmed that all of this traditional order was foreign to the law, these disagreeable responsibilities were considered as merely social duties in the eyes of those who were subject to them. The seigneurs used force to constrain the peasants not to claim the execution of these social duties, from which they meant to free themselves, and to respect their rights, which they extended as far as possible, thanks to the resources of the new jurisprudence.

The French nobility was obliterated at the end of the eighteenth century by a revolutionary government of common landowners who wanted no longer to support the obligations arising from feudal times. The third estate maintained that these obligations did not have any juridical origin; they considered them, consequently, as being social duties that had been imposed on them by force. The new force suppressed these duties, and the civil law alone remained to regulate relationships.

Today, the bourgeoisie, the state, and the church rival in zeal to proclaim the social duties the rich should fulfill towards the poor. For the first time, perhaps, the masters want to become the benefactors of the people. But the people revolt against these benefactors, ridicule social duties, and intend to obtain a rule of law. It is proletarian violence that alone permits the development of such a revolt, a revolt that seems so paradoxical at first sight. The historical value of this violence thus appears to be of extreme importance.[34]

The explanations given above on the role of war in the formation of law allows the hope that the organization of combat, dear to

---

[34] Sorel, *Insegnamenti sociali*, pp. 42–44, 53–55.

present-day syndicalism, could induce the beginning of a new juridical system. While the solidarists seek to jumble everything up, violence tends to separate, and we have seen that law is regarded as being all the more perfect when the schisms established between the subjects of the law are deepened.

IV

Each idea has a proper domain in which we find examples to help understand its origins, conceive of its functioning in detail, and judge its historical significance. The ideas of greatness and decline are linked, according to common opinion, with those of genius and mediocrity. Their proper domain is thus the one in which human activities are particularly sensitive to personal values. Economics tends to blend the individual works into a mass whose transformations resemble those studied by naturalists. Thus it is not in economics that we should look for the direct application of the concepts of greatness and decline. The more we get away from economics, the more we have the possibility of finding the ground that we are seeking. We are thus led to think that the concepts of grandeur and decline apply specifically to the activities of the free spirit— that is, to art, religion, and philosophy.

Chance favors some periods of history that have an abundance of superior men. When we compare the times that have preceded and those that have followed periods of greatness, we are surprised to see that some striking similarities exist between the two. Though the manner of presenting things may be greatly changed, it is the same spirit of mediocrity that is the moving force of both periods. The law of apparent regression is therefore not without foundation, but it has a completely different meaning than its originators have attributed to it. It signifies that sometimes humanity emerges from mediocrity under the energetic pressure of certain constraints but that it returns to this state whenever it is left to its own devices. Thus it would not be impossible that the future of society, refined and fallen into complete decadence, would resemble a distant, primitive past.

There exists no irreproachable nomenclature on the arts. In examining the question at hand, we may settle for distinguishing three classes, according to whether the purpose of the artist is entertainment, education, or an affirmation of power. If one attributes values to these groups based on the position that each one would hold in a statistical evaluation, the first would be the most important. The entertaining arts are the only ones truly known by savages. The latter show their sometimes rather remarkable taste in their dances, songs, and ornamentation, but their magic images seem extremely grotesque to us. In the course of civilization, man has not stopped inventing new ways of amusement, and often it has even happened that the educational arts and those affirming power have been corrupted under the influence of ideas engendered by the arts of entertainment.

Wagner probably was right when he said that opera constitutes the most advanced form of dramatic art, for opera constitutes a renaissance of the splendors of the barbarian celebrations and those of Roman decadence. It is true that we need a long apprenticeship in order to follow the complicated music used today in lyric drama, and this complexity can appear to many people as proof of the superiority of the contemporary theater over the traditional entertainments. But the technical differences can be enormous between two manifestations of artistic expression without there being a difference in genius. The complexity of contemporary music serves only to increase the spectators' interest for the work.

Often, nineteenth-century Catholicism has been reproached by people for its barbaric aesthetic values.[35] The technical differences here are not such that one can contest this judgment. This is because the clergy introduced a number of decorative elements into the churches which appeared to them to be charming in the processions, the only celebrations they know. The merchants who sell these horrors called "Saint Sulpice art" also sell excellent casts of ancient statues,[36] but their clientele prefer the figures that remind them of the good young people who inspired them in the religious procession.

The educational arts are seeing their domain circumscribed more

---

[35] Cf. André Hallays in the *Débats*, June 27 and July 4, 1902.
[36] André Hallays (*Débats*, July 18, 1902).

every day. Nowadays it is difficult to understand the importance the Greek philosophers attached to music as an educative art. They wanted the spirit of entertainment to be kept out of those cities that had to live with an eye to war.[37] Wagner must have been extremely naive to suppose that his theater could be educational. The men who go to Bayreuth never even dream of becoming Germanic heroes. No one goes to see a comedy with the idea that it can correct his morals, or to a tragedy in order to attain virtue. Attempts to introduce religious drama into France have failed ludicrously. Everything scenic means for us entertainment and only entertainment.[38] The men of the Revolution believed that official solemnities would be effective in forming good citizens. We know now that they served only to favor the liquor trade. It seems that in 1907 Marcel Sembat proposed to a Masonic convention that they create lay ceremonies to compete with Catholic ceremonies. He clearly regarded all the celebrations as entertainments between which competition is possible.

Catholic liturgies are practically the only examples of the educational arts in our country. But we should note that the clergy does not much like to perform the venerable Gregorian music that the Holy See recommends, for the congregations are not very apt to understand an art that embodies the most noble traditions of antiquity. They want to hear concerts in the churches, concerts that would be a diversion for them.

The important place manifestations of power have in the history of art is shown by the Greek acropolises; the public works of the Romans; the fortresses, communal buildings, and cathedrals of the Middle Ages; Versailles; the Place de la Concorde; and the Arc de Triomphe. But very few periods have truly achieved an esthetic conception of power. It is hard to admire the innumerable paintings the great personages of ancient Egypt have left to us; these are monumental statistics that give us a knowledge of the economy of Egypt. Asiatic kings often wished to immortalize their victories by

---

[37] Aristotle, *Politics*, Bk. V, Chaps. V, VI, VII.

[38] Modern Persia has created mystery plays concerning the misfortune of its holy men, and Renan found these creations to be admirable (*Les Téaziés de la Perse*, in the *Nouvelles études d'histoire religieuse* ["New Studies of Religious History"]). Persia is a country that possesses a very refined literature and cruel customs: we can ask if such customs are not necessary for the success of religious theater.

picturing, on stone, war episodes and triumphant marches; these representations are usually interesting only to the scholars. In periods of decadence, we see, just as we did in barbarian times, collections of sculpture and frescoes[39] intended to show that their creators were rich.

Gigantic works are greatly pleasing to mediocre societies and, accordingly, to decadent as well as primitive peoples. In the *Débats* of July 18, 1902, André Hallays points out the statue of Notre-Dame de France erected in Puy in 1860 as "one of the most disastrous monuments to the bad taste of the French clergy." He is astonished that no one thought of crowning the Rock of Corneille with a chapel similar to that constructed near it at the Rock of Aiguille in the Middle Ages. Skillful criticism did not understand the thinking of the clergy, who wanted to erect a trophy of the victory they believed to have definitely gained over liberalism.[40] The gigantic is generally displeasing; modern religious art, completely oriented toward pleasing the mediocre, could hardly express itself in an esthetic manifestation of power.

Théodule Ribot distinguishes four elements that contribute to the fostering of religious sentiment in primitive peoples: the emotion of fear, a certain feeble attraction for a God, the desire to propitiate a power superior to man by prayers and offerings, and the need to reinforce social bonds.[41] We can unite the first three elements in a single group, and, consequently, we could say that the ancient religions fall into two systems: they are intended, by means of their rites, to protect men against the evil that never ceases to threaten them; they are social disciplines whose action successfully complements that of the laws.

The history of Christianity has added something new: it shows us that repeatedly saints, who had learned to live the spiritual life in the monasteries, found themselves capable of leading the people towards devotions rich in results. Protestantism taught that exceptional graces very similar to those enjoyed by these mystic leaders

---

[39] Cf. Müntz, *Histoire de l'art pendant la Renaissance* ("History of Art During the Renaissance"), II, 79.

[40] It was Father Combalot who in 1850 started on the statue project. We know what a great part he had taken in the battle of the clergy against the university in the period of the July monarchy.

[41] Th. Ribot, *Psychologie des sentiments* ("Psychology of Attitudes"), pp. 301–303.

of the masses are accessible to all the faithful.[42] William James drew
the logical consequences of this theology in maintaining that the
supernatural experience is the essence of religion. We can characterize the principle of the first system as selfish,[43] since the believer
is concerned only with the interests of himself or his group. The
second principle is political. That of William James is at the same
time individualistic and social: the American philosopher supposes
that man begins by pursuing his own regeneration and that he next
shows prodigious (one could even say superhuman) activity in the
world with a view to changing the morals of his contemporaries.

William James founded his theory on Catholic hagiography and
on observations of certain American sects. We might be tempted
to say that it applies only to exceptions. But these exceptions are what
constitute the grandeur of religion. Greek Christianity, from the
general opinion, is inferior to Roman Christianity because it is not
served by men formed to the spiritual life who zealously attempt to
conquer the secular world. The exceptional value of Catholicism is
due to the fact that its monasteries continually prepare such heroes.

What we know of the prophets of Israel allows us to say that biblical Judaism owed its glory to religious experience. Modern Jews no
longer see in their religion anything but rites resembling those of
ancient magic superstitions. Thus, as soon as they receive an education they abandon their traditional practices with contempt. Having
been raised in a milieu almost totally devoid of spiritual life, they are
scandalously incompetent when they speak of Christianity, which
is completely nourished from the spiritual life.[44] The continual conquests Islam makes in black countries are obviously due to the fact
that its priests make known the general idea of high religion to populations previously bent under the yoke of fetishism. Buddhist monks
have no doubt known religious experience.

Thus William James's principle would serve to clarify the four
great universal religions in which, according to the opinion of every
competent person, the religious idea manifested itself in a truly

---

[42] Georges Sorel, *Réflexions sur la violence*, 4th ed., pp. 399–400. [*Reflections on
Violence* (New York: Collier, 1961), p. 255.]

[43] Th. Ribot said with regard to the three first elements that I have grouped to
form the first system: "The religious sentiment is the direct expression of a narrow
egoism" (*Psychologie des sentiments*, p. 302).

[44] Salomon Reinach has given a rather amusing example of this incompetence in
Orpheus.

striking way. In pagan civilizations, it only plays a very small role, and consequently, it usually can be neglected by the historian.

William James's principle is constantly threatened in Christianity, even in Catholicism, by the forces that give satisfaction to the mediocrity of men totally devoid of the mystic *élan*. Many educated Catholics today have undertaken to raise the church to the level of the lay spirit, without concerning themselves with the mystic principle that enlivened its tradition. Rites that furnish the soul with means of consolation, of hope, or even of calming certain sorrows,[45] a more or less unbelieving clergy that works in concert with public administration to better the lot of man—this very well satisfies the mediocre.

The modernists reason almost as did Madame de Warens, if we believe Rousseau's account of her in the sixth book of his *Confessions*: "Faithful to the religion she had embraced, she sincerely assumed complete profession of the faith. But when it came to a discussion of each article, it seemed that she believed completely otherwise than the Church, but submitting to it all the while." She explained this discrepancy to her confessor by reasons very like those we find used by our most subtle modernists: "I am not mistress of my faith, but I am mistress of my will. I submit it without reserve, and I want to believe everything. What more can you ask of me?"

We witness this spectacle that at first appears to be paradoxical: scholars who have rejected everything the church considers as forming the repository of faith nevertheless claim to remain in the church. Almost until the day of his condemnation, ex-Abbé Loisy gave prominent Catholics the impression that he remained a good priest. These modernists repeat verbatim words contained in orthodox dogmas while attributing to them meanings the orthodox theologians reject in horror. They devoutly receive the sacraments while admitting not at all or only with many reservations the theories concerning these sacraments given by ecclesiastical teaching. What does their Catholicism consist in, then?

For the advanced modernists, religion is reduced to a series of rites believed necessary to gain entrance into heaven. We are thus

---

45 In an address delivered on April 10, 1910, at Saint-Chamond, Aristide Briand said that the republic has shown the most liberal spirit toward Catholicism, since it has permitted the faithful to go to church "to draw some consolation from religious sources."

brought back to the pagan mysteries into which one was initiated to chase away the terrors of life in the next world. Although there is a great difference between the intellectual level of the modernists and that of the superstitious Romans of the decadent period, the same emotional basis is found in all these men.

The "Social Catholics" seem to have wished to adopt, at the present time, the ideas of Napoleon and of Auguste Comte: the great emperor believed that the priests would be, under the rule of the concordat, excellent auxiliaries to his prefects. The philosopher hoped to control popular sentiments by using neofetishist displays. Today the Social Catholics would like the clergy to organize associations that would be educational and economic at the same time and effective in bringing all classes to an understanding of their social duties. According to their small minds, the order that the excesses of capitalism gravely upset would thus come to reestablish itself.

Their illusion makes one think of what Renan wrote on Hellenic worship: "Essentially municipal and political at its beginning. . . . Athenian religion was at first only the religious consecration of patriotism and the institutions of the polis. This was the cult of the Acropolis; Aglaure and the oath that was taken on his altar by the young Athenians had no other meaning—almost as if in our country religion consisted in conscription, drilling soldiers, and saluting the flag. This would soon become rather tiresome. It had nothing infinite, nothing which touched man in his fate, nothing universal."[46] Finally, all this social religion lacked religious value. The Social Catholics dream of making Christianity regress to this mediocrity.

Catholicism will be able to renew itself only if a crisis produced by men conditioned to the spiritual life in the monasteries takes place in its bosom. It would thus react against mediocrity. Numerous historical experiences show us that such crises are able to stimulate tremendous effects of greatness. We should not, however, conceal the fact that the difficulties are particularly great today: if, as Hegel maintains, art, religion, and philosophy form the triology of the free spirit, it is indeed very difficult to believe that one of these elements could elevate itself to the sublime when the others remain stricken with complete impotence. The extreme baseness of the present Catholic esthetic will greatly hinder any attempts at a religious renaissance at the present time.

---

[46] Renan, *Saint-Paul*, p. 183.

Philosophy is much more sensitive to the individual's personality than art and religion, which are generally supported by social organizations appropriate for assuring the permanence of a trend. As extraordinary as are the religious experiences of the great mystics, there exist many men who ardently desire to imitate their type of life. Monasteries are created in order to perpetuate their examples of piety, and they keep the faith above the level of mediocrity for greater or shorter periods of time. When decadence intervenes, innovators are not long in appearing; as a result, Catholicism is able to surmount all the successive blows inflicted by human weakness.

During the Gothic period, the arts had an organization as solid as a system of production can have. At that time, they were integrated in the most intimate way with the trades. The Renaissance completely changed the position of the artists, who were no longer mixed with artisans and who were elevated to the status of the *literati*. According to good authors, the new order had a disastrous effect on the destiny of art.[47] The latter depended much more than before on personality. The history of the masters replaced the history of art. Often the schools of men of the first rank had for representatives only extremely decadent personalities. Only architecture continued to produce results offering a certain regularity, because it depends strictly on the traditional methods adopted by the builders.

In philosophy, what is truly essential is what totally escapes transmission by teaching. The masters point out to their contemporaries new ways of making contact with reality. The disciples pervert these institutions, because they purport to incorporate them into theories of a "rigid and dead metaphysic." The true greatness of an original philosopher is apparent when he views the world without sectarian spirit. But these moments are rare in his life. "The master, insofar as he formulates, develops, and translates into abstract ideas what he conceives, is, in a way, his own disciple."[48]

Thus greatness is only accidental, even in the great majority of the most illustrious philosophers. Academic mediocrity tends at once to falsify their ideas. I think that one could describe philosophy by the following metaphor: several fires, lit by men of extraordinary genius in moments of successful inspiration, flicker in the midst of

[47] Müntz, *loc. cit.*, pp. 79, 194; *Raphaël*, pp. 80–82.
[48] Bergson, *Introduction à la métaphysique* ("Introduction to Metaphysics"), in *Cahiers de la Quinzaine*, 4th ser., bk. 12, pp. 22–23.

fog. Very few people think of making their way by the light of these beacons. The mediocre mass navigates haphazardly, jabbering all the while.

The theory of mediocrity is well illustrated by the changes Marxism has undergone. The social-democratic writers who have purported to explain, apply, or extend the doctrine of their supposed master were men of notable vulgarity. Moreover, it appears that Marx did not have any illusions about the talent of those who passed for the authentic representatives of Marxism. Usually they attached a major importance to parts of his work which were already shown to be invalid. They did not understand the value of those ideas that are destined to assure Marx's glory.[49]

Marx's great error was in not realizing and taking into account the great power of mediocrity in history. He did not suspect that socialist sympathies (as he conceived them) are extremely artificial.[50] Now we are witnessing a crisis that threatens the ruination of all the movements capable of being ideologically connected to Marxism. Gustave Le Bon, who alone observes the common forms of political socialism, maintains that it reproduces old superstitions: "The socialist faith gives to the simple folk the hope the gods no longer gave them and the illusions science had taken away from them."[51] This regression of socialist ideas towards archaic illusions shows us once again the victory won by mediocrity over genius.

There will be no dearth of sociologists to claim that this study draws a conclusion in favor of a scientific justification of democracy. Here is the reasoning they will offer: In order to establish laws that best assure men's happiness, that have the most chance of lasting, and that best satisfy the minds of the realistic philosophers, it is necessary to observe how the nature of social things is revealed in the greatest number of cases in the course of history. The laws

---

[49] One is sometimes tempted to compare the doctors of social democracy with the harpies who soiled everything they touched.
[50] Georges Sorel, *Insegnamenti sociali*, p. 342.
[51] Gustave Le Bon, *Psychologie politique* ("Political Psychology"), p. 359.

must adapt to the least painful, strongest, and most general tendencies of the human spirit. Now, in proportion as we have considered areas in which our intelligence is most freely revealed, we have seen that mediocrity exerts its influence more completely. What is called by the pejorative term mediocrity in this study is what the political writers call democracy. It is thus demonstrated that the course of history calls for the introduction of democracy.

In 1848 the provisional government was naive enough to proclaim that it hoped to see the power of mediocrity reinstated. Proudhon indignantly denounced a circular that the ministry of public education had addressed to the rectors to explain this lovely doctrine to them. He said on March 22, 1848: "The minister expresses the desire that the primary schoolteachers stand as candidates to the Assembly, not because they are sufficiently enlightened, but despite their being insufficiently enlightened. . . . Who does not see that in the thinking of the minister, the primary schoolteacher is the envious mediocrity, who has invented nothing, who will invent nothing, destined to serve, by his silent votes, arbitrary democracy, and war on the rich. On this score, I protest against this candidacy; let us speak plainly, against this prostitution of the teachers. Just as the constitutional monarchy, seeking to surround itself with an aristocracy of talent and fortune, appeals to the notables, so democracy comprises its privileged class with mediocrities."[52]

Nowadays, many intellectuals find it to their own advantage to defend democracy. Thanks to their classical education, they are used to considering history as a sort of epic. Consequently, they put their wits to thinking up sophisms capable of demonstrating that democratic mediocrity engenders social grandeur. We have seen in the course of this study one of the most shameless of these sophisms, that of the law of apparent regression. Thanks to it, plunges into decadence are supposedly transformed into bold flight toward the loftiest summits that the mind could wish for.

This apology for democracy is not without serious dangers. About twenty years ago, it led many young men to anarchy; they intended to laud the grandeur of democracy in the most grandiloquent style, and they only encountered democrats mediocre from the moral as well as the intellectual point of view and completely

---

[52] Proudhon, *Solution du problème sociale* ("Solution of the Social Problem"), pp. 58–59.

alien to any idea of art. This former anarchist movement had a value by virtue of its foresight. It showed that intellect, in France, wanted to find greatness. We need not be astonished that numerous anarchists threw themselves into a revolutionary syndicalism, which appeared to them to offer the possibility of realizing greatness.

In May 1899, I published in *Rivista italiana di sociologia* an article on Marxism and social science. I ended it by expressing the wish that socialism be transformed into a moral philosophy. This change would have infused with greatness a movement that at that time lacked it almost to the same degree as democracy itself. Only several years later was I able to outline a solution to the problem I had posed: the *Reflections on Violence* is a moral philosophy based on the observation of what took place in revolutionary syndicalism. It is hardly necessary to say that this book has remained unintelligible to democrats and, in general, to all people who do not understand the laws of greatness and decline.

The present time is not favorable to the idea of grandeur, but other times will come. History teaches us that greatness cannot be absent indefinitely in that part of mankind which possesses the incomparable treasures of classical culture[53] and the Christian tradition. While waiting for the days of awakening, men who are aware ought to work toward becoming enlightened, disciplining their minds, and cultivating the most noble qualities of their souls,[54] without worrying about what democratic mediocrity will think of them.[55]

---

[53] We know what importance Proudhon attached to classical culture.

[54] This is why Proudhon ought to be regarded as a master whose glory, without doubt, is destined to grow a great deal.

[55] While completing the correction of the proofs on this book, I am reminded of a letter in which Flaubert expressed the hatred he felt for the prevailing mediocrity. In 1852 he wrote that he wanted to compose a dictionary of accepted ideas: "The preface in particular excites me strongly; it would be the historical glorification of everything that is approved. In it I would demonstrate that majorities have always been right while minorities have always been wrong. I would sacrifice all the great men to all the imbeciles. . . . Thus, for literature, I would establish . . . that mediocrity, being within everyone's reach, is alone legitimate and that it is necessary thus to banish every form of originality as dangerous, stupid, etc. . . . From this line of argument, I would arrive at the modern democratic idea of equality" (*Correspondance*, II, 157–158).

CHAPTER VII

The Advance toward Socialism[1]

I. *The three types of capitalism. Usury. Commerce. Supremacy of industry. Simultaneity or succession. Hegelian bias of Marx.*

II. *Manufacturing. Reduction of the worker to the role of insect. Marx's free cooperation. Vocational education.*

III. *Stages of capitalism traced by Kautsky. Trusts and cartels according to Paul de Rousiers. The American's penchant for isolation. Illusion of the trusts. Trusts and socialism.*

IV. *The conditions under which Marx's predictions are relevant. Inefficacy of social democracy. Disintegration according to Proudhon. Rebirth of socialism under the influence of Bolshevik ideas.*

 I

The ideas expressed by Marx on the advance toward socialism are closely connected with the considerations I have presented on historical evolution (pp. 130–137). Until the past few years they were thought to be of interest only to the commentators of *Capital*; today they play an important role in discussions that have been begun on the historic legitimacy of Bolshevism. Lenin is violently accused by the mediocre experts of social democracy of acting in contempt of laws Marx supposedly established. There is thus a serious practical interest in examining the economic stages in the advance toward socialism.

---

[1] This chapter was written in September 1920. I have abundantly used ideas that I had put forth in the *Saggi di critica del marxismo* ("Critical Essays on Marxism") and in the *Insegnamenti sociali della economia contemporanea*; but Sec. IV is new. [The chapter was presented as an appendix in the original French.—*Trans.*]

According to Marx there are three types of capitalism. "Usury and commercial capital are secondary forms present in history before capital in its fundamental form, which determines the economic organization of modern society."[2] Elsewhere he calls them the two brothers.[3] And here is another essential text: "In precapitalist society the usurer can take possession of everything that surpasses what is absolutely necessary to the existence of the one to whom he loans. . . . The usurer capitalist [can then] take possession of the total surplus value; the result is that usury capital paralyzes the productive forces instead of developing them and perpetuates the miserable situation in which, contrary to what happens under capitalist production, the social productivity of work is incapable of developing by means of work at the expense of work itself."[4]

Earlier philosophers were not in a position to reproach usury capitalism the way Marx does; they thought that interest constituted an economic paradox that could not be legitimized according to the principles of societies of workers, artisans, or small merchants, for the production of usury profit does not appeal to the responsibility of man.[5] The usurer very much resembles the keeper of a gambling house: the latter speculates on the folly of customers who, after having lost, persist in trying their luck in the hope that the future will bring them the means of restoring their loss. The usurer speculates on the naïveté of poor people who imagine that by causing themselves much privation they will succeed in reimbursing, even with large additional charges, the loan the capitalist makes them in order to permit them to await the sale of their products. One of the

---

[2] Karl Marx, *Capital*, I, 70. It is a general principle in the Marxist theory of knowledge that the phenomena on which scientific explanation is based appear last (*ibid.*, I, 30, col. 1). In the same order of ideas, Marx writes: "The problem comes forth simultaneously with the means of resolving it" (p. 36, col. 1). When one admits this principle, one must find very naive the contention of the Neo-Scholastics that an eternal philosophy can be founded on the small quantity of data that Aristotle and St. Thomas had at their disposal.

[3] Marx, *Capital*, III, pt. ii, 164.

[4] Marx, *Capital*, III, pt. ii, 166–167. Industrial capitalism never ceases in increasing its equipment—a state that permits it to increase its profit and often also to dominate the worker more completely.

[5] A popular Greek theme established a connection between the generating of gold by usury and the production of the precious metal that was attributed to the sun; thus was introduced a materialism difficult to reconcile with the tendencies of post-Socratic philosophy.

most opprobrious practices of the usurer is the forcing of payment of debts in times when economic difficulties overwhelm the debtor. The usurer can then either make him accept more inequitable contracts or even seize his wages.

When the usurer limits himself to helping a prosperous business instead of tyrannizing peasants and artisans, he quickly acquires the respectability that the metropolises (especially the seaboard ones) concede to the great merchant himself. Moralists go to great lengths to justify his operations.[6] Finally, there comes a time when politicians, enlightened by the economists, regard as an accomplishment of the greatest social utility the establishment of banks that, as a matter of course, put capital at the service of business.[7]

In countries where economic activity is weakening, we see a remarkable resurgence of usury capitalism. It finances the operations of foreigners who are less lethargic than the natives of the country. France has often been reproached for being more concerned with lending its money than investing it in native industries. It is good to study modern history from this point of view: "The depradations and violence of the Venetians," says Marx, "form one of the bases of the abundance of capital in the Netherlands, to whom Venice in its decline lent substantial amounts. In its turn Holland, fallen from its industrial and commercial supremacy near the end of the seventeenth century, saw itself compelled to make its great capital productive by lending it abroad, and from 1701 to 1776 particularly in England, its victorious rival. And the same situation now exists with regard to England and the United States."[8]

The present-day swindlers of the stock exchanges are not unlike the old usurers: they exploit in the well-to-do bourgeois the same illusions that put the poor people at the mercy of the rapacious money-holders. The great material differences between these opera-

---

[6] Marx, *Capital*, III, ii, 165.

[7] The creation of the Bank of England in 1694 was regarded as a masterpiece that resulted in making userers' operations less profitable (Marx, *Capital*, III, ii, 176).

[8] Marx, *Capital*, I, 338, col. 1. A stockbroker in New York said to Paul de Rousiers: "Associations of small English capitalists come here to buy already established and operating industries, breweries, packing houses, etc., but the money they bring is used by the Americans to set up new businesses under the form of private firms; the creative talent remains individual" (*La Vie américaine. Ranches, fermes et usines* ["American Life: Ranches, Farms, and Factories"], p. 350).

tions should not prevent us from recognizing their psychological similarities. The stock market is a true gambling house, where the most fantastic hopes are stimulated in actuality for the sole profit of the speculator, who does not share the hopes. The promoters have the habit of introducing shares at a price appreciably higher than their face value, and the good bourgeois, who has spent his life in saving, lets himself be trapped by misleading promises. On the faith of misleading brochures, he imagines that the future will bring enormous profits.[9] As the financial markets often undergo sudden changes, the great speculators have many opportunities to put in their own coffers the shares that they covet and that enable them to control the best businesses.

Formerly there were many rather unsuccessful laws against usurers. The modern laws that aim to regulate the operations of the stock market do not seem to have had very good results up to now. It does not seem likely that the swindlers can be prevented from deceiving their victims by means of very cleverly worded prospectuses. The only effective thing the state has succeeded in doing up until now has been to intervene in times of crisis to aid the large banks in cooperating to limit the effects of disasters.[10]

We can say that, as usury plays on the fantasies of its victims, fantasies which are basically identical in the most enlightened bourgeois and in the most backward people, in the same way commerce plays on probable increases in price. The price might appreciate because of different locales (between which transport of merchandise would be established), seasonal differences (which the storming of goods makes ideally contemporary in the books of commerce), or different ways of presenting articles to the public (in wholesale or retail form, for example).

---

[9] The huge gains realized on the shares of the Suez Canal have contributed a great deal toward turning the heads of that segment of the bourgeoisie least disposed by its habits to launch out into risky operations. It does not matter that de Lesseps committed the most extravagant madness in his Panama venture—he was always the great Frenchman, the glorious piercer of isthmuses, the man who made the name of his native land shine throughout the world. This adventure is all the more strange because the reputable Paris banks gave it only feeble support.

[10] In general, the large banks with huge capital do not indulge much in speculation, a practice that could compromise the absolute confidence that the public must have in them. We could thus say that they play a moderating role on the stock markets, as formerly they moderated the demands of the old usurers. The swindlers often start periodicals to attack our powerful banks, which stand in their way. Thus we must be wary of the campaigns led against these institutions.

Usury and commerce have many points in common; I will point out a few that are very obvious. In general, they do not create very lasting establishments. It is rather rare that the son of a usurer or merchant possesses the quality of sangfroid, of proper appreciation of the probabilities, or of constant attention to business which has assured the successes of the founder of the enterprise. The children almost always are ruined by wanting to live like aristocrats. Factories, on the other hand, thanks to a bureaucratic organization always being perfected, can continue to prosper after the disappearance of the founder. In order to make large profits, the usurer and the merchant need high prices.[11] That is why mortgagors demand protective rights. The American trusts and the German cartels have contributed very much to causing the increase in tariffs. The usurer and the merchant often undertake to bring about scarcity so as artificially to create high prices.[12] The true nature of capitalist industry is to create abundance; thus is affirmed in a very clear way the opposition between industrial capitalism and the old capitalisms.

"Before capitalist production, it was commerce that dominated industry; the reverse is true in modern society," says Marx.[13] And a little above he writes: "The law according to which the autonomous development of commercial capital is in inverse proportion to the development of capitalist production can be seen most clearly in peoples whose commerce consisted in carrying trade. The Venetians, Genoans, and Dutch realized a profit, not by exporting their own products, but above all, by assuring trade between nations or communities that were only slightly developed commercially and economically; consequently, by exploiting the producing countries. Their commercial capital had an existence independent of and clearly separate from the branches of production to which it served as intermediary. The monopoly of this role of intermediary and the trade to which it gave rise declined in proportion as the peoples on whose exploitation it lived developed economically. This fact

---

[11] In the middle of the 19th century, many old commercial houses abandoned business in France because large banks started to practice discounts, railroad and steamship companies offered their services to everyone, and transport fees were reduced. Formerly, by contrast, long-distance transport had been difficult to organize, and the rebates had been qualified by a thousand precautions.

[12] According to King's law, a deficit of 10 percent would increase the unit price by 30 percent and the total value by nearly 12 percent.

[13] Marx, *Capital*, III, pt. i, 363.

that is indicated, not only by the falling off of several branches of commerce, but also by the decline of purely commercial states, proves incontestably that the development of capitalist production results in the subordination of commercial capital to industrial capital."[14]

Thus is established the Marxist view of the progression of capitalism starting from usury, developing through commerce, and culminating in large-scale modern production. We should now ask ourselves an important question about which orthodox interpreters of Marx do not seem to be too much concerned: should the three stages be considered as successive (or at least designed to push former stages back into a region of historical impotence), or rather should they be considered as capable of indefinitely preserving their right to existence, conditions of which being determined by national events?

We know that a similar problem divides the interpreters of Hegel: same say that, according to the sage of Berlin, the first two forms of the free spirit (art and religion) must disappear when philosophy is entirely developed;[15] others maintain that art, religion, and philosophy can coexist. Marx accepted the first interpretation, for we read in *Capital*: "The religious world is only the reflection of the real world. . . . The religious reflection of the real world can only disappear when the conditions of work and practical life present man with clear and rational relations with his fellow men and with nature."[16] Thus Marx obviously supposes that the philosophies of spirit and nature, as conceived by Hegel, would be called on to reveal themselves completely at the expense of religion.

This interpretation of Hegelian thought led Marx in *Critique of the Gotha Program* (1875) to forecast that at the end of the overthrow of the capitalist regime there would arise first an order under

---

[14] *Ibid.*, III, pt. i, 361–362. This development still finds expression in the history of England by the fact that "the merchant class and the mercantile cities were politically reactionary and allied with the landed and financial aristocracy against industrial capital. To be convinced of this, one must only compare the political role of Liverpool to that of Manchester and Birmingham. The mercantile capitalists and the English moneyed interests (finance aristocracy) refused to bow to the facts and did not recognize the supremacy of industrial capital until the suppression of the Corn Laws" (p. 360).

[15] This first interpretation has been adopted by Benedetto Croce, *Ce qui est vivant et ce qui est mort dans la philosophie de Hegel* ("What is Living and What is Dead in the Philosophy of Hegel"), p. 106.

[16] Marx, *Capital*, I, 31, col. 2.

which would reign the so-called collectivist principle, according to which each producer would receive a remuneration proportional to his work, and then a communist regime, under which each citizen would be able to satisfy his needs. Those are personal opinions that could be discussed endlessly. It should be observed, however, that the Marxian concept of the free spirit has all the findings of history against it; all evidence tends to show that art and religion are not destined to disappear. Saverio Merlino was thus justified in maintaining that the collectivist and communist principles are not mutually exclusive and that both are destined to be found in capitalist society, since all nations are undertaking social reforms.[17]

The same Hegelian biases inspired in Marx the idea of a technological development in modern production resulting in the disappearance of small enterprises, which would be crushed by industrial giants. It is certain that, in many cases, industrial concentration represents a superior stage in technology. But I have said earlier (p. 154) that the Marxists generally failed to examine the basis for this superiority.[18] They reasoned in an abstract way in admitting the superiority of what impressed them by the enormity of its dimensions. The socialists seem to be in agreement today in recognizing that concentration does not make sense for agriculture as it does for metallurgy. But by the way in which they talk of small rural property, it is obvious that they understand very little about the reasons for its prosperity: they remain slaves to the biases that Marx had borrowed from Hegelian teachings, whose nature they do not understand.

The biological idea found in the romantic notion of evolution makes any return to the early forms of society improbable.[19] Marx

---

[17] Saverio Merlino, *Formes et essence du socialisme*. The French edition is of 1898. The socialists who rejected Marx's catastrophic theory should have eagerly accepted the doctrines of Saverio Merlino, but our "reformists" were not intelligent enough to understand the ideas of the Italian socialist.

[18] This superiority is remarkable, as I have said on p. 154, whenever one wants to conserve heat. This is a point to which I have often called attention.

[19] The obstinacy with which Kautsky defended the law of increasing proletarianization results from the fact that he did not want to admit a setback to a social organization, which Marx pointed out as forming an important step in the march toward socialism. In *The Poverty of Philosophy*, Marx says that cotton has driven out wool and linen; potatoes, bread; spirits, wine; and that "cotton, potatoes, and spirits are the pivots of bourgeois society" (p. 82). Probably he regarded the usage of these three products of inferior quality as characterizing an irreversible step of bourgeois evolution.

thought that, when production had reached the stage where commerce is subordinated to industry, the forms he called antediluvian would never again appear in a country in the course of serious progress. In America, however, we have seen usury conquer under the name of trusts a large place in the economy. He never would have thought that the great factories could be replaced by the work of small family workshops; at the present time, however, we wonder if the use of small electric motors is not likely to produce (in certain regions at least) this transformation.[20] It is advisable to make a less rigid model of capitalism than Marx has done.

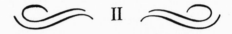

We are now going to examine how Marx understood the development of the organization of work in modern times.

At the very beginning, merchants bought the raw materials and entrusted them to family workshops for a scale of charges which gave rise to great dispute due to the bad faith of the entrepreneurs.[21] Then they sold them, sometimes in the regional open markets, sometimes to powerful merchants established in the commercial centers. This regime, to which Le Play gave the name of the regime of "collective manufacture," shows in a particularly crude manner the role of commerce in this old-fashioned industry. The merchant (who is usually called a manufacturer, although he manufactures nothing) is the man who does the thinking for a whole group of producers, whose horizon is limited to the execution of manual operations.

An immense social revolution was accomplished when the entrepreneurs of collective manufactures united the formerly scattered workshops into one factory. The old artisans did not let themselves be conquered easily. "The small textile producers of Leeds as late

---

[20] Reuleaux long ago affirmed that engines using hot air, waterfalls, or gasoline, and easily usable in applications of from 1 to 3 horsepower, should be included "among the most important modern machines and regarded as carrying the seed of a complete transformation of a part of industry" that would return to a regime of craftsmen (*Cinématique*, pp. 559–561).

[21] Intentional errors on the measurement of yarn and the arbitrary appraisal of defects gave rise to scandalous abuses that provoked worker revolts several times.

as 1794 sent a petition to Parliament demanding a law to forbid all merchants from becoming manufacturers. Thus the new manufacturing concerns were established by preference in ports, export centers, or places in the interior situated outside of the control of the municipal regime and its trade guilds. Henceforth there was a desperate battle in England between the old privileged towns (corporate towns) and these new seedbeds of industry."[22] The producers who had acquired their right to work according to the old laws of apprenticeship found it intolerable that men without any technical qualification should compete with them.

For a very long time the chief question for the leaders of industry was to obtain an iron discipline, to which the working classes opposed the most stubborn resistance. Thus it was not surprising if at the head of these establishments were often placed men without any technical knowledge but endowed with those qualities of command one so often sees among officers who have come up from the ranks. Severe regulations were established to punish by heavy fines every violation of the regulations, however small. The application of the detail of this private legislation was entrusted to foremen who abused their power like real noncommissioned officers of disciplinary companies. For a century, all the literature relating to industry has been full of the laments of humanitarians who are shocked by a system so little worthy of nations that, in their constitutions, seem most concerned with assuring liberty to all their citizens. This reigning system is what I call "forced cooperation"; it is opposed in a very clear way to the free cooperation of which Marx dreamed.

"Ignorance is the mother of industry as well as of superstition," wrote Adam Ferguson, the teacher of Adam Smith. "Thought and imagination are liable to be lost for a moment, but the habit of moving one's foot or hand depends on neither. Thus we could say that perfection with regard to manufacturing consists in being able to do without the mind so that, without any intellectual effort, the workshop can be considered as a machine whose parts are men."[23] The advance of the worker toward a completely mindless life seems to be the ideal of the leaders of this forced cooperation. The skill

---

[22] Marx, *Capital*, I, 336, col. 1.
[23] Reported by Marx, *ibid.*, I, 157, col. 1.

the worker acquires can, in the long run, be compared reasonably enough to the instinct of an insect.[24] The stupefaction of the people was so well regarded as the normal rule in modern times that the first French translator of Adam Smith found unfortunate the latter's idea of combatting by education the disadvantages presented by the division of labor.[25]

More than once I have explained the reason for the success of the division of labor in manufacturing. Since it was not yet possible to construct rapid and precise machinery, it was necessary to have men trained to a very advanced degree of automation, carrying out what mechanical devices could not yet do. Provided that tasks were reduced to a little movement of the hand or foot, one could succeed in obtaining a prompt and exact execution when habit had surpassed all thought. Man had also passed from the sphere of intelligence to that of instinct, yet naturalists are always astonished in discovering the extreme perfection with which an insect executes the tasks ordered by instinct. One could say that this system of production illustrates in an amazing way the theories of Bergson on intelligence and instinct.[26]

In contrast to this system let us reproduce the sketch of free cooperation Marx made on the page of *Capital* where he speaks of the disappearance of religion: "Social life, of which material production and the relationships that it implies form the base,[27] will not be disengaged from the mystical cloud that veils its appearance until the day when we will see the work of freely associated men acting consciously and masters of their own social movement."[28] It is not by promulgating laws that we can attain such a state; it is not a matter of giving men the power of association according to their whim.[29] But it is necessary to lead the producers to think without ever being

---

[24] Marx compares the Indian weaver to a spider (*ibid.*, I, 148, col. 1).

[25] Marx, *Capital*, I, 157, col. 2.

[26] The training in sports also aims to lead men to carry out movements with a mechanical precision and rapidity. They mechanize the individual and can only succeed if the intellectual faculties are more or less extinguished. It has already been observed that sports are not very favorable to intelligence, but I believe the reason for this vice has not been given.

[27] Marx obviously alludes here to juridical and political relationships.

[28] Marx, *Capital*, I, 31, col. 2.

[29] Marx would certainly not have approved this declaration of Ledru-Rolin which Proudhon reports at the end of the first part of *L'Avertissement aux propriétaires* ("Notice To Property Owners"): "If, after the electoral reform the people are still unhappy, they will no longer have the right to complain."

slaves to errors of reasoning, prejudices, or instincts.[30] We should not take Marx's text entirely literally; in this instance, as in many others, he wrote under the influence of Hegelian ideas. In order to be usefully applied, his words should be interpreted; one must understand that the socialist workshop would bring together producers whose minds would always be alert to criticize the techniques being learned, who would be guided by foremen similar to assistants of chemistry professors and who would be supervised by engineers who would speak to their men as a teacher speaks to his pupils.

In order to arrive at this economic state, production will have to have acquired the qualities that the progressive workshop develops under the capitalist system. This scientific cooperation calls for workers who have received a good vocational education; gives them as direct bosses foremen capable of taking hold of the smallest idea for improvement thought of by the workers, conveying them to the less skillful men and thus accumulating the very small progress of experience; and puts at the head of the factory engineers whose ability is quickly recognized by everyone. Marx has defined in strong terms the opposition between this cooperation and that which industry has created: "Large industry obliges society under the pain of death to replace the fragmented individual, burdened by a productive function of detail, by the integral individual who will know how to handle the most diverse necessities of work and in various functions gives a free scope to the diversity of his natural or acquired capacities." From instinct, then, we revert to intelligence.

Marx complained that the bourgeoisie, which created polytechnical, agricultural, and other schools for its children, has given the proletariat only a mere shadow of vocational education. He hoped that by dint of the increasing political influence of the working classes, "the teaching of technology, in both theory and practice, would be introduced into the schools of the masses,"[31] and he added this important reflection: "It is without doubt that such ferments of transformation, whose end is the suppression of the former divi-

---

[30] In Marx, liberty is always more or less synonymous with rationality; Engels said that by means of the social revolution the world will pass from the reign of fatality to the reign of liberty. This means that rationality will succeed irrationality.

[31] Marx says in a footnote that productive work should not be separated from education.

sion of labor,[32] are in flagrant contradiction to the capitalistic system of industry and the economic condition in which it places the worker. But the only true way by which a mode of production and its corresponding social organization advance toward their dissolution and metamorphosis is by the historical development of their innate conflicts."[33] There is no better way of pointing out the importance of the role vocational education must play in the march toward socialism.

In *Matériaux d'une théorie du prolétariat*, I have tried to give a sketch of what mass education could be in line with modern needs. The most difficult problem seems to be that of perfecting the men to whom supervision is entrusted. It would be necessary for foremen to have the qualities of observation found in the best laboratory workers. One cannot succeed in the first attempt at forming a good overseer. Consequently, it has been asserted that schools do not produce good results for these "noncoms" of industry; it would be preferable that they be forced to work all their life.[34]

It is generally thought today that the preparation of engineers is greatly in need of improvement.[35] I doubt that we are arriving at significant results in France, because our experience with the history of the polytechnical school is not encouraging. At the end of the eighteenth century, military engineers who through the fortunes of revolution had participated in the dictatorship of the Convention wanted to create an institution intended to teach the ideas on which they had been nourished during their years of apprenticeship. But the men who represented their tradition were persecuted by the pure scholars, in whose eyes there is nothing superior to the art of playing with intricate mathematical functions. Today, Carnot's institution exists only in name. A known popularizer, despairing

---

[32] By this we should understand that the enslavement of the alienated workers, who have been reduced to the role of insects, would disappear—instinct having given way to the intelligence formerly monopolized by the owners.

[33] Marx, *Capital*, I, 211.

[34] Elsewhere I have said that all the supervisors and workers are compelled to undergo perpetual apprenticeship in an industry in progress (Georges Sorel, *Matériaux d'une théorie du prolétariat* ["Materials of a Theory of the Proletariat"; Paris: Marcel Rivière, 1919], p. 137). The foremen have more trouble in accepting this condition than the engineers and workers.

[35] At the end of 1919 an engineer in a chemical products factory whom I know to have an extremely prudent mind wrote to me: "As for the supervisors of production (of which I am one), their ignorance is so widespread that in reality they are only nominal bosses who let themselves be reduced to the routine and sometimes excellent methods of the older workers, who are the mainstays of the factory."

of our country ever rising to the technological level of Germany, asked that the defeated be forbidden to develop their scientific learning establishments to the same level as before (*Effort*, April 5, 1919). I am persuaded that if we have wanted to occupy the left bank of the Rhine for fifteen years, it is much less in consideration of military guarantees than in the hope of *stealing* manufacturing secrets from the Germans.[36]

At the time of the old systems of cooperation, work was conducted under the supervision of leaders who monopolized all thinking; to the degree in which the merchant character of industry disappears, however, this situation is only maintained by routine. And, often, the former role of the merchant-masters of production is held by men who are only good at acting the part of important personnages. Adapting St. Simon's famous parable to the present, I will say that all of the administrators of our railways, of Saint-Gobain, or of the coal mines could be dismissed without having the production cost of the merchandise go up one penny. These proud official representatives of economic France are as useless as the members of the *Académie française*, the sociologists, and the heroes of the national defense.

There is no scarcity of bourgeois representatives who maintain that the Russian Revolution proved that a country can not do without intellectuals; they say that Lenin had to offer substantial salaries to the organizers of the enterprises he wanted to revive and to engineers and foreign specialists of all kinds. But I have not heard it said that he felt the need of appealing to the intellectual powers of the deputies of the Duma, to the financiers who formerly established the connection between the Russian treasury and the financial community in Paris, or to the innumerable Jouhaux who offer themselves so generously everywhere in order to restore the economy of Europe.[37] Thus I believe I was correct in maintaining in the *Avenir socialiste des syndicats* that socialism would be a catastrophe for the intellectuals.

---

[36] The *Débats* of October 31, 1920, complain of the English General Masterman, who does not permit French officers to obtain access to the workshops where German airplane builders are applying or studying secret procedures.

[37] The seriousness with which this general secretary of the General Confederation of Labor plays his role of busybody, makes him a noteworthy example. His enemies accuse him of betrayal, but certainly they are wrong; it is not easy for a former worker to preserve his composure when so many bourgeois tell him that he is called on to be one of the saviors of France.

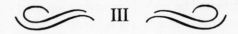

In 1912 Kautsky presented ideas on the development of capitalism
which are in complete contradiction to those of his master. Marx
had taught that England was the classic country for the modern
economy and consequently the one in which it was possible to find
facts useful for developing theories; going much further, he had
dared to write that "the most industrially developed country only
serves to show to those who follow it on the industrial path the
image on their own future."[38] As a result industrial capital was destined to prevail everywhere, just as Marx observed it happening in
England shortly after the middle of the nineteenth century. On the
other hand, Kautsky maintains that England has ceased to be the
classic land of capitalism, that Germany and America are developing
with much more vigor, and that it is in these two latter countries
that one must study the future of England.[39] The experience of the
trusts shows that high finance is each day becoming more the master
of industry;[40] it supports militarism, the politics of violence at home
and abroad, and the struggle against the working classes. Thus we
would be mistaken to expect a progressive reduction of social conflicts similar to that which took place in England in the time of
Gladstone.[41]

Immediately we notice something paradoxical in Kautsky's doctrine; he conceives the future of the country in which industry has
made the boldest development in terms of the remnants of Prussian
feudalism: "The great landed interests today are enthusiastically
in favor of strong power—if possible, monarchical; as court nobility
they think they can exercise personal influence on the monarch and
through him the government. They are crazy about militarism, for

---

[38] Marx, *Capital*, I, 10.
[39] Kautsky, *La Révolution sociale* ("The Social Revolution"), pp. 79, 81.
[40] *Ibid.*, pp. 76–78.
[41] Kautsky, *La Révolution sociale*, p. 82. Here Kautsky contrasts Chamberlain
and Gladstone. But is not the former the representative of metallurgical, rather
than financial, industrialists? It seems very probable that the English metallurgists
had a large responsibility in Japan's 1904 decision to enter abruptly into war against
Russia. The cotton manufacturers, on the contrary, were pacifist.

it opens to their children the career of officer to which the sons of bourgeois seem less suited. Thus they constantly recommend a violent policy at home and abroad. Likewise, high finance is very predisposed to favor militarism, a strong government, and a policy of war. It has nothing to fear from a strong power independent from the parliament and the people; it controls this power by personal influence exerted at the court, and besides, the power is its debtor. Men of money do not see militarism with an indifferent eye: public debts are viewed by them not only as creditors, but also as providers of the state."[42] It is extremely difficult to believe that America, or even England, resembles the picture drawn by Kautsky.[43] I will limit myself to examining here what he says about the new forms of the capitalist economy.

According to this expert on social democracy, the German cartels and the American trusts belong to the same economic type. This is not the opinion of Paul de Rousiers, who is an excellent observer. In his view, the cartels were born out of reasons of a commercial nature: to avoid the lowering of prices by the overproduction of a factory directed too boldly; to better the utilization of transport systems that would no longer encroach on one another's territory; to conduct a joint search for new trade outlets.[44] "The realization of common interests among several producers would inevitably result in the formation of a highly disciplined association, assuring the defense of these interests in return for exact obedience."[45] Many times in his book Paul de Rousiers returns to the fundamental psychological principle of the cartels: this "conservative character [of the Germans] disposed to compromises, concerned with security rather than triumph."[46] "The moderation of the German character would not suffice to assure the survival of these leagues of producers

[42] Kautsky, *La Révolution sociale*, pp. 74–75.

[43] Kautsky does not dare to predict that America will imitate Germany, but he wrongly believes that England is imitating the Prussian policy in Ireland. It does not seem to me that the social policy of the English was brought about for the same reasons as that of the Germans. Kautsky says: "Only one trait mars this description: the English army is not yet organized in the Prussian way" (*ibid.*, p. 81). The analogies are very secondary.

[44] Paul de Rousiers, *Les Syndicats industriels* ("Industrial Unions"), pp. 272–276. This author points out the difficulty of establishing cartels in branches that do not manufacture mass consumer goods, because these branches are dependent on the whims of the buyers.

[45] Paul de Rousiers, *Les Syndicats*, p. 279.

[46] *Ibid.*, p. 136.

if the spirit of discipline—of a meticulous and exact discipline—did not reign among the members. Here again we find the effect of the social habits of a nation."[47]

Paul de Rousiers contrasts the cartel and the trust in an unusually clear way. "The former," he says, "is a league of allies in which each one preserves a certain liberty of action, but forbids himself the usage of certain weapons against the others. It represents a temperament more or less brought out in the economic struggle. On the other hand, the trust is the result of a struggle to the death. One is the German solution, the other the American solution of a problem posed in Germany as in America by the industrial system. . . . These two solutions are as different from each other as the economic, social, and political conditions of the German empire are different from the economic, political, and social conditions of the American republic. They are not of the same nature."[48] "On the one side, there is defense of common interests; on the other, domination, a despotic domination over the members of the trust and enterprising against the nonmembers. The German remains moderate; he does not dream of resounding triumph. . . . The American is ambitious, ambitious of power much more still than money, which he loves as a conqueror loves his troops and his cannons, because it assures him power. The trust is an instrument of domination for him. The difference between the cartels and the trusts is not a difference of degree, as is often said, it is a difference in kind."[49] I believe the trust is related to usury capitalism[50] and the cartels to commercial capitalism.

In order to understand fully the procedures followed by the Americans in the conduct of their affairs we must remind ourselves often that these are men of the independent sort. "The American of Anglo-Saxon origin," says Paul de Rousiers, "is self-sufficient, and if he likes the company of others this liking is limited to his home, that is, to his wife and children. . . . Neither his sisters, brothers, nor cousins are, for him, anything else but neighbors.[51] He does not have

---

[47] *Ibid.*, p. 160.
[48] *Ibid.*, p. 125.
[49] *Ibid.*, p. 108.
[50] Kautsky rightly says: "The financial capitalist is the old userer in a more modern form" (*La Révolution sociale*, p. 74).
[51] Paul de Rousiers observes humorously: "The neighbor whom one should love as himself, but of whom, because of the weakness of human nature, one always thinks of much less than oneself" (*La Vie américaine. Ranches, fermes et usines*, p. 137).

the clannish spirit that characterizes certain peoples of Europe; he does not feel any particular attachment to his relatives."[52] And even more, he habituates his children to fend for themselves at a very early age, to prepare themselves to try their luck, so well that many Frenchmen established in the United States reproach the Yankee fathers for their selfishness.[53] The rural life predominant for such a long time in America favored this spirit of isolation. "Formerly the nation, almost entirely agricultural, was comprised almost totally of independent landowners: few tenant farmers, few large fortunes, many farmers; such was New England then.[54] We have seen in certain states of the West very similar conditions. Independence was the normal condition.[55] The old character still exists in the new states because they are settled under the leadership of Yankees. "The large landowner of the West nine times out of ten comes from the eastern states; he is a Yankee who has made himself a farmer, perhaps only temporarily. . . . It is he who upholds the American tradition and imposes it on the incoming group."[56] "What sustains the Americans in these enterprises so full of hardship is the innate love of independence. In order to succeed in becoming their own masters, in living in their own house, they accept everything—solitude, absence of the most elementary comfort, and the dangers of a wandering life in an uninhabited region."[57] I think one could say the American population preserves to an extraordinary extent the peasant qualities of being combative and dominating, which give it a certain similarity to the old equestrian orders. An old Civil War colonel expressed the same opinion when he declared to Paul de Rousiers: "We are an imperious race."[58]

The instinct of association is very old in Germany and is directly

---

[52] *Ibid.* On page 145 he says that the American phrase "Home, sweet home" can be interpreted by this phrase: "It is so pleasant not to be in someone else's home."

[53] *Ibid.*, p. 139, and *La Vie américaine. L'Education et la société* ("American Life: Education and Society"), pp. 9–10.

[54] Many Americans in these old states still have a taste for farming today (Paul de Rousiers, *La Vie américaine. Ranches, fermes et usines*, p. 265).

[55] Paul de Rousiers, *La Vie américaine. Ranches, fermes et usines*, p. 281.

[56] *Ibid.*, p. 111. Cf. p. 121.

[57] *Ibid.*, p. 144.

[58] Elsewhere, he finds the United States a "country of intense struggles, indomitable energy, and excessive ambitions" (*Les Syndicats industriels*, p. 278). We should not neglect the spirit of national exclusiveness, which originates from the Puritans and which, according to Paul de Rousiers, explains the harshness with which the North treated the South as well as the illusions that make protectionism so easily accepted (*La Vie américaine. Ranches, fermes et usines*, p. 318).

opposed to the quasi-feudal sentiments of the Yankee; historically the instinct of association seems to be connected to customs of serfdom.[59] The extreme discipline always exercised by the German state has only served to develop ideas of individual weakness, submission, and moderation in ambition which Paul de Rousiers points out as characteristic of the cartels. The history of Andrew Carnegie is particularly suited to show the contrasting feudal character of the trusts. American industrialists who wanted to make agreements with him "sometimes perceived that they had promoted his schemes without participating in his profits."[60] With such a man, born for domination, there is no possible equitable association. I believe that the preceding explanations are sufficient to show that trusts and cartels have as their foundation historic national conditions. Thus, they cannot be thought of in abstract terms as economic systems capable of universal application.

The large American bankers have an obvious interest in making their customers believe that trusts represent the best type of industry. In this way, they can widely practice what economists in their country call "watering." They take advantage of the illusions of small capitalists in issuing many more shares of stock than necessary. They create two types of stock: preferred stock generally receives an advantage of 7 percent before other stock is paid, and if there is a year when the profits do not allow giving them this remuneration the holders of these stocks exercise their rights on the profits of following years. The common stock receives something when the masters of the trust believe it useful to interest the public in speculating on this paper. The preferred stock serves to pay the industrialists whose companies are bought; the common stock is supposed to represent "the savings due to consolidation."[61] Thus the speculators must urge their publicists to entice the public by these problematic savings.

---

[59] The spirit of association is highly developed in America, but it is not related to serfdom, or the convent life, or military custom. No one abandons his personality in the American association, which obtains such a remarkable success in the pursuit of the public good.

[60] Paul de Rousiers, *Les Syndicats*, p. 80.

[61] Paul de Rousiers, *Les Syndicats*, pp. 85–87. The administrators are often disposed to use the sums that should revert to the common stock for expenses destined to increase productive capacity. In July 1900 the best common stocks of the metallurgical group (those of the iron-wire trust) were assessed at $32; two years previously, they had been issued at $100 (pp. 87–88).

This literature succeeds rather well because the American is very easily dazzled by the colossal. When Paul de Rousiers visited the United States for the first time people spoke to him with admiration about mammoth farms where wheat was cultivated by the methods of large industry; after many peregrinations he ended up by discovering a farm of 22,000 hectares and one of 16,000. They came from concessions made to railroad companies, and the owners cultivated only a part of them for purposes of advertising in hopes of attracting settlers. On the largest farm only 6,000 hectares had been worked by means of modest horse-drawn ploughs, and this surface was divided into five centers of cultivation.[62]

The Americans have been impressed by the success of the Standard Oil Company and of the sugar trust. They believed too easily that every attempt at large monopoly must produce great benefits: Paul de Rousiers has told how the whiskey and rope trusts lasted only a short time.[63] The success of the sugar trust depends almost entirely on tariffs that prevent foreign competition and on the fact that the bosses had to pay off the politicians very dearly.[64] Havemeyer, who is the mainspring of this monopoly, affirmed before an inquiry commission that the origin of all the trusts was tariff protection.[65] That is surely not the case for the Standard Oil Company. But this company knew how to make arrangements with the railroad companies so that the latter would transport the petroleum of its competitors at a very high price or with great delays, and would not permit pipelines crossing their tracks, which these competitors might be tempted to build.[66]

If we agree with the historical philosophy of Marx, we must say that in spite of all the talk of Kautsky and of the admirers of Pierpont Morgan, the trusts do not characterize an era of superior capitalism unless it can be demonstrated that these organizations, so deplorably usurious, give rise to incontestable progress in the instruments of production. Now here is the opinion of Walker, president of the

---

[62] Paul de Rousiers, *La Vie américaine. Ranches, fermes et usines*, pp. 104–110.
[63] Paul de Rousiers, *Les Industries monopolisées aux Etats-Unis* ("Industrial Monopolies in the United States"), pp. 218–223, 230–239. In the rope trust, the embezzlement of funds was enormous.
[64] Paul de Rousiers, *La Vie américaine. Ranches, fermes et usines*, pp. 324–325.
[65] Paul de Rousiers, *Les Syndicats*, p. 41.
[66] Paul de Rousiers, *Les Industries monopolisées aux Etats-Unis*, pp. 39–54.

Massachusetts Institute of Technology: "The trusts destroy competition and the 'invention-power' of the people. I consider them
absolutely pernicious. They constitute a veritable tyranny, and
America will rid herself of them as she knows how to rid herself of
all tyrannies. By what means this will take place I do not know, but
I have confidence in the enormous force of public opinion in this
country."[67] Against such an authoritative opinion the admirers of
trusts would have to bring solid proofs, but they have not done so.
In order to utilize all the byproducts of the refining of petroleum,
large establishments are necessary. But it is a long way from such
a concentration to the monopoly of the Standard Oil Company.
We do not see what technical progress an "ocean trust" could introduce into naval art.

Numerous American socialists have greeted the success of the
trusts with enthusiasm because it seemed to them that the trusts
constituted a forward step on the path to the nationalization of the
large industries.[68] The matter seems simple enough to people used
to resolving historical problems with abstract formulas. But when
facts and men are considered such as they are in reality the socialist
beneficence of the trusts no longer seems as evident as it does to
Kautsky. According to Marx's hypothesis the bourgeoisie will de-
liver to the revolution an industry in which the factories will be
subject to truly scientific direction. One can say that in current
scientific work individuals are just about interchangeable. Thus it
will be easy for the socialist regime to maintain good management
over production, thanks to the cooperation of groups whose members will have received a serious scientific education—a management
under which the good methods learned in the schools will be con-
tinuously applied and in which esprit de corps will eliminate the in-
efficient workers. Thus the transition will be brought about by an
economic bridge, whose solidarity we must be careful not to undermine during the years of preparation for socialism. According to
Kautsky's hypothesis this economic bridge does not exist, since until
its dying day industrial capitalism would not be able to give a predominant place to science in its factories. After a system in which
the wills of the imperious masters are made so apparent, only a state

[67] *Ibid.*, p. 5.
[68] *Ibid.*, p. 327.

socialism could succeed[69]—in which politicians would rule in place of financiers. But the men whom the latter had chosen as auxiliaries would certainly not be replaced by bureaucrats to advantage. For a kind of small feudal baron would be substituted people possessing finesse, flexible docility, and contempt of honor, which qualities were formerly displayed by aristocrats protected by the kings.

IV

The preceding considerations tend to show us that the march toward socialism will not come about in a manner as simple, as necessary, and, consequently, as easy to describe in advance as Marx had supposed. Marx's Hegelian leanings led him to admit, without being generally aware of it, that history advances (at least with regard to peoples considered to be blessed with a superior civilization) under the influence of the force of the mysterious *Weltgeist*. This ideal agent imposes on matter the obligation of realizing ends whose logical order is finally discovered by men of genius. Like all romantics, Marx supposed that the *Weltgeist* operated in the heads of his friends. There is a certain amount of truth in this doctrine. Fortunate happenings (which have often been called providential) lend themselves rather well to a division into periods[70] that can be defined, each one by a characteristic that can enter into a logical order. Such an arrangement gives substance to a group of past events that philosophers find too interesting to admit could completely escape

---

[69] In the course of the First World War, the bourgeois governments let themselves blindly create a quantity of institutions that have familiarized populations with the idea of state socialism. It is against state socialism, much more than against capitalism, that true Marxists should battle. This fight is all the more necessary because it cannot be seen how the transition could be made from state socialism to proletarian socialism.

[70] Proudhon wrote to Michelet on January 23, 1860: "We are beginning the second phase of our revolution. I consider the first as having occurred from the time of Voltaire, Rousseau, and Turgot and ending in 1848; from Descartes to Hegel" (*Correspondance*, XIV, 192). The new quality of 1848 would thus come from Hegelian influences; undoubtedly, Proudhon meant here to claim his share in this revival of the revolutionary idea. This is an opinion that must seem very scandalous to our patriotic sociologists, who, since 1914, have never ceased to spew forth curses against the philosophy of Hegel.

the intelligence. But we must be careful not to mistake such scholastic schemes for laws operative in the future.[71]

The pretension displayed by Marx in speaking scientifically of the march towards socialism is very defensible if, like him, we admit that we are on the eve of a catastrophe that will put an end to the bourgeois regime, whose continuation would cause great social harm. After 1847 capitalism seemed to be so exhausted to Marx that it had become incapable of producing new stages in its economic development. Thus all that could happen until the hour of the revolution must belong to the last of the stages recognized in the study of the past. The utopians, who believed that an ardent sermon by properly cultivating the will of good citizens would lead the world to the realization of fantasies dear to their hearts, seemed to Marx to be ignoramuses incapable of perceiving the forces acting around them. The social mechanisms[72] that were to enter into play at the moment of the revolution and immediately afterwards were those that critical observation could perceive in Marx's own time. To reason on the effects of mechanisms, whose laws were given by the movements of his time seemed to Marx to incontestably comprise a true work of science.

Thirty-five years after the publication of the *Communist Manifesto*, Marx did not yet perceive any essential change in the social economy of Europe. Long before the American trusts were spoken of, the great financiers had gained millions by merging mine companies or railroads. Thus, it was demonstrated that usury capitalism had not spoken its last word. A number of businesses that could have been excellent vegetated as a consequence of the enormous sums levied on them by their organizers. It does not seem that Marx discerned the important reasons that were to give Lassalle's ideas supremacy over his in Germany. He did not understand much about the consequences that followed the end of the War of 1870, which extended to all the countries of Germanic culture the principles of Frederick the Great. These illusions would be difficult to explain if it were not admitted that Marx easily abandoned the terrain of the materialist philosophy of history in order to let himself be guided

---

[71] Cf. what I said above on p. 134 and especially in the *Matériaux d'une théorie du prolétariat* (pp. 23–24).
[72] On social mechanisms, cf. G. Sorel, *ibid.*, p. 80.

by the doctrine of *Weltgeist*. Social mechanisms were no longer empirical data, but agents of the mysterious force of history. There was no longer a need to examine history, since a scholarly study of the past had led to the discovery of the modern method of action of *Weltgeist* without a determination of the duration of this method of action.

The war of 1914 upset every conceivable idea on the future of social democracy. The German army was probably defeated less by the strategy of the generals of the Entente than by the anti-nationalist propaganda that Lord Northcliffe had succeeded in having spread in Germany by independent social democrats.[73] The emperor abandoned the fight without wishing to engage in civil strife, believing that social democracy would be better managed by western democracies than the monarchy of the Hohenzollerns could be. The social democrats believed that they were not buying too dearly the right of making the happiness of the German people by accepting great territorial losses, endless humiliations, and the disappearance of military institutions before which our politicians had so long trembled.[74] From the standpoint of the working class, the record of the socialist government is not brilliant: it massacred masses of workers as Cavaignac had done in 1848 and Thiers in 1871; it signed a treaty that condemned the German proletariat to work, perhaps for a century, in order to enrich the bourgeoisie of France and England. This government does not dare to enter into friendly relations with the Soviet Union because the Entente does not permit it do draw near to Russia. According to the Entente, Russia has the audacity to defy democratic principles. Kautsky, accustomed to making sovereign decisions in international congresses, thought he would be the supreme arbiter of peace, but he fell to the level of a third-rate *folliculaire*. He had to content himself with executing suspicious tasks to suit the enemies of his country and of the proletariat. No one declaims with as much violence against

---

[73] I was told by a Frenchman who had been a prisoner in Germany that from the end of 1917 a military catastrophe could be foretold because authority was no longer respected.

[74] In 1814 and 1815, the Bourbons did not have to undergo as harsh conditions, and yet people never ceased reproaching them for the treaties of Paris as long as they were on the throne. It is this fear of our politicians which explains the rage with which they humiliate a defenseless enemy today.

the Bolsheviks, whom our diplomats are so afraid of seeing appear one day on the Rhine.[75]

So many new things have been introduced into the world that great value can no longer be attached to the categories that, according to Marx, were to remain unchangeable until the revolution. Henceforth, everything is given in to disorder; nothing is necessary any longer; no predictions are possible. I think it is useful to bring to the attention of my readers an important passage from a letter written by Proudhon on October 29, 1860, to a doctor of his region: "Under Louis-Phillippe, social dissolution had already begun, and philosophical minds could not doubt that an immense revolution had commenced. . . . Today civilization is very truly in a crisis of which we can find only one analogy in history: that which determined the rise of Christianity. All traditions are worn out, all beliefs abolished. On the other hand the new program is not *made*: I mean that it has not entered into the conscience of the masses. This is what I call dissolution. It is the most atrocious period in the existence of societies. All factors unite to distress good men: prostitution of conscience, triumph of mediocrity, confusion of truth and falsehood, compromising of principles, baseness of the passions, despicability in customs, suppression of truth, rewards for lying, base flattery, charlatanism, and vice. . . . I have few illusions, and I do not expect tomorrow to see in our country a resurgence—as if by a wave of the wand—of liberty, respect for law, public honesty, frankness of opinion, good faith in the newspapers, morality in government, reason in the bourgeois, and common sense in the plebeian.[76] No, no;

---

[75] The Independent Socialists follow the same path as Kautsky; while the workers wanted to prevent passage of arms and ammunition into Poland by the Entente, the Independents betrayed Soviet Russia (*Humanité*, Sept. 2, 1920, according to the *Rothe Fahne*). While correcting this manuscript, I read in *Information* of Jan. 27, 1921, that Serrati accuses Lenin of strangling the Independent Socialists of Germany for the benefit of the partisans of a war of revenge and that Moscow "has not ceased to denounce the Independents as being valets, licking the boots of French generals." It is not very unusual to see in the large Italian newspapers that the Independents would serve as informers to General Nollet.

[76] One of Proudhon's great sorrows was to see the workers let themselves be taken in by the chauvinistic claptrap of the *Siècle* ("Century") and the *Opinion nationale*. On October 27, he wrote to Chaudey: "Be very careful not to let yourself be seduced [in the *Courrier du dimanche* ("Sunday Courier")] by what I will call the patriotic mood and what is actually the downfall of patriotism. Everything you do from which the empire might benefit, or which is in the same direction as the empire, helping it, is bad for France, bad for civilization: silence, always silence!" (*Correspondance*, X, 187). True patriotism would have consisted in fight-

decadence—and that for a period of which I cannot see the end and which will not be less than one or two generations—that is our lot. . . . I will see only evil; I will die in complete darkness, marked by my life's record with the seal of reprobation in a rotten society."[77] The situation is even more serious than in 1860, because we are coming out of a war that is the source of innumerable ills. Supposing that Napoleon III could once again launch France into adventures, Proudhon said to Chaudey on October 27, 1860: "My profound conviction is that we are entering more and more into the era of dissolution and trouble. . . . Mass slaughter will come, and the prostration that will follow these blood baths will be dreadful. We will not see the work of the new age; we will fight in the dark. We must brace ourselves to endure this life in doing our duty without too much sadness. Let us help each other. Let us call out to one another in the darkness, and each time that the opportunity presents itself, let us do justice: that is the consolation of persecuted virtue."[78] Let us not then be astonished to find a frightening prostration everywhere at the present time. This phenomenon is in the nature of things.

We can say of our time what Proudhon said to Michelet on January 23, 1860: "We will not be extricated from this state of affairs except by a sweeping revolution in ideas and in men's hearts. You and I are working toward the revolution; that will be our honor in the eyes of posterity if she remembers us."[79] Social democracy is being cruelly punished today for having fought with so much tenacity the anarchists who intended to make a revolution arise in men's minds and hearts.

It must be observed that today there exists an overwhelming historical fact that can reaffirm the courage of the revolutionaries.

---

ing Napoleon III, according to Proudhon. On August 4, he wrote to Delhasse about demonstrations in Belgium against the emperor's projects for annexation: "I rejoice in it, considering everything anti-Bonapartist as eminently liberal, just, humanitarian, republican, and even French" (p. 124). The idea of "sacred union" would undoubtedly have seemed very strange to Proudhon.

[77] Proudhon, *Correspondance*, X, 205–206. In 1864, in writing the *Capacité politique des classes ouvrières* ("Political Capacity of the Working Classes"), he felt renewed hope in his heart; on October 9, he announced to Delhasse that he hoped to see the collapse of the bourgeoisie (*Correspondance*, XIV, 65).

[78] Proudhon, *Correspondance*, X, 187–188.

[79] *Ibid.*, XIV, 192. On May 3 he wrote to an old friend: "Let us give all our thought; let us give it with calm serenity, and then we must leave things alone. We can do nothing more" (*ibid.*, X, 47).

Everywhere the workers feel a sense of solidarity with the republic of the soviets, while the bourgeoisie feels an affinity for the anti-Bolsheviks. The Pope, after having taken so many precautions in order not to be accused during the war of deviating from the neutrality which to him seemed required by his position as father of all Catholics, intervened on the day that Poland was seriously threatened by the Red Army. In his eyes it was not a question of a disagreement between two republics about entirely temporal interests. The Bolsheviks seemed to him to be the destroyers of all the civilization to which the church had adapted, just as the Albigenses had been viewed by orthodox sages of the Middle Ages. For want of daring to preach a crusade against the new heretics, the leaders of the hierarchy engaged the faithful to pray that heaven intervene in favor of Poland.[80] A number of great men of the bourgeoisie, like the heroic burgomaster of Brussels and cartloads of other heroes, have expressed their horror at the conduct of the workers who refused to give their labor for the sending of arms or ammunition to Warsaw. Moreover, the proletariat—even in England, where the Third International of Lenin is not very popular—felt a sense of solidarity with the Soviet republic. They did not listen to the "competent" people who purported to show them that in the Russo-Polish conflict right was on the side of Poland. For them, as for the Pope, it was not a matter of international politics, but of the social question posed in all Europe by the development of economic conflicts.

Many workers until that time wondered how correct writers were who represented the absolute proposition of socialism as false literature, but for almost three years the Bolsheviks have resisted Europe under far more difficult conditions than those in which our Convention found itself. Thus we must admit that under normal conditions socialism could be applied without too much difficulty.

In a letter of May 21, 1858, Proudhon said to his doctor, Crétin, that his book, *De La Justice*, while being too difficult to become popular, would still have considerable influence: "The profundity of

---

[80] The French clergy is certain that heaven clearly manifested its strategy during this war: first, at the end of July, 1918, after Foch had consecrated his armies at the Sacré-Coeur, and in the month of August, 1920, in giving the victory at the gates of Warsaw to the Poles. It is empirically established that heaven detests the Germans and the Bolsheviks. Our reactionary publicists have no doubt that the infernal powers of Germany and the Soviet Republic do not cease to plot against civilization.

science henceforth guarantees its certitude, and it is certitude that assures the rapidity of the advance. Now how many readers are needed in order to have this certitude pass from theory in itself into the public consciousness? A few dozen, no more. The rest will catch what they can and what they learn from science will guarantee them the rest."[81] The importance for the future of socialism of this certitude (so effectively shown by Proudhon) is possessed today by the people in a far more solid way than could be done by the more or less direct effects of a book. It results from the example offered to us by the Soviet republic. The sentiment of the sublime, which never dies in the popular soul,[82] moved by the account of the prodigious voluntary sacrifices of the Bolsheviks, sanctifies the certitude of socialism already admitted by intelligence.

The example of the Soviet republic has the effect of giving an unusual confidence to the partisans of socialist intransigence, who have so much difficulty in fighting against the *Reformists*. The latter take their stand on the not very sublime sentiments that are found most often in our souls,[83] and they are supported in varying degrees by the political leaders of the bourgeoisie. The advice that Proudhon gave to Chaudey on June 24, 1860, concerning the publication of the *Courrier du dimanche* is still useful to contemplate today: "Beware of the small opposition. Do not argue with despotism; do not let it be believed that you take its legality seriously, and that you are thinking of overcoming it by means of the imperial law. You would humble yourself, and one fine day unbeknownst to you, you would find yourself caught in the trap and humiliated.[84] In France's present

---

[81] Proudhon, *Correspondance*, VIII, 46. Proudhon observes that the philosophy of the Revolution is not subject to the scholastic conditions that rule the propagation of the doctrines of an Aristotle or a Kant. "The People," he says, "do not read me, and without reading me, they hear me. Their hearts swear by the Revolution." Proudhon affirms here that his doctrines are in perfect agreement with the sentiments of the working class. An author cannot be called great among socialists if he is not entitled to such a judgment.

[82] That is why the popular soul has always accepted the sometimes clumsy but strongly felt songs of poets whom bourgeois criticism has neglected.

[83] On October 27, 1860, Proudhon wrote to Beslay: "I do not contribute to the *Courrier du dimanche*; I do not find it forceful enough against imperial France" (*Correspondance*, X, 196).

[84] In a letter of October 27, 1860, he said to Chaudey: "Nothing is easier, you know, under a despotic power, than to speak about things in which blame is forbidden and in which one has only the resource of silence. One wants to express an opinion, even an opinion of opposition; one congratulates oneself for remaining independent; one has recourse to a thousand ruses, a thousand little rubrics. One

state, if one starts in earnest to attack the Empire with equal weapons, it could go on for a hundred years. By that time, as the storyteller says, everyone would be dead and the country in full decline. What is necessary is an energetic war, a clandestine press, open disapproval—conspiracy, if need be—[85]and finally, when there is no way to do anything else, silence. Yes, silence: what silence would not weigh a hundred times more on the subject than the harangues of the Olliviers and the Jules Favres?"[86]

I believe it worthwhile to reproduce here the last lines of the *Insegnamenti sociali della economia contemporanea*: "Early Christianity could very probably have obtained toleration, like so many other exotic cults, as did Judaism,[87] but it sought to isolate itself. Thus it provoked distrust and even persecutions. It was the intransigent teachers of doctrine who prevented the new religion from taking a normal place in Roman society. There was no lack of wise men who treated Tertullian and all those who refused to accept any conciliation as madmen. Today we see that it was thanks to these supposed madmen that Christianity was able to form its ideas and become the master of the world when its hour had come."[88]

takes oratorical precautions; one makes concessions; finally and always, after having said too little and very badly, one ends up by giving the advantage to the adversary" (*ibid.*, X, 183–184).

[85] Proudhon would not have been scandalized by articles 1 and 8 of the conditions of loyalty to the Third International put forth on July 26, 1920, to the French Socialist Party by the office in Moscow: Change the character of propaganda by giving it a frankly revolutionary tone. Combine legal action with illegal action.

[86] *Correspondance* X, 85–86.

[87] It seems that could have happened all the more easily because Christianity had protection in Rome and even had adherents in high society very early. If the great authors, like Juvenal, do not speak of the Christians, or, like Tacitus, speak of them in a summary and embarrassed way, it is in my opinion because they were anxious to spare the sensibilities of the group in which their readers were recruited and in which friends of the new religion were found.

[88] When I wrote *La Marche au socialisme*, I had on hand neither the *Introduction à l'économie moderne* ("Introduction to Modern Economy") nor the manuscript of my book on pragmatism. I ask the reader to excuse the repetition he will observe in comparing the present work to these two works.

Index

215